European Media

Global Media and Communication

Arab Media, Noha Mellor, Khalil Rinnawi, Nabil Dajani and
    Muhammad I. Ayish
European Media, Stylianos Papathanassopoulos and Ralph Negrine

European Media

Structures, Policies and Identity

STYLIANOS PAPATHANASSOPOULOS AND
RALPH NEGRINE

polity

First published in 2011 by Polity Press

Polity Press
65 Bridge Street
Cambridge CB2 1UR, UK

Polity Press
350 Main Street
Malden, MA 02148, USA

ISBN-13: 978-0-7456-4474-5
ISBN-13: 978-0-7456-4475-2 (pb)

A catalogue record for this book is available from the British Library.

Typeset in 11 on 13 pt Adobe Garamond Pro
by Servis Filmsetting Ltd, Stockport, Cheshire
Printed and bound in Great Britain by MPG Books Group Limited, Bodmin, Cornwall

For further information on Polity, visit our website: www.politybooks.com

Contents

Detailed Contents

List of Illustrations

Tables

Figures

Boxes

Abbreviations

ACT	Association of Commercial Television in Europe
ADSL	asymmetrical digital subscriber line
AER	Association Européene des Radios
AMS	Audiovisual Media Services
ARD	Arbeitsgemeinschaft der Öffentlichrechtlichen Rundfunkanstalten der Bundesrepublik Deutschland
BBC	British Broadcasting Corporation
BSkyB	British Sky Broadcasting
CFI	Court of First Instance
CLT	Compagnie Luxembourgeoise de Télédiffusion
DAB	digital audio broadcasting
DMB	digital multimedia broadcasting
DMP	digital media player
DRM	digital rights management system
DSL	digital subscriber line
DTH	direct-to-home
DTT	digital terrestrial television
DVB	digital video broadcasting
DVB-H	digital video broadcasting - handheld
DVD	digital video disk
EBU	European Broadcasting Union
EC	European Commission
ECJ	European Court of Justice
EICTA	European Information and Communications Technology Industry Association
EPC	European Publishers Council
EU	European Union
GATS	General Agreement on Trade in Services
GDP	gross domestic product
GPS	global positioning system
HDTV	high definition TV
IDATE	Institut de l'Audiovisuel et des Télécommunications en Europe
IP	internet protocol

IPTV	internet protocol television
ISDN	integrated services digital network
ISP	internet service provider
LAN	local area network
NOS	Nederlandse Omroep Stichting
Ofcom	Office of Communications
PDA	personal digital assistant
PSB	public service broadcasting
RAI	Radio Televisione Italiana
RTE	Radio Telefís Éireann
RTL	Radio Télévision Luxembourgeoise
RTVE	Radio Televisión Española
SHDSL	single-pair high-speed digital subscriber line
STB	set top box
TWF	Television without Frontiers
VCR	video cassette recorder
VDSL (VHDSL)	very-high-bitrate digital subscriber line
VHS	video home system
VoD	video-on-demand
VRT	Vlaamse Radio en Televisie
WIPO	World International Property Organization
WTN	World Television News

To Katia, Thanassis and Aphrodite for their continuous support, good humour and patience

To Angie

Acknowledgements

Many people helped in the making of this book. In particular, we would like to thank the National and Kapodistrian University of Athens for its financial assistance at various stages of the research in the last three years. Our thanks go also to the many journalists who helped us with our research and patiently answered our questions, as well as the two anonymous readers at Polity for their valuable comments and thoughts on our typescript.

Our special thanks go to John Thompson and Andrea Drugan at Polity Press who have enthusiastically supported the whole project. We would like to express our sincere thanks to Caroline Richmond, who has shown professionalism and patience throughout the process of putting this book together. Needless to say, all responsibility for shortcomings and inaccuracies are ours.

Stelios Papathanassopoulos, Ralph Negrine

1 Introduction: The Media in the European Context

The media in European states have experienced a period of continuous change from the 1980s onwards. This period has been associated with changes in media policy as well as a series of technological developments which have, either directly or indirectly, had an influence on policy choices towards the media sector, and especially television. Emerging channels, including the internet, mobile and other interactive media, are outperforming their traditional counterparts and seizing market share from them. In the past, European media systems were characterized by simplicity – there were usually only a small handful of public-owned TV and radio stations, newspapers were available at specific times of the day and distributed in specific places. Today's media systems, however, are characterized by complexity: processes of technological convergence and digitalization have dramatically changed the media landscape. Cable and satellite services deliver hundreds of channels; broadband links and websites allow anyone to distribute video to millions of people; and mobile phones connect subscribers to each other but also to television and to web services. The simplicity of yesteryear has given rise to a multiplicity of services that connect to one another but also compete with one another for shares of subscribers. To give one obvious example, internet service providers supply services to customers but also supply news – thus competing with traditional news outlets – and business information.

Although much has changed, there is also a sense that everything has remained more or less the same. We still (mostly) watch TV at home, listen to radio in many cases in our cars and read newspapers, especially on Sundays. But at the same time, the younger generations watch TV on their PC monitors, barely turn on a traditional TV set, and very often exchange messages and videos via their mobile devices and the internet, on social networking sites. They don't read newspapers but they frequently visit web versions and are also informed by blogs. In reality, there is no simple explanation for these complex processes of change. Neither can we say that there is a common universal trend, even a common model, across Europe. In fact, each country has dealt with the developments of the new media and the surrounding issues and the pressures for change in different ways. What has united them is the sense, as in the 1980s, that these issues are common to all and that the

European Union has an increasing role in media affairs. Among the common issues are uncertainty over the course of future technological innovation with respect to 'new media'; the decline of the traditional media, especially newspapers; renewed pressure on public broadcasters' finances, either the licence fees and/or advertising revenues; the new and more active role of the European Commission; and a concern over the effect of inward and outward investment on broadcasting and communications systems, especially in the aftermath of the financial crisis. Despite these common issues of concern, it is important to observe also that radical changes in the media system in post-communist Eastern European countries have brought about transformations in the ways in which they are organized and run. The old communist-style of control has given way to competitive media systems, though there is evidence to suggest that these transformations have not necessarily given rise to plural-ist media. In fact, linkages between businesses formed out of the collapse of the communist era and media power appear to constitute obstacles to reform and freedom (see Vidal-Hall, 2009).

Some of the changes which have taken place came about as a result of many interconnecting factors and can be understood as part of larger processes that have rendered the media global. They are global in the sense of being better understood when contextualized within larger transnational processes. These include international, national and domestic politics, technology and busi-ness but they have also been affected by 'diplomacy' and 'industrial policy', since negotiations among states and between states and regional organiza-tions (such as the negotiations around GATS, the WTO and the EU) have become, at least since the mid-1980s, part of the modern media (see also Puppis, 2008). Moreover, the current financial crisis may foster protectionist behaviour and bring back industrial policy as the main initiator of communi-cations policy in Europe, especially as regards the new media and audiovisual programme production.

In this respect one has to consider the role of the European Union and the processes of European integration leading towards the Europeanization, or EU-ization, of the whole communications sector on the continent. In effect, there is common agreement that the process of European integration has called into question many features associated with more traditional models that explored the state of individual national politics and policies (Cole and Drake, 2000; Ladrech, 1994). In the 1950s and 1960s, a common approach was to consider the impact of spillovers from economic integration into the political realm, but it is now accepted that it is necessary to examine (and understand) the 'transformative power of Europe' (Risse, 2003). The EU, through its very existence and its actions, may thus be seen as help-ing to reshape the nature of Europe itself. Although it is often difficult to disentangle the impact of European integration from other causes of policy change, such as economic globalization, changing policy fashions and endogenous political reforms, Europe is, for many, more than just an ill-defined and ill-conceived idea. Ulrich Beck, for example, sees it as a bulwark against globalization and the power of the USA – 'without Europe there is no answer to globalization' (Beck, 1999) – and Zigmunt Bauman believes that 'Europe still has much to offer in dealing with the great challenges that face us in the twenty-first century' (Bauman, 2004). In their eyes, and in the eyes of many, Europe stands for something – and something that is quite different from other states and state systems.

Within European and international relations studies, there is a fast-growing and vast academic literature on the development and transformation of the EU polity and policies and on the impact of European integration and international regimes and organizations on the domestic structures of member states and non-members alike. In particular, processes labelled as 'Europeanization' have come under scrutiny from different theoretical perspectives (Goetz and Hix, 2000; Kohler-Koch, 1999; Ward, 2004; Humphreys, 2007), though the discussions have not yet given rise to 'a single and precise definition' (Lenschow, 2006: 57; Olsen, 2002: 923; Graziano and Vink, 2007).

In essence, the idea of 'Europeanization' touches on the ways in which national 'domestic policies, politics and polities' (Börzel and Risse, 2000: 1), as well as institution-building or institutional change, policy-making procedures and styles at the member state level, are, or have been, affected by policies created at EU level. It can thus be understood as a complex process of political change – i.e. of 'transfer' of policies across member states (Featherstone and Radaelli, 2003). A suitable working definition of Europeanization remains that offered by Ladrech, namely: 'Europeanization is an incremental process reorienting the direction and shape of politics to the degree that EC political and economic dynamics become part of the organizational logic of national politics and policymaking' (1994: 70). An example of such a reorientation would be the 'large-scale policy transfer . . . involved in . . . the body of European legislation that candidate countries must accept before joining the Union' (Radaelli, 2000: 26–7; see also Bauer et al., 2007). But, beyond such obvious examples of transfers of policies, it has been argued by Green Cowles, Caporaso and Risse that 'there has been very little systematic study of why, how and under what conditions Europeanization shapes a variety of domestic structures in a number of countries' (2001: 3). There remains, in other words, much more detailed research to be done so as to be able to identify specific processes and flows, particularly as these take different shape in different member states.

Some commentators have therefore argued that public policies within the EU can be understood as a two-way process in which member states 'upload' their preferences to Brussels via negotiations and 'download' them from various EU policy menus (Bugdahn, 2005: 178). In this way, the EU is recognized as a 'complex organization where the national and European levels are increasingly intermeshed in a pattern of multi-level governance. No longer is the EU necessarily destined to develop teleologically towards a unified political community: its outcomes and impact at the national level are much more contingent and uncertain' (Buller, 2003: 528). Within these processes of change, it becomes possible to recognize that it is not only the European Commission but also its individual member states and commissioners who can serve as 'agents for change' working towards the creation of a single market in political and strategic ways (Jabko, 2006).

These wide-ranging discussions about the meaning of Europeanization suggest that the complexity of the process and its outcomes are by no means predetermined. Europeanization has numerous dimensions, and it is worth considering these and how they have impacted on the creation and transfer of audiovisual media policy.

Dimensions of Europeanization

It should be obvious that there is much more to Europeanization than the idea that it concerns the process of 'domestic adaptation to the pressures emanating directly or indirectly from EU membership' (Featherstone, 2003, quoted in Smaele, 2007: 129). On the one hand, there is a matter of structural and institutional alignment with the EU governance structure; on the other, there is a broader question of the implementation of policies deriving from the EU. There needs to be recognition of the duality of the process in question.

In his work on Europeanization, Johan Olsen (2002: 923–4) distinguishes five possible uses of the term in respect of structural considerations:

- *changes in external boundaries*: This involves the territorial reach of a system of governance and the degree to which Europe as a continent becomes a single political space. For example, Europeanization is taking place as the EU expands through enlargement.
- *the development of institutions at the European level*: This relates to the creation and operation of bodies to coordinate and enforce policies that draw on the EU's principles.
- *the central penetration of national systems of governance*: Europeanization here involves the division of responsibilities and powers between different

levels of governance. All multilevel systems of governance need to work out a balance between unity and diversity, central coordination and local autonomy. Europeanization, then, implies adapting national and sub-national systems of governance to a European political centre and European-wide norms.

- *exporting forms of political organization*: Europeanization as exporting forms of political organization and governance beyond European territory. It signifies a more positive export–import balance as non-European countries import more from Europe than vice versa and European solutions exert more influence in international forums.

- *a political unification project*: The degree to which Europe is becoming a more unified and stronger political entity is related to territorial space, centre-building, domestic adaptation, and how European developments impact and are impacted by systems of governance and events outside the continent.

While these dimensions of Europeanization point to the creation of a more integrated governance structure, in practice there are possible disjunctures between them: a politically stronger Europe does not, for example, lead to a closer cultural Europe. More pertinently, as the EU has expanded outwards it has created a larger infrastructure at the same time as having allowed for greater differences. As Smaele has observed in this regard: 'More Europe, therefore, basically adds more of the same: more diversity but also unity in diversity' (2007: 131).

But the concern with Europeanization as an issue about structures – i.e. What new structures or forms of governance does it bring about? – has to be complemented by a concern with Europeanization as an issue about policies. Namely, how are policies created and how do they then become (or not) part of the policy regime of member states? In this respect, one has to take into consideration a narrower dimension of Europeanization, so-called EU-ization (Flockhart, 2010). EU-ization differs from Europeanization on account of its

> focus on the EU and because it is predominantly concerned with 'political encounters', where specific political entities such as the EU and Member State representatives engage in the transfer of institutional and organizational practices and policies. EU-ization is a small, but important part of the much broader and longer term process of Europeanization, which is predominantly concerned with 'cultural encounters'. (Ibid.: 790–1)

Changes in EU laws and treaties have undoubtedly modified national traditions of policy-making and the freedom of manoeuvre of national decision-makers. This can be seen in many areas of economic and social life, although national traditions do often reassert themselves strongly in the form of strategies for resisting change and in the details of implementation. That tension is well described by Peter Humphreys:

> collectively . . . member states have sought to retain primary responsibility for media policy, with the EU relegated to a supportive role. The Commission, on the other hand, acting as a 'purposeful opportunist' . . . and as a 'policy entrepreneur' . . . has sought both to expand its competences and to coordinate a European response to the new international market and technological challenges. (Humphreys, 2007: 185)

The outcomes of these interplays have obviously varied from one sector to another. While the processes of Europeanization have modified the public policies, political agendas and governing styles of national political actors, they have also had to meet the challenges to those changes from within member states (see Ward, 2004: 121). As Bugdahn (2005: 178–9) notes, one should thus be able to assess whether and to what extent EU policies have been implemented; implementation could be considered as a first stage of Europeanization, since the member states 'have the option of adopting new or preserving existing domestic legislation that influences also the operational context of the transposing legislation'. Bugdahn therefore defines the 'Europeanization of a policy area as a situation in which actors at the EU level have taken a policy decision with the intention . . . to prescribe or influence the choice of a member state's policy/administrative option in a policy area' (ibid.: 180).

This can be likened to what Cole and Drake (2000: 27) refer to as *independent variable*, whereby it can be demonstrated that the EU has produced change in specific policy sectors and that national institutions and actors participate more intensively in the EU decision-making process. Another form of Europeanization mentioned by Cole and Drake is one of *emulative policy transfer* – i.e. as a process by which policies and practices are copied by one member state from another (see Humphreys, 2002). Europeanization is perhaps a misnomer here, since it could be seen as a process whereby member states are influenced by strong national models rather than a European one, though it is possible that such a model may provide a framework for EU policies. Policy transfer, however, is constrained when there are no national cases to be imitated, as in the case of media ownership. For example, EU member states such as the UK, Italy, the Netherlands and, to a certain extent, France and Germany, one after the other, have started forming regulatory authorities which have been strongly influenced by the example of the US Federal Communications Commission.

As Cole and Drake (2000: 27) also point out, Europeanization has been used as a *smokescreen for domestic political strategies* and as a powerful domestic political resource for driving through change. A controversial example here would be the way in which a particular construction of Europe can be used as a means of blocking or encouraging change in candidate member states. For instance, the EU, through the Commission, asks, if not demands, that candidate countries align their media systems in general and broadcasting in particular with the EU directives (Rosenbaum, 2003). Eastern European countries were also given prerequisites for EU membership, including, for example, adjusting their broadcasting systems to the 'Television without Frontiers' (TWF) Directive and transforming their state television companies to Western-style public service broadcasters.

If the broad outlines of Europeanization have been explored at some length – here and elsewhere – are the outcomes of Europeanization straight-forward and unproblematic? The immediate response is to accept that, despite the tangible outcomes (Radaelli, 2000) or impacts (Lodge, 2002), neither its pace nor its direction is entirely predictable. Sometimes the EU can influence domestic administrative arrangements (Lippert et al., 2001: 981–2) and may trigger domestic change by prescribing concrete institutional requirements with which the member states must comply. This can be seen as a form of *positive integration*. At times, by changing the distribution of power and resources between domestic actors, it may have less of a direct and positive influence. This can be termed a form of negative *integration*. A third possibility is that the EU influences national arrangements even more indirectly, by *altering the beliefs and expectations* of domestic actors. For example, as Humphreys notes:

> the Europeanization of telecommunications policy and regulation has occurred less because of the Europeanizing policies of national policy makers or the European Commission, but rather as a result of the strategies of key private economic interests reacting to the challenges presented by . . . globalisation, technological change and the 'crisis of Fordism'. (2002: 65)

Interestingly, Humphreys adds another layer of analysis of EU policy-making that needs to be considered, and this touches on the content of policies per se. As he points out (Humphreys, 2007: 199), EU policy can lower barriers as well as raise them, can bring things down to a lower common denominator as well as seek to 'improve' matters. For this reason, he terms the former *negative integration* and the latter *positive integration*. The inability of the European Union to deal with the plethora of issues surrounding the maintenance of pluralism in media he sees as 'highly illustrative of the EU's liberal bias towards negative integration. It exemplifies the difficulty that the Commission encounters in pursuing more interventionist cultural and social policies (positive integration) that confront powerful vested economic interests and challenge member states' claims of primary competence for media policy' (ibid.).

In making such judgements about the *aims, objectives and content* of EU policies themselves, Humphreys opens up a debate about the ways in which they are open to interpretation. For example, his conclusions about the 'liberal bias' of the EU are not shared by David Ward, who suggests that, though its policies are painted as being 'overly economically liberal', in fact they have 'a dualism between the economic benefits of developing a common market for television and certain fundamental human rights' (2004: 122). One of his examples is that of the support for media pluralism at a pan-European rather than a national level, where liberal strategies often dominate. The same sorts of differences of views can be found in respect of the EU's position regarding public service broadcasting, where some see the unwillingness to confront 'state aid' as a sign of support while others, such as Harrison and Wood (2007), are less sanguine.

However one sees these kinds of discussions, it should be clear by now that we are looking at an extremely complex set of considerations. There is, first, the matter of the direction of influence: it could be 'bottom-up (that is, from member state→EU), top-down (EU→ member state), horizontal (state→state) and round about (member state→EU→member state)' (Lenschow, 2006: 57). One can also envisage Europeanization as *a two-stage process*: one from above, orchestrated from Brussels, and confined to formal members (in this case it could be said that it could be narrowed to either *EU Europeanization* or *EU-ization*); and one from below, covering the whole European continent, where an equally large number of countries are still non-members (which does not make them any less 'European').

The second matter to consider is how influence is reconstituted into some form of impact, be it a new structure of governance or rules, a new way of implementing directives or perhaps even stalling on these. The third matter to consider is whether the influence and transference into some measurable impact is positive or negative in the sense that Peter Humphreys has set out. Do these lead to a 'better' and 'higher' and more 'laudable' policy regime or do they simply lower the barriers?

The real problem in trying to deal with these complexities is that the EU, though unified, has to balance competing interests. There is a rich diversity in language, culture, economic preferences, administrative methods, and political and social priorities across the twenty-seven member states. These have tended to be magnified by the intense and often conflictual bargaining process in Brussels. The latter creates what is a dominant feature of the EU's policy-making procedure – i.e. its emphasis on finding a balance between the opinions of interested parties in order to arrive at a consensus and then a common approach towards the international environment (Thatcher, 2004; Michalis, 2007). This is almost certainly what has happened in the communications field: larger European countries created pressure for change and therefore for new policies; the negotiation process that followed brought forth a compromise which, in turn, led to a directive that was intended to be applied in all the member states. We can trace this process in respect of the EU's involvement in the communications field, initially in the television system, then in telecommunications and finally in information and communications technology and digitalization. While the question of its competence in these matters has continued to fascinate many commentators, there is now no doubt that the EU has fully embraced the entire communication sector – from old 'audiovisual' media right through to the 'global information society' (see also Humphreys, 2007; Harrison and Woods, 2007; Richardson, 2006).

The media seem to provide a good example of the process of EU-ization and of policy transfer, since they reflect and reveal a 'permanent state of reconstruction and reconstitution' (Flockhart, 2010: 805). The EU, through the European Commission, has both initiated a number of initiatives in the media field and assumed that, since the new convergent communication landscape raises a number of questions with a pan-European dimension, it is the appropriate body to deal with these (see chapter 4).

On the other hand, the European media are part and parcel of the global media. In effect, as Jeremy Tunstall notes (2008: 8–10), the world's media can be seen as operating at the following five levels:

1 the world or global level;
2 the world region (or group of nation-states) level, such as South Asia, East Asia, the Arab world and Euro-America (including the entire European and American continents);
3 the national level;
4 the national region level, such as the cases of Germany, Spain, Pakistan and recently China and India;
5 the very local level.

For Tunstall there are many media connections, big and small, between Europe and the Americas, and this is especially noticeable in international news, entertainment formats, news channels, advertising agencies, magazines, music, radio and TV station ownership, book publishing, and satellite and cable TV, as well as internet platforms (ibid.: 8–9, 282–4, 410–11).

The case of European media belongs to what Tunstall calls a world region, yet the media systems can also be considered at the national level, since there are many nationally bounded systems as well as smaller states within the European continent which communicate with each other despite their differences. In effect, there is a dialectic relationship between the national and the international, the global and the local, the European and the regional, and the old media and new media. These are not simply a consequence of processes of globalization but also outcomes of technological change, policy-making and economics which help give shape to the new world and to the media order. Nevertheless, as Humphreys and Padget (2006: 384) have noted:

> Globalizing technology intensifies international competition and renders ter-ritorially defined markets indefensible. The more intense these pressures, the more likely it is that political and economic actors will accept the rationale for regulatory reform on the basis of the need to remain economically competitive. Market dynamism leads actors to accept liberalization more readily. In growth markets, competition is a 'positive sum game,' and attention is focused on the opportunities of liberalization rather than the threats.

The case of the European media is unique for one other reason. Although the aim of policy-makers is to increase European interactions and trans-border communication, what one sees is an increase of communication at the local/national rather than the European level. This is even the case with the internet, since there is much more internet traffic within national borders than across member states, and in some cases the traffic is higher with the USA.

We wish to argue, therefore, that the process of Europeanization and of European integration can be seen as an extension of the globalization debate, since the EU offers a set of unique mechanisms for enabling its member states to manage their relations within the Union and the global order. In the case of the media, Europe in general and the EU in particular has provided institutional and financial support for promoting research and development, innovation, education, and other skills that could insulate the media industry from the dislocations of globalization. In effect, the EU operates as a regional international organization that manages the processes of globalization for its member states and works tirelessly to prevent the processes and impacts of globalization being defined either by the United States or by other regional powers. For its newer members, in particular the post-communist Eastern European countries, the European Union is not so much a defensive mecha-nism as a means of becoming more global and participating in processes of globalization. The EU thus not only opens up new markets to these member states but provides structural funds that enable them to emerge from their relative isolation.

By and large, the EU has managed to affect the pathways of globalization in ways that are not against the interests of member states. It can make a difference in respect of global issues (Laïdi, 2008). As Castells (2000: 339) has noted, Europe is 'the network state', with competing visions mediating between global and local spaces, while

> European integration is, at the same time, a reaction to the process of globalization and its most advanced expression. It is proof that the global economy is not an undifferentiated system made up of firms and capital flows, but a regionalized structure in which old national institutions and new supranational entities still play a major role in organizing economic competition, and in reaping, or spoiling, the benefits of it. . . . while most economic activity and most jobs in the world are national, regional, or even local, the core, strategic economic activities are globally integrated in the Information Age through electronically enacted networks of exchange of capital, commodities, and information. It is this global integration that induces and shapes the current process of European unification, on the basis of European institutions historically constituted around predominantly political goals. (Ibid.: 348)

Within this framework, the media in Europe are being increasingly forged by forces that are outside national geographic or political borders, yet there are important questions about the extent to which they can be seen as *European* media. In what ways do they represent the commonness of the European 'project'? Do they begin to reflect something unique and European or are they no more than separate media systems within a geographic and political entity that is defined as European? These sorts of questions are becoming increasingly important, as the framework of the EU has now expanded to include a range of countries that have often been considered to be at the fringes (or outside) of commonly understood notions of what Europe means or is.

The media in Europe still function as national media, despite attempts to bring them closer in terms of either regulatory systems or content. This is understandable. What is more of a puzzle is why the media in Europe – and often the public in Europe – lack a European orientation. In the 2009 European Parliament election, for example, the Euro-sceptic and Euro-phobic tendencies made some important gains in numerous countries – for example, Austria, the UK and the Czech Republic – without encountering any proactive or positive countering moves from European policy-makers. Even the negative public responses towards the ratification of the Lisbon Treaty have been met by somewhat feeble and unconvincing actions. Europe thus continues to offer the best place for examining processes of technological and cultural change within a regional and global context.

But this is not quite the end of the story. There is also the question of the underlying infrastructure over which all media content must travel (Noam, 2008). Europe in general and the EU countries in particular have entered a new era of challenges which have to be faced. They have to compete once again for both hardware (networks and infrastructure) and content. As in the past, consumer demand has been taken for granted, with the 'consumer choice' argument once again playing a dominant role in all new media developments. In the 1980s, cable TV was considered the ideal technology to end centralized television systems as well as a technology that would encourage interpersonal communication and democracy. In the last decade, the same arguments have returned but are now applied to different technologies or conceptualizations of communication, such as the 'wired society' or the 'information society'. But this rhetoric has paid little attention to the citizen-viewer, even though policies are meant to take him/her into consideration. Yet, as the trends in European media consumption show, Europeans appear to pursue a different path from the one the media industry would wish for. The rapid decline of the press and the increased use of blogs and videos on websites is an indication of this, with European households spending as much as 20 per cent of their budgets on media and entertainment for internet access and mobile media.

The organization of the book

This book seeks to present an account of the contemporary media field, focusing on the trends as well as on the problems faced by the media in Europe. It covers a broad spread of media markets, highlighting the new sectors that are emerging and outlining the factors driving the media business into the twenty-first century. It examines the current structure of the various sectors that make up the European media market (broadcasting, the press, the internet), identifies and assesses the major players and issues, and provides an overview of each sector of the industry.

The argument here is that Europe continues to offer the best place for examining global media processes. In doing so, it aims:

1 to describe the issues, the dynamics and the realities of the European media sector by synthesizing the most up-to-date information on developments. Although much of the focus will be on the Western European media, attention will also be paid to the media of the newer member states;
2 to critically assess whether we are seeing the emergence of European media or simply the continuation of separate national media in a European context;
3 to explore debates about the role of the media in the formation of a European public sphere and a European identity.

The book is divided into three parts. The first part deals with the *structure of the European media*. Chapter 2 aims to describe some of the basic structural dimensions of the media in Europe. It provides an overview of the common characteristics as well as those that distinguish systems one from the other, and from the rest of the world. It examines how the media in Europe operate alongside one another and explores developments in the face of global competition and global deregulation.

Chapter 3 discusses developments in the new media in Europe, and in particular in the areas of digital television, internet penetration, internet protocol television (IPTV) development and mobile television. It argues that, as with the case of analogue cable and satellite television in the 1980s, the development of digital media is associated with industrial policy considerations rather than with realistic estimates, and, most importantly, it does not often take into account the reactions of viewers – although all interested parties argue that this time they have taken consumer demand seriously into consideration.

The second part of the book focuses on the *Europeanization of the media*. Chapter 4 argues that, in the last thirty years, the EU has sought to initiate policies to 'Europeanize' the whole communication sector of its member states, if not the European continent. These policies, also discussed at length in this chapter, with their strong industrial policy elements and considerations, have sought to harmonize as well as to protect the media sector and to make it competitive both in the internal European market and in the global market. Additionally, they have tried to protect European cultural identity from the 'American challenge'. Chapter 4 argues, therefore, that, as with other sectors of European economy and society, the EU, through an incremental policy process and ongoing modernization of its regulatory framework, has expanded its *acquis communautaire* to most aspects of the communication landscape, from TV advertising and programme quotas to production, distribution and training, from the definition of European works to cultural and linguistic diversity, from copyright protection to the protection of minors, from telecommunications to the convergence of the media and digital television.

Chapter 5 argues that the proliferation of media outlets in relation to the convergence and digitalization of the media communications sector has already transformed the European sector. One witnesses not only changes in the number of media experiences, with more choices and more content for consumers, but also many new patterns of content production and consumption. Nevertheless, the traditional media, principally television, continue to work in traditional ways, and the concerns within Europe, especially within the EU, are related to imports of content from foreign countries, especially the USA. The first part of the chapter discusses new developments in industries producing content and taking advantage from convergence and digitalization, while the second focuses on aspects of television programming.

The last two chapters of the book form its third section, which deals with the political and cultural dimension of Europe and the EU. Chapter 7 examines the arguments as to whether there is a European public sphere. It sets out the key debates surrounding this question and the evidence that seeks either to support or to deny its existence. In seeking to do this, the chapter deals with broader questions relating to what is common – or different – across Europe. Chapter 8 explores the concept of 'Europe' and 'Europeanness' and asks how the media cover subjects that raise issues about the boundaries – physical, cultural, political – of Europe. The sorts of questions that are raised include not only what, or where, the 'West' and/or 'Europe' is, but also how the 'West' or 'Europe' crystallized as an idea, as an identity. It draws on contemporary research on a range of topics that highlight the ways and means the media use – or do not use – to enable the construction of a European identity. Topics treated are accession talks (of Turkey, for example), the coverage of the EU in the media, the organization of journalists in European political centres, and so on. By focusing on these issues, the chapter draws attention to key concerns about the nature of the European media and the extent to which they play a part in defining the meaning of Europe.

The final chapter, Chapter 9, summarizes the arguments developed in the book and provides a way of answering the key question that underpins this analysis: Are there different and separate media sectors in Europe or can one say that there is an emerging European media sector?

Part I

The Political Economy of Media in Europe

2 The Structure of (Old) Media in Europe

The media in Europe have changed dramatically over the past two decades. The principal media have experienced different fortunes: while the number of television channels has undoubtedly multiplied within an increasingly commercial environment, the newspaper industry is showing signs of serious decline. The media in Europe are being reshaped, as elsewhere, by technological change, increased competition and consolidation and, though perhaps to a lesser extent, a process of 'Europeanization'. These developments are essentially altering the dynamics of the long-established and existing media systems and helping to give a new shape to the emerging ones.

This chapter will provide an overview of media systems in Europe.

Media models

It is always tempting to seek to create classificatory frameworks that neatly parcel out different elements under different categories, and the case of 'the media in Europe' is probably no different. When seeking to make sense of the latter, a schema that can place different countries under different headings and so create meaningful groupings for the purpose of comparison would be extremely useful. Unfortunately, such a schema does not really exist and, in truth, has never really existed. In the 1960s, and even up to the 1980s, there were classificatory schemes that, though simple, adequately summed up differences between models of broadcasting systems in respect of state direction and involvement – i.e. too much or too little – or commercialization – i.e. public or private. There were similar models concerning newspapers, as state direction and aid was permissible in some countries but not in others. But subtle, and sometimes not so subtle, differences between media systems across countries remained.

That said, one useful point that was often made – if exaggerated, perhaps – in distinguishing between *Western* European broadcasting, as if it had some sort of unitary character, and the American commercial system was that the former sought to reflect some notion of the public good and the *public interest* (Bertrand and Urabayen, 1985: 25). The European model differed from the American one in a number of ways: in terms of state intervention, in terms of ownership (public or private), in terms of the nature of the competition between the broadcasters, and in terms of the duties and responsibilities of the broadcasting services. But creating points of contrast from the commercially driven, privately owned media system in the USA (see, for example, Brown, 1995) did little to mask the differences that existed between the countries of Western Europe, where the processes or mechanisms of 'oversight' varied according to individual political and cultural traditions. (The differences between the Western and Eastern European countries – i.e. 'old' and 'new' Europe – were even more marked. By and large, before 1989 all the media in the Eastern European and Soviet countries were owned, supervised or controlled by the Communist Party, and fully subsidized from the state budget (Vartanova, 2002; Stevenson, 1994: 194–5).) As Sparks notes: 'The media before the fall of communism were large-scale, hierarchically organized, bureaucratic establishments in which there were elaborate procedures for ensuring acquiescence to the will of the directorate' (2000: 45).

In general terms, though, in the period before the 'deregulatory turn' in the 1980s, one commonly used way to characterize the different broadcasting systems that existed in Western Europe was to draw attention to the importance of the public broadcasting organizations, such as the BBC, TF1 (France), ARD (Germany) or RAI (Italy), and to their relative strengths *vis-à-vis*, on the one hand, the state as regulator and controller and, on the other, commercial services as competitors. Three models were then used to account for similarities and differences between the broadcasting systems across Europe.

- In the 'integration' model, public service broadcasters were funded mainly through a licence fee and enjoyed a *de jure* monopoly. This model has its roots in the idea that broadcasting could be treated as a natural monopoly and the belief that only this sort of structure could uphold the 'public interest'. Such a model did not rely on either journalistic or advertising competition for the provision of diversity but was based, in theory, on the notion of 'internal pluralism'. That is, the councils or committees which were directly or indirectly responsible for programming would be made up of representatives of various political, social and cultural groups in society ('internal pluralism') and this would ensure that a wide variety of perspectives were represented by the broadcasting authorities. Despite the political influence that was exerted on these organizations, there was a basic consensus on this form of regulation and this structure of broadcasting. Most countries in Europe chose this model – a funding structure that mixed commercial advertising revenue and licence fees.

- The 'duopoly' model, favoured by Britain from the 1950s onwards, was a hybrid model. Here one finds both public and private broadcasters competing for audiences but not for the same sources of revenue: thus, the BBC relies solely on the licence fee, while the commercial companies rely solely on commercial funding. However, the nature of the duopoly requires some mechanism to ensure that a full range and variety of genres and opinions are transmitted and that the competition between the services does not standardize the output. This has been achieved by the setting up of regulatory agencies for the commercial sector, with the BBC overseeing the public sector. Significantly, both private and public authorities pursue broadly similar public service broadcasting obligations.
- A third model is worth taking into account because it has implications for the discussion of the processes of deregulation which swept across European broadcasting systems in the 1980s. According to Dyson and Humphreys, 'as early as the inter war period, Luxembourg had seen the advantage of creating an appropriately lax regulatory environment so that its national private commercial operator (CLT/RTL) could cream off advertising from its neighbours' (1988: 7). It was a policy which inevitably brought it into conflict with countries that wanted to preserve their cultural dominance and their programming policies (e.g. the UK).

With the onset of a wave of deregulatory policies being implemented across European broadcasting systems in the 1980s and beyond – in part because of technological developments such as cable and satellite TV, which made a mockery of any efforts to limit (some would say stunt) developments in broadcasting – the models of the pre-1980s were obviously deficient. As more and more countries introduced greater elements of commercialism in their systems and/or undermined the pre-eminence of the public broadcasting service by cutting back on funding or making advertising revenue part of their funding structure, the Western European broadcasting scene began to look much more commercial than it once did (see table 2.1). Oddly enough, the creation of so many commercial broadcasting systems led to some sort of convergence and greater similarities than had existed previously. And so what had initially been a fairly closed, state-controlled system characterized by a small number of public broadcasters now became a large competitive environment, with a knock-on effect on the nature of the public broadcasters, funding systems, cultures, and so on (Brants and De Bens, 2000; Papathanassopoulos, 2002). The pace of broadcasting liberalization in Europe followed various waves. According to Tunstall and Machin (1999: 190), the waves affected:

1 Italy, Luxembourg, France and Germany, all four of which had committed themselves to massive deregulation by 1986;
2 (around 1988 to 1992) Britain and some heavily cabled nations such as the Netherlands and Belgium;
3 (in the early 1990s) most of the smaller nations of Scandinavia and the Mediterranean, including Sweden, Greece, Portugal, and Spain;
4 a number of newly independent and ex-communist nations in Eastern and East-Central Europe.

The restructuring of European broadcasting has not only brought about an increase in the number of private channels in operation, it has also changed the relationship between the private and the public broadcasting sector. Where once only a few channels existed, there are now many – and many more to come. Although the processes of liberalization and the impact of those change has varied from country to country (Papathanassopoulos, 2002), the effects are now being felt across Europe, with new commercial players and forces coming into play. This represents the 'triumph of the liberal model' (Hallin and Mancini, 2004: 251) that prevails in its purest form in North America, since its 'structures, practices and values [have displaced], to a substantial degree, those of the other media systems'. To this we can add that the former communist nations have also become more like their Western counterparts, absorbing elements of commercialism, both good and bad. As Vidal-Hall notes:

> As local capital ran short, the entry of many of the major western European media corporations, dominantly German, Swiss and Austrian, into CEE [former communist bloc countries] was warmly welcomed. It brought huge and much needed injections of cash plus technical and professional innovation. In the absence of adequate legislation, media concentration, vertical and horizontal, proliferated to the point of saturation in some countries. As some of the incoming corporations extended ownership into more than one country, cross border concentration also became an issue. . . .
>
> As the old state media assets were sold off, local media oligarchs were born and any separation of powers was lost in the determination by politicians to retain control by other means: the multiple roles of 'bizniss', politics and the media frequently ended up in the same hands; where the market or politics collided with attempts to build a democratic media akin to a 'fourth estate' watchdog on power, the latter deferred. (2009: 2–4)

Indeed, a new media landscape has emerged in the former Eastern bloc, the 'new democracies', which, as with the rest of the society and economy, was modelled upon the Euro-American system. Splichal (1994: 145–6), for example, has referred to the 'Italianization' of the Eastern European media

Table 2.1 Typology of national broadcasting systems in Western Europe

System	1980	1990	1997	2007
Public monopoly	Belgium Bulgaria Czech Republic Denmark Hungary Latvia Norway Poland Slovenia Sweden Romania Russia			
Public monopoly/ mixed revenue	Austria Finland France Germany Greece Iceland Netherlands Portugal Switzerland Turkey	Austria Denmark Iceland Ireland Netherlands Portugal Switzerland	Austria Ireland Switzerland	
Private monopoly/ advertising only	Luxembourg	Luxembourg	Luxembourg	Luxembourg
Dual system (public service; commercial broadcasters)	Italy (1976) UK (1954)	Belgium (1988) Finland (1991) France (1986) Germany (1984) Greece (1989) Italy Latvia (1990) Netherlands (1989) Norway (1991) Portugal (1992) Spain (1982) Slovenia (1991)	Belgium (1994) Bulgaria Czech Republic (1992) Denmark (1997) Finland France Germany Greece Hungary (1997) Italy Latvia Netherlands Norway	Austria (2001) Belgium Bulgaria Czech Republic Denmark Finland France Germany Greece Ireland (1998) Italy Latvia Netherlands Norway Poland Portugal Spain Slovenia

Table 2.1 (*continued*)

System	1980	1990	1997	2007
Dual system (public service; commercial broadcasters)		Sweden (1988) Romania (1989) UK	Poland (1992) Portugal Spain Slovenia Sweden Turkey (1993) Romania Russia (1993) UK	Sweden Switzerland (1999) Turkey Romania Russia UK

Note: The year of the liberalization of the TV system in individual countries is given in parentheses.

Source: Adapted from Siune and Hultén (1998: 27), Papathanassopoulos (2002: 15), and Hardy (2008: 58).

– namely, the politicization of the media and the integration of media and political elites – a form which has similarities to the Mediterranean model (see below, and also Sukosd, 2000; Iordanova, 1995).

Some have argued, though, that the differences across European national media systems 'are clearly diminishing' (Hallin and Mancini, 2004: 294) and that, even in the Eastern European countries, 'the media have become less dependent on political parties, politicians, and political systems for their finances, for their legitimacy, and for their primary and exclusive news sources' (Gross, 2003: 80). Homogenization of media systems, in this respect, is the outcome of a number of factors, including the influence of the USA, technological innovation and the forces 'that are essentially internal to European society, such as modernization, secularization and commercialization, though certainly linked to the process of globalization' (Hallin and Mancini, 2004: 294).

The argument for a degree of homogenization emphasizes the similarities – in the commercial nature of broadcasting systems – across European media systems, but there are still important differences that need to be taken into account in any discussion of 'the media in Europe'. According to Tunstall (2008: 247–83), the media systems of the twenty-seven EU member states can be divided into three categories, which principally take into account the size of the media market and population size – factors which create their own dynamics internally and externally.

- The first consists of the big five countries (with populations averaging 60 million), France, Germany, Italy, Spain and the UK, where public broadcasting institutions remain strong and important. Daily newspaper sales, at least in the recent past, have been quite substantial in both the provincial and the national market, and these countries have important magazine and book industries.

- The second consists of twelve countries with populations between 16 million (the Netherlands) and 400,000 (Malta). They are, in most cases, strongly influenced by their much larger neighbours, though there is a heavier consolidation of the media.
- The third consists of nine former communist countries (Bulgaria, Romania, Estonia, Latvia, Lithuania, Hungary, the Czech Republic, Slovakia and Slovenia) with average populations of 5 million. Poland, with a much larger population (38.5 million), is, in effect, striving to join the first team. In terms of advertising expenditure, these countries have been growing steadily for more than a decade, a fact that explains why channels emerge all over the region and why major Western European companies develop enterprises and buy media assets there. One could also add Russia, which presents similar trends (Vartanova, 2002), though some argue that it follows its own system (Becker, 2004). After the collapse of the communist system in 1989, most of these countries experienced rapid development of their outlets, the entry of foreign owners and the consolidation of their media systems into the hands of a new ruling class (Gross, 2004; Vidal-Hall, 2009).

These three categories provide a useful framework for exploring media systems and differences. Interestingly, they also set out a challenge for us: where would we place countries that are seeking to join the EU, such as Ukraine, where there have been recent concerns about the treatment of journalists and issues of pluralism in the media (Julliard and Vidal, 2010), or Turkey, which has been criticized for its human rights record? An important consideration, however, is that the framework incorporates countries from the former communist bloc as part of the overall structure: these countries represent a significant addition to the 'core' of the EU and often bring with them media systems that are very different from those more common in Western Europe.

These sorts of challenges can also be raised in the context of a different framework, this time from Hallin and Mancini's (2004) seminal book on media systems. This work, which seeks to move beyond simplistic comparisons of media systems of the 'social responsibility' versus 'communist' variety, is built around four variables that, the authors argue, produce three models of media systems: polarized, liberal and democratic corporate. Unlike the categorization of media systems, which takes into account such things as the size of the population and the media market, Hallin and Mancini's models seek to incorporate historical trends – for example, when the mass press developed – alongside considerations such as relations between media and the state. While these models have been criticized for being concerned less with culture and entertainment aspects of media structures (Hardy, 2008: 20), they have nonetheless been widely referenced. The four variables that underpin the models are:

- the development of media markets, and particularly the mass circulation press;
- political parallelism – i.e. the degree and nature of the links between the media and political parties;
- the development of journalistic professionalism;
- journalistic autonomy and the role of the state, including with respect to policy and regulation. (Hallin and Mancini, 2004: 21)

The first model, the *polarized pluralist model or Mediterranean model*, in which the media are integrated into politics and the state, has a strong role. The media systems of Spain, Italy, France, Greece and Portugal fit into this model, though one could also probably add Turkey, Malta and Cyprus (Papathanassopoulos, 2007). According to Hallin and Mancini (2004: 89), the mass media in these countries were intimately involved in the political conflicts that mark the history of this region, and there is a strong tradition of regarding them as means of ideological expression and political mobilization. The media also share some major characteristics: low levels of newspaper circulation, a tradition of advocacy reporting, *instrumentalization* of privately owned media, politicization of public broadcasting and broadcast regulation, and limited development of journalism as an autonomous profession (Hallin and Papathanassopoulos, 2000).

The second model, the *liberal model*, is the one in which market mechanisms predominate. It is characterized by the early development of press freedom and the mass-circulation press. As Hallin and Mancini (2004:75) note: 'commercial newspapers dominate, political parallelism is low and internal pluralism predominates'. There is a strong professionalization of journalism, although journalistic autonomy is more likely to be limited by commercial pressures than by political interference. The countries in Europe which best represent this model are Britain and Ireland. Moreover, although the role of the state is limited, public broadcasting and the regulation of commercial channels has traditionally been very strong.

The third model is the *democratic corporate model*, in which commercial media and politicized media coexist and the state plays an important role. The Scandinavian countries, Germany, Austria and Switzerland, as well as Belgium and the Netherlands, represent this model. According to Hallin and Mancini (2004: 67–8), the features of the democratic corporatist media system are high newspaper circulation and the early development of a mass-circulation press; a tradition of a strong party press, thus providing external pluralism (especially in the national press) and substantial autonomy in political issues; strong professionalism and institutionalized self-regulation; and strong state intervention at a structural level, press subsidies, and strong public service broadcasting

In most of the above countries one finds a moderate form of pluralism, which in practice means a high level of political stability based on strong parties with long traditions and a diverse media (Hallin and Mancini, 2004: 68). At the same time they are, by and large, 'strong welfare states', as the state traditionally played a strong role in the economy. Moreover, the broadcast media in particular are to a certain extent regarded as social institutions 'for which the state has responsibility, and press freedom coexists with relatively strong support for and regulation of media' (ibid.: 74). It is no coincidence, therefore, that in these countries public broadcasters have a strong presence. As Hallin and Mancini point out , 'broadcasting has been treated as part of the *res publica*, as an institution whose influence on society is too great to be left under the control of private interests' (ibid.: 164).

Yet, by and large, all the broadcast systems that have been so central to Western European countries continue to face challenges from a number of different sources. While in the past they may have been regarded as part of the infrastructure of informed democratic polities, untouchable and permanent, they have long ceased to be the only organizations of broadcasting that matter. Even the BBC, the ideal type, was confronted by commercial rivals (ITV, Channel 4) from the mid-1950s onwards, and commercial rivals that became an important part of the broadcasting landscape. As these others provided news, sport and entertainment, the position of the public broadcasters began to erode, as they often lost their share of the audience, and their sole access to sources of public funding could be questioned.

Challenges to once dominant public broadcasters have thus come from a variety of directions but have been principally about funding – Should they continue to have state aid? Should commercial broadcasters meeting regulatory and civic requirements also share state funding? Is such funding 'unfair'? – with related concerns about the consequences of limiting public broadcasters' funds on their ability to buy in, or produce, high-quality programming. Following Hallin and Mancini (2004), then, the commercialization of the media brought about by deregulatory activity has weakened public broadcasters, more so as the audience share of the commercial broadcasters has increased and the audience as a whole has fragmented. However, as Hardy observes, their analysis is in line with critical scholarship . . . which examined the erosion of PSB [public service broadcasters] and increasing marketization. In addition, changes in technology and modes of consumption and payment for content challenge the financial arrangements and identifications on which PSB has traditionally depended. Yet the analysis needs stronger qualification than Hallin and Mancini offer. In particular, it overestimates the weakening of PSB institutions and institutional support for public media. (2008: 233)

These are points which fit in with our analysis of the EU's position with respect to public broadcasting systems in general. Clearly, no two countries are identical and so different media systems face different problems, and it would be unwise to suggest that some common pattern prevails. Nevertheless, and despite differences, the attempt to create a European governmental structure through the EU *is forcing individual countries to come to terms with European regulatory frameworks.* So there are, as we shall see in chapter 4, attempts to bring European countries closer together by harmonizing the rules that operate in different contexts, and by ensuring that a common regulatory framework exists so that trade, including the trade in television, is carried out unencumbered by unnecessary national rules and regulations. What is interesting about this is that it creates a tension between trends leading to greater diversity and trends leading to greater unity. Indeed, both exist side by side, albeit at different levels, so that a common regulatory framework may be in place yet countries act independently and separately. More significantly, perhaps, while that common framework may exist or come into existence at the level of trade, for example, it does not necessarily extend to such matters as diversity or indeed the philosophies that underpin the operation of media. Public broadcasters (and print media) may thus coexist and be regulated at the EU level in similar ways but may operate in very different ways given the sorts of considerations – professionalism, autonomy, parallelism – to which Hallin and Mancini (2004) have drawn attention.

In spite of EU activity, therefore, differences between media and between the media of different countries present a mosaic: newspapers remain within their geographical and political boundaries, as does a considerable amount of terrestrial television. By contrast, satellite TV can cross geographical and political boundaries but in practice it faces linguistic and cultural barriers. Yet most countries in the EU import heavily from the USA. Consequently, any cross-border alliances that can be found are alliances where those obstacles – language, geographic boundaries, cultures, etc. – can easily be overcome (and where there are sound economic reasons for attempting to do so). It is on such grounds, therefore, that the EU seeks to operate, though these may turn out to be those that are of least importance and least objectionable rather than those to which the EU, in theory, aspires.

The next sections explore, separately, the changes impacting on the broadcast and print media.

The challenges to public broadcasting systems

If Europe remains distinct from the other media systems around the world, especially from the USA, it is due to the existence and operation of the public service broadcasters. In the last two decades, public broadcasters have faced the erosion of both their viewing share and their revenue. Although a number of European public broadcasters have responded to the challenge from commercial broadcasters, in general, their futures are dependent on secure and appropriate funding mechanisms for their continued operation.

With a few exceptions, European public broadcasters used to have two main sources of revenue: the licence fee and advertising. Although, in the past, there have been many objections to these two sources of funding being made available to public broadcasters, it is only since the early 1990s that private broadcasters have made complaints to the European Court of Justice (Papathanassopoulos, 2001; Harrison and Woods, 2007). In March 2004, the leading private media associations, the Association of Commercial Television (ACT), Association Européenne des Radios (AER) and the European Publishers Council (EPC), released a White Paper, *Safeguarding the Future of the European Audiovisual Market* (2004), in which they argued that years of overfunding and under-regulation of public broadcasters have undermined the competitiveness of the television industry as well as adversely affecting multi-channel television, TV programme production, radio broadcasting, internet content and the press. They also accused the European Commission of taking over ten years to deal with some of the complaints against the public broadcasting funding system. This delay, compounded by inadequate financial transparency in publicly funded broadcasting and the failure of EU member states properly to define the remit of publicly funded broadcasters in receipt of state aid, resulted – in the view of the private sector – in 'an unprecedented level of market distortion'. They also called on the EU member states to initiate the process of migration to a single funded model of public broadcasters and to implement correctly and in an impartial manner the existing competition as provisioned by the EU Treaty, as has been applied to other sectors with a significant public sector element (see also chapter 4).

Some public broadcasting systems, though, face other internal problems that create different challenges. In Europe, only Spain and Portugal were funded mainly by advertising and to a lesser extent by public subsidies.

However, in recent years, the licence fee has been replaced by public funding in the Netherlands (in 2000), the Flemish community of Belgium (2000) and Hungary (2002). But in the cases of Portugal and Spain the respective public broadcasters have faced a financial crisis brought about by the progressive loss of their market share and the increased costs of production and acquisition of TV products, at the same time as their revenues from advertising have decreased and the public state subsidy has proved inadequate. To compound matters, the private broadcasters also complained to the European Commission and the European Court of Justice that they were losing advertising revenue because the public broadcasters were lowering their rates so as to attract advertising (Papathanassopoulos, 2002).

Although the above examples derive from different cases, they can be seen as an indication that the challenge to the public broadcasters can come from many quarters and can be fought out in many countries. As with Spain and Portugal, the Netherlands has been affected by changes to its core funding scheme for public broadcasters, with consequences. Since the replacement of the licence fee by a levy on income tax, the budget of the Dutch public broadcaster NOS has been fixed by law at the 1998 level, with yearly indexing. But since then there have been complaints against various aspects of the financing regime for the Dutch public service broadcasters from several commercial broadcasters and other media undertakings. The European Commission also received these complaints, which raised concerns about the lack of a precise definition of the public service task, its entrustment, and the proportionality of the financing, including the financing of online activities. After a preliminary investigation, the Commission expressed concerns on a number of points, notably the proportionality of the financing, as regards both adequate mechanisms to prevent overcompensation for public service activities and the respect of market principles. The Dutch government passed a new media law in 2008 and a year later submitted to the European Commission commitments to amend the new financing regime so as to ensure its compliance with the state aid rules. Among its commitments to the EU, the Dutch government promised to limit the compensation of public service broadcasters to ensure that funding does not exceed what is necessary to fulfil the public service tasks. In January 2010, the European Commission approved the new financing regime of NOS (Europa, 2010).

Even in the UK, the location of one of the most successful public broadcasters in Europe, there is an ongoing debate about whether the BBC should be the sole beneficiary of the licence fee or whether a general fund should be created – possibly out of the licence fee. This would be a 'contestable fund', allowing producers to bid for resources to make public service programmes (Cox, 2004).

The underlying point of these examples is that what the public broadcasters do and how they do it is inextricably linked to their sources and systems of funding. Tinkering with the funding system, though, risks tinkering with the public broadcasting system itself. Furthermore, once the licence fee system is either abolished or replaced, or some limitations are imposed upon it, it is extremely difficult to reinstate it. But if the level of the licence fee stays unchanged and the costs of production and broadcasting rights inexorably rise as competition intensifies (Molsky, 1999), public broadcasters may either have to cut some of their organizational expenses or decrease their production costs (with obvious consequences for 'quality') (Iosifidis, 2007b). For policy-makers at all levels, then, the challenge is whether or not – and how, if at all – to maintain the presence of the public broadcasters in the twenty-first century.

The financial dimension of the problems faced by public broadcasters cannot be de-linked from the changes now taking place in the digital media landscape. In the past, public broadcasters may have had to face competition from a small number of rivals, but today their number has increased, and channels have proliferated terrestrially, digitally and on the web. These changes will further fragment the audience, thus both undermining public broadcasters' legitimacy and claim to the full licence fee and decreasing advertising revenue – if they remain unchallenged, that is. The introduction of digital television also means higher costs in the short and medium term as public broadcasters try to upgrade their infrastructures and purchase new equipment, buy or produce more competitive and thus more expensive programming, and launch new channels – all this at a time when their revenues are essentially stagnant.

Questions about the nature and importance of public broadcasters cannot be easily answered, but nor can they be ignored. Maintaining them in robust health means actively supporting them and not eroding them financially or in any other way; to do so, though, requires political and regulatory will, as well as an ability to withstand criticism of favouritism from private broadcasters (see chapter 4). How best to maintain a healthy public broadcasting sector and a competitive and adventurous private one is the challenge for the twenty-first century.

The consolidation of the media industry

The liberalization of the rules governing the television sector has led to the creation of larger and fewer dominant groups. The trend towards a complex form of cooperation between media and telecommunications groups in Europe has long raised fears of excessive concentration of ownership (Murdock and Golding, 1999). Mergers, acquisitions and common shareholding, led in many instances by telecommunications groups, have created a web of common interests across the European media, though even here the pattern is not uniform. Although the EU has failed to harmonize ownership regulations, its interest in this area indicates a concern with the economic forces behind media and the risk that these may pose for diversity and pluralism. But, as Peter Humphreys also notes, 'there is every sign that oligopolistic developments in the mainstream European industry are the price to be paid for the sector's growth and for the development of new technologies' (1996: 304). The same may also be true in respect of consolidation of industries in order to meet global challenges (see Siune, 1998: 24).

In the digital era, the growth of vertical integration strategies can be seen as 'defensive moments in the face of uncertainty and convulsions brought about by digital networks and their challenge to the power distribution' (Bustamante, 2004: 813). But the rationale behind such integration is clear: the advantage of owning a distribution system means that a service provider will have a secure outlet for programmes/content and/or TV channels. This allows them to dominate the small and medium companies, 'both established and new, over the mass and niche markets both global and local' (ibid.).

This coupling of media giants, characterized by 'a strong sense of continuity from the analogue era' (Iosifidis et al., 2005: 3), will certainly cause new problems in terms of media ownership, concentration, media diversity and quality (Barnett, 2004). At the same time, the economic recession of the last few years and the downturn in advertising may lead to further consolidation; companies such as RTL have already developed a pan-European strategy, usually launched in league with local partners – RTL in Germany, M6 in France, Antenna 3 TV in Spain, Alpha TV in Greece, RTL4 in the Netherlands and RTL Klub in Hungary. The failures or bankruptcies in the digital TV sector have affected competition in the pay-TV services, leading to consolidation and vertical integration. As IDATE observed, 'in most European countries, there are now between two and four major players on each market; whereas five years ago there could have been anywhere up to a hundred' (IDATE, 2003). If issues of pluralism and diversity are seen to be critical for democratic polities (Golding, 2000; Schiller, 2000), then these trends, at the same time as they raise issues about the production and the distribution of information and communication goods and services, do need to be confronted at a European level.

Yet the last two decades have also shown that it is extremely difficult for the EU to develop a coherent policy on mergers and concentration of activity, as measurements of market strength are extremely problematic (see also chapter 4). Large diversified conglomerates cannot easily be classified under any single category (George, 2007; Garcia and Surles, 2007). For example, processes of convergence and digitalization have given rise to telecommunications companies that can provide television, telephony and internet access – the so-called triple play option. They can thus enter the audiovisual field and begin to play a powerful role in the communications sector. The main European companies, such as Vivendi, Kirch or BSkyB, are to a larger or lesser extent controlled by US interests, and over 90 per cent of the fifty largest European media companies are located in just seven member states – France, Germany, Italy, Luxembourg, the Netherlands, Spain and the UK (Harcourt, 2008: 13–14). RTL, which is owned by Bertelsmann, has interests in ten European countries. The merger of the German ProSiebenSat.1 TV station with the formerly Scandinavian SBS Group in 2007 led to the formation of a second Europe-wide TV alliance, which operates in thirteen countries across Europe.

Such consolidation has not necessarily been seen negatively by the EU, and there is a view that, in practice, it has looked favourably at mergers and acquisitions on a European rather than on a national level (see chapter 4).

The foundation of new regulatory bodies

With the deregulation of the broadcast media in the 1980s and the expansion of the sector as a whole – including the emerging alliances with the telecommunications sector – older forms of regulation were superseded by newer ones – ones supposedly better able to deal with the new broadcast environment. In many cases *new regulatory bodies* were established (to license new, mainly commercial broadcasters) alongside new and more formalized procedures for overseeing their operations (see table 2.2). The emergence of such regulatory bodies, almost non-existent in Europe before the 1980s, is often seen as the outcome of 'regulatory capitalism' and is grounded in the delegation of regulatory competencies to authorities that are partly independent from direct political control (Gilardi, 2005). Nonetheless, such bodies can also lead to political uncertainty if a government loses power, say, and they fitted in well with the process of Europeanization, which favoured the creation of independent regulators.

In practice, though, one can sometimes find a multitude of regulators even within one media sector. Broadcasting regulation usually encompasses the power to license broadcasters, to monitor whether broadcasters are fulfilling their legal obligations, and to impose sanctions if they fail to carry out those

Table 2.2 Broadcasting regulatory authorities in selected European countries

Country	Regulatory authority	Supervision of private broadcasters	Supervision of public broadcasters
Austria	Kommunikationsbehörde (Communications Authority)	✓	
Belgium	Vlaamse Regulator voor de Media (Flemish Regulator for the Media)	✓	✓
Belgium	Conseil Supérieur de l'Audiovisuel de la Communauté Française	✓	✓
Bulgaria	СЪВЕТЪТ ЗА ЕЛЕКТРОННИ МЕДИИ (Council for Electronic Media)	✓	✓
Cyprus	Arxi Radiotileorasis Kyprou (Cyprus Radio-Television Authority)	✓	✓
Czech Rep	Rada pro rozhlasové a televizní vysílání (Council for Radio and TV)	✓	✓
Denmark	Radio and Television Board, c/o Media Secretariat	✓	
Estonia	Eesti Rahvusringhääling (Estonian Broadcasting Council)	✓	✓
Finland	Viestintävirasto (Finnish Communications Regulatory Authority)	✓	✓
France	Conseil Supérieur de l'Audiovisuel	✓	✓
Germany	Direktorenkonferenz der Landesmedienanstalten	✓	
Greece	Ethniko Symvoylio Radiotileorasis (National Broadcasting Council)	✓	✓
Hungary	Nemzeti Média- és Hírközlési Hatóság (National Media and Communications Authority)	✓	
Ireland	Broadcasting Commission of Ireland	✓	
Italy	Autorità per le garanzie nelle comunicazioni (Authority for the Supervision of Communication)	✓	✓
Lithuania	Lietuvos radijo ir televizijos komisija (Radio and Television Commission)	✓	✓
Netherlands	Commissariaat voor de Media (Commission for the Media)	✓	✓
Norway	Medietilsynet (Media Authority)	✓	✓
Poland	Krajowa Radę Radiofonii i Telewizji (National Broadcasting Council)	✓	✓
Portugal	Autoridade Nacional de Comunicações (National Authority of Communications)	✓	
Slovenia	Agencija za pošto in elektronske komunikacije (Communications Council)	✓	✓
Spain	Consejo Audiovisual de Navarra (CoAN)	✓	✓
	Conseil de la comunicació audiovisual de Catalunya		✓

Table 2.2 (*continued*)

Country	Regulatory authority	Supervision of private broadcasters	Supervision of public broadcasters
Spain	Comisión del Mercado de las Telecomunicaciones – CMT	✓	
Sweden	Myndigheten för radio och TV (Swedish Broadcasting Authority)	✓	✓
United Kingdom	Office of Communications – Ofcom	✓	

Source: Data based on European Platform of Regulatory Authorities (www.epra.org).

obligations. To these traditional functions, one needs to add those of organizing and coordinating the broadcasting landscape. Since 1998 regulatory authorities have started cooperating in order to coordinate their approaches and so avoid divergent policies. The function, structure and jurisdiction of such authorities vary, and in most countries there are separate regulatory bodies for supervising broadcasting and telecommunications.

We should note, however, that regulatory authorities in the media and communication sector are a relatively recent institutional innovation in Europe, with the exception of Britain. Although one finds the model of the regulatory authority much earlier in the USA, in the shape of the Federal Communication Commission, Europeans until recently have adopted the British way which separates broadcasting from telecommunications. It is an irony, therefore, that the British have since adopted the US model – though Ofcom does not fully regulate the BBC!

Most European governments have chosen to form a broadcasting authority along the lines of the old British Independent Broadcasting Authority, but without the same powers. In effect, such regulatory bodies act as a buffer between the partisan interests of the government of the day and the broadcasting companies. In most cases, such authorities have been used to provide an illusion of liberalization by permitting politicians to show their distance from the media, yet exercising some control by appointing the members of their boards.

The newspaper sector

The variables to which Hallin and Mancini (2004) drew attention, in particular those relating to the early development of the mass press, political parallelism and journalistic autonomy and professionalism, are in the background of any discussion of the press in Europe. Countries have different histories – political, social, etc. – and thus the patterns of press development are quite varied. If we look at the overall structure of the press, a number of differences become apparent, in the past as in the present.

In general terms, newspapers remain a largely national medium. This can be accounted for by referring to language but also to differences in news agenda (see chapter 8, for example, re coverage of Europe). But there are other disparities.

- The consumption of newspapers in Southern Europe (Greece, Spain, and Italy), for example, is much lower than that in Northern Europe (Norway, Finland, and Sweden);
- Whereas Britain has a strong national press, in France, for example, it is a regional paper that sells more copies than any of the best-known French dailies. In Germany, the biggest newspapers are regional, based in Frankfurt, Munich and Hamburg (Sidel and McMane, 1995). However, it seems, as Gustafsson and Weibull note, that 'the countries with a high newspaper penetration all have the same kind of newspaper structure, with a strong local press, besides a fairly strong national press' (cited in Host, 1999).
- Most countries have a preference for morning dailies. Greece seems to be an exception, since most of its leading newspapers are evening dailies.
- In some countries, the Sunday press is very popular (Britain, Sweden, Greece), with many titles and colour supplements, while in some others it is virtually non-existent (Germany, France);
- In some countries the tabloid 'sensationalist' press is very popular (Britain, Germany, Norway) but in others it is much less so (France, Greece). The British *Sun* and the German *Bild Zeitung* have the highest circulations.
- In some countries the tabloid press is the 'yellow' or 'sensationalist' press, whereas the broadsheets are seen as 'respectable'. Yet in others the tabloid press is associated with the physical size of a newspaper rather than the content, and some of these can present very serious journalism (Spain, Italy, and Greece). None would consider *Ta Nea* (Greece), *El Pais* (Spain) and *La Repubblica* (Italy) as sensational newspapers because of their tabloid format.
- As Humphreys notes, 'a related factor for the comparative strength of the Northern European press industries and the weakness of the Southern press has been the share of advertising expenditure received by the press' (1996: 36). In fact, the lion's share of media advertising in the Northern European countries has tended to be reserved for the press.
- Europe has a large number of strong and established newspaper

publishers. Newspaper groups tend to operate solely in their domestic market, although a few have interests in several countries.

Within the European Union, Germany, France and Britain remain the strongest markets for newspapers. Between them they supply 60 per cent of Western Europe's daily sales, 71 per cent of its paid-for weeklies and 78 per cent of its free papers. But all the signs of market saturation and long-term decline are in evidence. Another sign of difficulties for the press is its gradually declining share of total media advertising expenditure, as television and local free newspapers increase in importance. Despite this trend, and though changing rapidly in an increasingly competitive environment, the press's share of advertising expenditure is still significant.

In the last two decades the newspaper markets in the European Union have suffered in terms of sales, titles and readers (see also chapter 3). Moreover, the shift of advertising revenue away from newspapers has created an urgent desire to review the 'old' model of revenue streams – i.e. sales and advertising. With both in decline, newer ways are being tested, including news organizations delivering news online, with or without a pay wall. The challenge is how to develop a new business model that will ensure that organizations can continue to raise revenues from (declining) sales of newspapers and from advertisers who are finding new ways to reach diverse audiences. The most urgent problem, though, is how to find ways of getting audiences to pay for the news product, especially as it has been traditionally collected within news organizations, dependent on expensive printing presses for newspaper production and employing full-time professional journalists.

Summary

European television used to be dominated by public broadcasters operating under strict national regulation, most of them being funded by a licence fee and limited advertising. Since the 1980s there has been a dual system, consisting of a strong private sector, exclusively funded by advertising in its various forms, such as conventional commercials, sponsoring and bartering, and a public sector, funded mainly by a licence fee and only to a lesser extent by advertising. By and large, this 'dual television system', largely recognized as a 'distinctive feature of the broadcasting landscape in Europe' and an integral part of the European model of society (CEC, 1998b: 37), seems to be challenged. This is on account of new developments in market forces as well as the development and application of new technologies, such as digital television. TV channels are now able to charge their viewers/customers on an individual basis, while the fragmentation of the TV market poses new problems for the funding of the generalist private channels. The latter developments also question the dual funding of public broadcasters, who at the same time have to face new competition from digital operators.

However, these are not new issues. In effect, they have been refocused by a number of contemporary trends (Sinclair, 2004: 1). At the beginning of the twenty-first century, European television faces a *déjà vu* situation – intense competition, the development and application of new technologies, further consolidation in the structure of ownership (Kelly et al., 2004: 2–3; Iosifidis et al., 2005: 1) – and at the same time it witnesses a process of Europeanization, as we shall discuss in chapter 4. These 'old' trends seem to be the main issues that will likely affect the structure of the European television industry, except that the media structures and systems are far more complex and intertwined than they used to be: digital and analogue, print and broadcasting, free and paid-for, web-based and free-to-air, professionally produced or audience generated, and so on.

The new developments in the European media field, such as digital television and online media, will become a reality for the simple reason that they are heavily influenced by the needs of the European industry, financial concerns and intense marketing. These trends have to be seen within the wider framework of the 'information society' in the EU, and the digitalization of communications seems to be part and parcel of a developing process leading to the 'information society'. It grants dominant status to business and technological change and it pulls together divergent systems of the communications sector. It operates alongside, and gains from, the advent of new global competition, which takes place on both the international and the local level. As in the past, this industrial need has been associated with the emergence of neo-liberal ideologies advocating the restructuring and modernization of the economy and, in effect, the marketization of the public communication sector (Murdock and Golding, 1999; Murdock, 2000), while consumer demand has been taken for granted. These are the issues we are going to address in the next chapters.

3   The New Media in Europe

The history of communication is, in many ways, a history of 'older' media being superseded by 'new' media, with each such occurrence being heralded as a revolution. The expansion of television in the 1980s – following the deregulatory 'turn' in Europe – was also a revolution in television, as cable and satellite services multiplied endlessly. Since then, television has continued to dominate most of our lives, but it has now been overtaken by a revolution in the ways in which programmes are made, stored, transmitted and received. This is the 'digital revolution', a revolution that is constituted by the internet – a 'new' technology per se – but that, in reality, is the outcome of a process of digitalization and convergence of all aspects of the communications sector. As Denis McQuail (2005: 137) has noted, the 'most fundamental aspect of the information communication technology is probably the fact of digitalization, by which all texts . . . can be reduced to a binary code and can share the same process of production, distribution and storage' and 'convergence between the existing media forms in terms of their organization, distribution, reception and regulation'. If convergence 'is understood as the technologically-driven fusing of the content (that is, media), computing (information technology) and com-munications (telecoms and broadcast distribution) industries', then it is digi-talization, rather than the internet, that truly enables it (Kung et al., 2008: 4).

Whether it is music or television programmes, telephony or text, the avail-ability of these – and more – in a digital format means that they can all be delivered and consumed in a variety of ways that do away with previously demarcated technologies. Convergence will therefore force all media sec-tors, if they wish to survive this latest of revolutions, 'to review their busi-ness models, technology choices and organization' (McQueen, 2007). Each sector, though, will face different sets of issues. There may be similar concerns but the ways in which the problems will be resolved will be different. But at heart is a situation whereby audiences/consumers can often obtain content – listen or make music, watch television programmes and films, make and get news – for free because, in this digitalized and converged world, content is available through so many different and uncontrolled ways.

As this chapter will argue, online services will drive the development of new (media) markets, since the whole sector is in transition. In this sense, new media refers to all new forms of communication (texts, images, audio and visual) combined in different ways (fixed, mobile, wireless). At an operational level, as Pavlik and Powel observe, 'new media include a variety of technologies that perform the following five functions: (1) information gathering, searching, sorting, and communicating; (2) production, editing, and design; (3) storage, representation, and retrieval; (4) distribution; and (5) access, design, and display' (2003: 225). These functions are frequently intertwined and integrated into single technical devices. This means that the scope of the new media extends beyond the TV set and includes PC, internet, PDAs and other internet devices as well as mobile phones. As Rob Frieden notes:

> Convergence as relates to content means that consumers can expect anytime, anywhere and any device access to preferred content. That means carriers, equipment manufacturers and content providers will have to work cooperatively to offer platforms, where users can access the same content via different devices, e.g., the cellphone, television set, personal assistant and personal computer. (2007: 82)

In spite of these changes, some of which, such as electronic book readers, are only now moving into the marketplace, the TV set and screen continue to dominate the communications landscape. Even here, though, there have been significant changes – for example, from analogue to digital to high definition – and in plans to produce a 'television monitor' that will be equipped to deal with traditional 'television' and such things as emails, games and the web. Given the continuing importance of television as traditionally understood but also in its promised guise, this chapter will seek to explore developments across Europe and pay particular attention to the ways in which the EU has sought to exploit this sector as part of its larger commitment to establishing both an industrial policy and a communications policy.

The new media and European industrial policy

Although 'there is no clear definition of industrial policy', Meyer-Stamer goes on to argue that 'almost any policy has some impact on industry and thus an industrial-policy component' (1996: 471). And, in the context of discussions about the EU, it is clear that it has been consistently engaged in actions that are intended to reshape and develop a range of sectors so as to make them globally competitive. This has certainly been the case in respect of the communications industry, where we can trace EU, formerly EC, involvement from the 1980s onwards (see Meyer-Stamer, 1996; Korres, 2007).

Since the 1980s, the importance of the new media to the communications industry and to the European economy has been widely recognized.

With the emergence of the idea of the information society and the knowledge economy, as well as the necessity of the European economies to remain competitive in the global market, the EU has increased its efforts to reshape the industry – more so, as the new media are often considered to be engines of growth. As the *Digital Britain* report notes, 'The communications sector underpins everything we do as an economy and society, to a degree few could have imagined even a quarter of a century ago' (DCMS and DBIS, 2009: 7).

The significance of the communications sector for the EU can be easily understood when looking at the amount of 'hardware' that it exports and imports. Figures for 2005 place it as the leading trader in high-tech products in the world, with €198 billion in exports and €230 billion in imports. While other countries, such as Japan, exported more and imported less, the significance of these figures lies in the extent of production and consumption that it signifies (Eurostat, 2007). But the 'hardware' dimension is only one aspect of the communications industry. In conceptualizations of the information and knowledge society, growth is understood as being driven by services, software, telecommunications and content rather than by industries with large investments in production facilities, plant and equipment, and other tangible assets. Here also, the levels of production and consumption are indicative of the importance of this sector: Ofcom (2006, 2007) estimated that, in 2005, the global communications market generated revenues of around £840 billion, equating to around £129 for each person on the planet. Other figures for the same year suggest that, at the EU-27 level, the telecom services sector provided jobs for 1.2 million people and generated €190 billion in value added; the production value of telecom equipment exceeded €17 billion (Vekeman, 2008); information and communication technologies (ICT) use accounts for 26 per cent of research efforts, 20 per cent of business investment and almost 50 per cent of all productivity growth (CEC, 2008a); and so on. Such figures emphasize the size and potential of the market and the fact that the communications sector forms an important part of most economies in the developed world. They also go some way towards justifying the EU's involvement in this sector and its desire to create the most competitive and dynamic knowledge-driven economy, as foreseen by the Lisbon Treaty. In the early phase of its involvement, in the 1990s, the EU sought to achieve its goals through policies of liberalization of telecommunications and information technologies; more recently, the focus has been on social aspects of information society developments (Servaes, 2000: 434), although, in practice, the boundaries between types of policy are often blurred (Pitelis, 2007: 366).

The EU continues to alert member states to the importance of this sector and to the dangers of lagging behind competitor countries or regions. For example, in a recent communication the Commission pointed out to the

European Council that, although 'productivity growth reached 1.5% in 2006, compared to an annual growth rate of 1.2% between 2000 and 2005 . . . Europe is still lagging behind other leading economies both in investment in information and communication technologies (ICT) and in terms of their use to enhance productivity' (CEC, 2007b: 6). In other words, the new media are an essential part of European economies, and they need substantial investment – in broadband and in telecommunications – if they are to gain a comparative advantage in the global market. In these processes, innovation – in hardware and in software – is often the key to expansion and competitive advantage, and every 'sector and activity needs to be constantly initiating, refining and improving its products, services and processes. The conditions to stimulate vigorous innovation have to be in place' (CEC, 2008a: 2). The danger is that, as the European Commission has warned, 'the gap between the EU's efforts and those of its main competitors is undermining its future ability to lead information society innovations' (CEC, 2008a). This is one of the reasons why the European Commission believes that the roll-out and development of high-speed broadband internet is so significant, as the potential for growth is huge (Reding, 2009).

The fact is that the EU has the world's largest developed consumer market and 100 million broadband internet connections and is thus well placed to reap the economic benefits of ICT (CEC, 2008a). Rich rewards will come if it is able to innovate in the field of digital communication, be it broadband and related technologies (discussed in the next section) or digital television (discussed in a later section).

The penetration of the internet in Europe

Across the world, consumers have been upgrading from old-fashioned dial-up internet access to higher speed broadband.[1] This is the biggest chance many telecoms operators have of delivering revenue growth, as audiences/consumers (and businesses) appear to be prepared to pay premium prices for what is a premium internet service. By July 2010, there were 825 million internet users in Asia, 475 million in Europe and 266 million in North America, with other areas representing far smaller numbers. In terms of the rate of penetration by population size, the picture is different, with a 77.4 per cent rate in North America, 61.3 per cent in Australia/Oceania and 58.4 per cent in Europe (www.internetworldstats.com, 2010). The number of internet connections increases annually and the strong pace of growth shows no signs of abating, as the heads of European governments know well. In effect, broadband internet access using fixed-wire DSL (digital subscriber line) or cable hook-ups has gone mainstream in the last few years, helping at the same time to transform the communications sector and the way digital content is distributed and consumed (Taylor, 2004).

However, internet availability is a good example of the disparities that can coexist in Europe. On the one hand, the EU is the homeland to some of the most internet-savvy nations in the world, such as the Netherlands, Denmark and Finland. Together with the UK, Belgium, Luxembourg and France, they had broadband penetration rates higher than the USA. On the other hand, the new member states have low levels of access and penetration (CEC, 2008a) (see also chapter 7). Similarly, internet use, as well as the price and the technology available to customers, varies widely across Europe (see also chapter 5). The European Commission has recently blamed governments for not doing enough to open up the market by forcing former state telecoms monopolies to face competition that would reduce prices and get more people online. More developed broadband markets offer faster speeds at lower prices, while those in EU newcomer states, mostly in Eastern Europe, tend to get a worse deal. In Slovakia, customers have to pay at least €49 for broadband access with a download speed of 1 megabyte per second. In the Netherlands, prices start at €14 (CEC, 2008a).

The goal of the Commission was to have internet broadband available to all Europeans by 2010 and high-speed internet broadband for all by 2013 (Reding, 2009). Some countries have already started implementing these targets: France, with the France Numérique 2012 plan, aims to equip all French households with an internet connection of at least 512 kbit/s by the end of 2012. The *Digital Britain* report wants governments to commit to providing all households with a broadband connection of at least 2 Mbit/s by the same time. In Germany, the federal government, in its *Breitbandstrategie*, calls for connections of 50 Mbit/s to serve 75 per cent of the population by 2014. Finland has even committed to a universal broadband service at 100 Mbit/s. These are examples of countries which have established clear priorities, if not always the means to achieve them!

The development of digital television

The European television market, as elsewhere, is on the verge of replacing the old analogue TV system with a digital one. Although the digital technology has been available since the 1980s, one could argue that the conditions are ripe for the changes that this entails, from replacing television sets to introducing a whole raft of new facilities so as to improve the production and consumption experience. In the process of switchover from analogue to digital, television set manufacturers will be able to maximize their revenues as they sell new equipment, and producers will have an opportunity to repackage libraries of old content as well as producing new programmes. The consumers, following their initial expenditure on new sets and set-top boxes, will be rewarded by a multiplicity of services. In effect, the arrival of digital television has slowly begun to alter the media landscape, even though it has not yet penetrated into all markets as fully and as deeply as its proponents had hoped.

Digital television provides a more efficient use of frequencies, 'which opens up bandwidth to allow more channels of existing technical quality (analogue) as well as the possibility of higher definition pictures (HDTV) or on demand services such as . . .Video On demand (VoD)' (OECD, 2007: 8). However, the full implications of the digitalization of television are still the subject of much speculation, hype and uncertainty. As the history of European television has shown, the successful development of any new technology has a great deal to do with the content and the perceived value added that is offered to the viewers.

The introduction of digital television is extremely costly, as it requires a new infrastructure for both operators (transmission equipment, studios, etc.) and consumers (TV sets, set-top boxes). Transmissions can be made by cable, satellite or terrestrial frequencies, each of which has its advantages and disadvantages.

- *Satellite* is the easiest way to transmit a large number of services and thus a wide range of choices, but it is limited by the number of homes under the satellite footprint, and further by the number of homes with receiving dishes. Digital satellite television requires the installation of a dish, which some consumers dislike (analogue satellite television subscribers also had to buy and install new set-boxes and a satellite aerial). Moreover, satellite transmission is dependent on the weather – for example, downtime can result from very wet and unsettled conditions.
- Digital *terrestrial* television (DTT) is potentially universally available (given appropriate TV sets) because it works with standard aerials, but it is more restricted than satellite in terms of its spectrum. The entry of DTT makes the longer-term replacement of analogue terrestrial distribution television technology inevitable. With DTT, a significant incentive will be offered for the mass-market general public to upgrade when the time comes to replace their old TV sets. The replacement cycle of sets will be a major driver for the penetration of DTT, since new sets will increasingly be capable of receiving DTT broadcasts automatically.
- Digital *cable* is positioned somewhere between digital satellite and terrestrial in terms of the number of channels it can offer. Since from their

Table 3.1 Digital TV in Europe (and timetable for DTT)

Country	Legislation	DTT Launch	Switch-off (estimated)	Expected range
UK	1996	1999	2012	2012–15
Sweden	1997	1999	2008	2008
Spain	1998	2000	2010	2012–15
Finland	1996	2002	2007	2007
Netherlands	1999	2003	2006	2006
Germany	2002	2004	2010	2006–8
Italy	2001	2003	2012	2012–15
France	2000	2005	2010	2012–15
Switzerland	2002	2001	2009	2009–12
Luxembourg		2006	2006	
Belgium	2002	2002	2010	2009–12
Austria	2001	2007	2008	2008
Norway	2002	2007	2009	2009–12
Denmark	2002	2007	2011	2009–12
Ireland	2001	2007	2010	2009–12
Greece		2006	2012	2012–15
Portugal		2008	2012	2012–15

Source: Adapted from European Media Consulting Association, 2008; EOA, 2007; e-Media Institute, 2008.

inception cable systems were designed as multi-functional networks offering their customers television and telephony services, they are better suited to providing interactive applications such as home banking, home shopping and computing, but they require a large investment in broadband fibre-optic cabling.

The years 2002 to 2005 saw digital television entering a new phase, with the introduction and success of primarily free-to-air terrestrial platforms. Since then, all European countries have announced their plans to switch over from analogue to digital by 2012 (see table 3.1 and figure 3.1). In the run-up to 2012, as we shall see below, other television technologies – HDTV, IPTV and even mobile TV – have been announced. By the middle of 2009, the UK was the most developed market in Europe, since the penetration of digital TV had climbed from zero in 1998 to about 25.7 million households, or 91 per cent. The digital penetration in the rest of Europe varies, from 100 per cent in Finland, 96 per cent in Sweden, 66 per cent in France and 56 per cent in Germany to 21 per cent in Greece and 17 per cent in Lithuania. Although pay television was often considered to be the driver for developments in digital TV in Europe, financial problems associated with pay-TV ventures

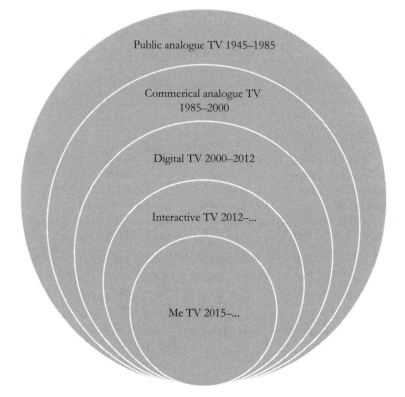

Figure 3.1 Stages in the European television industry

Source: Compiled from Meyer (2006), Papathanassopoulos (2002), Ellis (2000), Bughin and Griekspoor (1997).

and platforms have created a situation in which free-to-view services (e.g. the BBC-led Freeview service in the UK in 2002; the France Televisions-led TNT in France in 2005) (Iosifidis, 2007c) have moved ahead and exploited the technology. In effect, DTT in most European countries has been transformed into a free-to-air platform, with public broadcasters playing a key role (see figure 3.2).

The development of digital television – cable, satellite or terrestrial – depends on the existing analogue structure. European countries fall into four distinct groups:

- countries where the terrestrial reception mode dominates (France, Italy, Spain, UK and Finland);
- countries where cable infrastructure is the dominant mode (Sweden, Denmark, Benelux countries, Germany and Austria): it seems that the analogue switch-off is not a major issue in most of these countries;

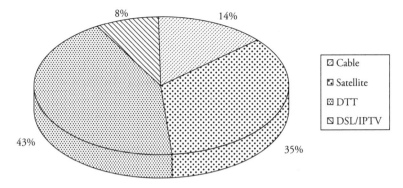

Figure 3.2 Digital TV households in Western Europe, by platform

Source: Compiled from EOA (2009), eMedia Institute (2009).

- countries with neither widespread cable penetration nor particularly advanced DTT plans, which look as if they will struggle to meet the deadline (for example, Greece, Ireland and Poland, where DTT is still in a trial phase). Digital DTH (direct-to-home) has recorded most success in countries, including the major markets of France, Italy, Spain and the UK, which, because of slow build-out, government intervention or poor marketing, have low cable penetration. A further factor could be the presence of long-standing terrestrial pay services in France, Italy and Spain and an established analogue DTH package in the UK;
- the Eastern and Central European countries, where the preparation for the digital switchover adds to the complexity of post-communist transformation in broadcasting. This reflects the slower growth and development of the television market in general. Digital penetration in the region is running at only 10 per cent, while DTT is still in its infancy; by 2012, less than 6 per cent of the region's homes will rely on DTT as their primary means of TV viewing. Regardless of the strong interest in Eastern European television, 'conversion to digital is hindered as consumer disposable income strives to match economic growth' (*TV International*, 2008a, 2009). Progress towards digital switchover in this region has been slow, with the majority of countries yet to launch digital terrestrial television. According to market forecasts, the region will have 52 per cent digital TV penetration by 2013 (*TV International*, 2009). For analysts the main problems are: (1) lack of sufficient understanding of the issues involved in the digital switchover, especially as regards the broadcasting, programming and market issues involved; (2) turf wars between broadcasting and telecommunications regulatory authorities; (3) the impact of politics on the process of preparation and execution of digital switchover strategies;

and (4), in some cases, launching the process prematurely, for inappropriate reasons. Depending on one's point of view, this is either a 'premature' digital switchover in countries not yet ready for it, or a case of countries needing a wake-up call to face technological and market realities to which they are not responding properly (see Jakubowicz, 2007).

Although financial and market uncertainties still surround the future of the digital television market, many consider that the switchover has already happened, with many people receiving digital television and those yet to convert – mostly the elderly and those on low incomes – not an attractive target for advertisers. The fact is that the transition is at present largely a preoccupation of the advanced economies of the world, and the major markets are the USA, Japan and Europe – and, within Western Europe, the UK, Spain, Germany, Italy and France. Others will inevitably follow in their wake.

Internet protocol television (IPTV)

Internet Protocol Television (IPTV) offers another way of accessing television programming. IPTV services are divided into two forms: one distributed via the PC ('web-TV'), the other via the TV using a set-top box on a closed broadband connection (IPTV). Thus, by and large, we can say that IPTV is delivered to a set-top box over a closed network, while web or online TV is available on the open internet and typically watched on a PC – in other words, IPTV services are offered over closed content distribution networks and are different from video streaming over the public internet viewed on a PC (*Screen Digest*, 2008a; Light and Lancefield, 2007; Rooney, 2006; Thomson, 2006). IPTV is considered one of the biggest opportunities in the converged communications market, as it opens up not only the broadcast TV market to telecoms operators but also a whole realm of possibilities around interactive video services and applications, as well as adjacent opportunities such as advertising (Philpott, 2007).

IPTV services were popular in Western Europe in 2009 – accounting for about 11 million households – but the picture varies tremendously from market to market. According to market research estimates, approximately 6 million households in Western Europe subscribed to IPTV – up from 3.8 million in 2006 – and this figure is predicted to increase to approximately 7 million by 2014 (Richard, 2008; *Screen Digest*, 2008a; *eMarketer*, 2008). These numbers are comparatively small when seen in the context of the TV market as a whole, so it remains to be seen what the eventual development of IPTV will be. The optimism of 2006 was replaced by scepticism in the large number of major operators who struggle to make their impact in a market new to them. The fairly limited penetration comes from having to move sub-scribers away from long-established cable and digital satellite services and, to a lesser extent, from the impact of digital terrestrial television. Nevertheless, 'IPTV still remains the fastest growing pay-TV platform, ahead of even satellite in both relative and absolute terms' (*Screen Digest*, 2008a: 20).

Mobile TV

IPTV is not the only way for a telecoms operator to enter the TV market. Since the beginning of 2003 most mobile telecommunications companies have been offering video via their multimedia portals and for downloading. Streaming services, which emerged at the end of 2003, were seen as a second stage in the development of mobile video. The third stage will be that of mobile TV broadcast on traditional TV networks designed for telephones or other pieces of mobile equipment, such as PDAs (Meyer, 2006). Mobile TV is an ambiguous term and differs from mobile video (Orgad, 2009). It is the transmission of traditional and on-demand audiovisual content to a mobile device and includes live and time-shifted TV. It follows a scheduled transmission timetable, emulating traditional TV services, and is delivered over cellular networks (streamed TV services) or broadcast networks, such as DVB-H. Mobile video is generally short-form content, delivered to the user's handset on demand, either downloaded or streamed over the cellular network (*TV International*, 2007; Urban, 2007).

In effect, mobile TV is a prime example of the digital convergence that unites personal mobile communications, which according to the European Commission is one of Europe's most dynamic markets, with the diversity and publicity of the audiovisual sector (CEC, 2007b). Needless to say, it represents a new opportunity for European industry to gain competitive advantage in the world market. Moreover, mobile TV allows consumers not only to watch TV while on the move but also to have access to personal-ized, time-shifted and on-demand audiovisual content. Last, but not least, it represents a tremendous opportunity for Europe to maintain and expand its leadership in mobile technology and mobile services. For example, it is esti-mated that there were 1.1 million subscribers to mobile broadcast TV services at the end of 2008, and at the end of 2009 these services were operational only in nine European countries (Austria, Spain, the Netherlands, Hungary, Finland, Germany, the Czech Republic and Switzerland (EAO, 2009: 95). As the European Commission points out (CEC, 2007b: 2), 'Mobile TV is at the frontier of high-value, innovative services. . . . [It] fits well with the

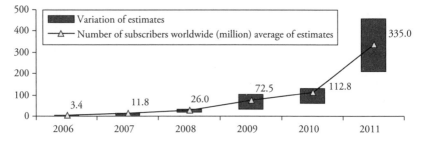

Figure 3.3 Broadcast mobile TV subscriber uptake

Source: Estimates by *In-Stat, ABI, NSR, Datamonitor, Informa Telecoms & Media, eMarketer, Strategy Analytics, Gartner.*
CEC (2007b).

objectives set out in the Commission's *Communication* . . . on an innovation-friendly, modern Europe' – hence the desire to encourage 'cooperation between broadcasters, mobile service operators and operators of transmission networks' (Reding, 2008).

In practice, there are issues about which models and technologies to use, viewing patterns and consumer interest, licensing procedures and spectrum availability and, more generally, the potential for growth. As with many new developments, the promise has sped ahead of the reality (see figure 3.3).

High definition TV (HDTV)

The launch of high-definition TV in Europe has come in the wake of developments in such places as the USA and Japan, but since 2006 it has become available in most European countries, mostly through pay TV but also in some cases through free-to-air television: 4.6 million European households (2 per cent of all TV households) can watch HDTV on a regular basis. The UK and France present the highest development, while Germany and Spain show little progress (*Screen Digest*, 2009a). As the technology develops (for example, television sets able to handle different formats) and programmes become available – in 2009 there were 274 HDTV channels in the greater Europe region on various platforms (EAO, 2009: 120) – it is expected that HDTV will establish itself in most television markets (see figures 3.4 and 3.5). The industry has already moved towards this direction with the launch of 3D television.

There are now HD-ready TV sets which are affordable for the average household, and they are installed in one in four European homes. There are also new DVDs (digital video discs) capable of recording HD signals, and their prices are falling. Moreover, the 'HD-ready' specifications and label for

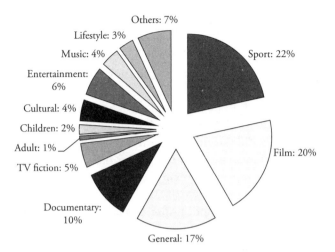

Figure 3.4 HDTV channels in Europe, 2009

Source: Based on data from *Screen Digest* (2008b, 2009a), EAO (2009).

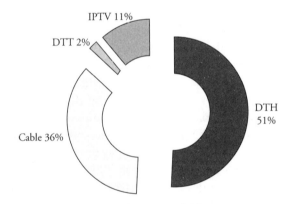

Figure 3.5 HDTV channels in Europe, by means of delivery, 2009

Source: Based on data from *Screen Digest* (2008b, 2009a), EAO (2009).

TV sets and STBs, set up by the European Information and Communications Technology Industry Association in the middle of the decade, have been widely accepted and promoted by consumer electronics manufacturers, retailers and broadcasters. The HD feature will increase the appeal of new-generation TVs (flat, widescreen, HD) and drive the transition. Indeed, sales of flat (now HD) TVs have outpaced predictions and prices have been dropped faster than expected.

However, the availability of content remains an issue. The consumers/ viewers have been attracted by falling prices and the impressive-looking sets for HDTV, but the content is not sufficient to fill the schedules. This is explained by two factors: in most European countries HDTV services were launched only in 2006 and, more fundamentally, HDTV is so far available mostly to pay-TV homes and not free-to-air (*Screen Digest*, 2009a).

Another obstacle in Europe is regulation. While legislation has helped the roll-out of HD in the USA, Japan and Australia, the approaches of national European authorities differ from country to country. In many cases there has not yet been a decision about what to do with the spectrum freed by digital switchover, with HD just one of many services competing to fill that space (*Television Business International*, 2007). Lastly, the format 'war' between HD-DVD and Blu-ray, an optical-disc format for storing high-definition video (as we will see in the following pages), may also be delaying processes of adoption.

From VCR to DVD

In the era of convergence and digitalization, the video cassette recorder (VCR) has given way to the DVD. DVD is smaller, lighter and more convenient, and the replication of discs is much more efficient than tape-copying. In effect, the DVD 'has rejuvenated the home video industry and has finally enabled television to achieve what film had by the mid-1980s, namely, a viable direct-to-consumer market for its programming' (Kompare, 2006). By the turn of the century, DVD players had become the fastest-selling product in the history of US consumer electronics, as the market grew twice as fast as it had done for the VCR (*Screen Digest*, 2002). In fact, the DVD player became a true mass market device in Western Europe in 2004 as penetration reached over 50 per cent for the first time. The five largest European video markets – the UK, France, Germany, Italy and Spain – account for more than three-quarters of consumer spending in Europe, while just under two-thirds was generated by the top three countries. The UK alone accounted for over a third – 34.6 per cent – of the total, while France generated 16.9 per cent and Germany 13.1 per cent. Moreover, European spending on DVD grew to €11.5 billion – more than eight times the amount spent on VHS during the same period. The falling prices provided a stimulus for DVD to penetrate rapidly into European TV households (*Screen Digest*, 2005b).

As average DVD prices continued to fall or even to stabilize in Europe (as they did in the USA), the growth in revenues, especially from hardware sales, started to slow down and decline. In 2006, for example, sales of players and recorders were down by 4 per cent in units. The manufacturers saw that hardware sales were boosted by the introduction of DVD recorders equipped with hard disk drives, suggesting that consumers would rather record content from the TV than buy pre-recorded discs from video stores.

It is not therefore a surprise that the industry turned to the next generation of recording devices, firstly to personal video recorders (PVR) and high-definition DVD (HD DVD). The PVR is a computer hard disk, either operated manually or tied to an interactive guide programmes service, giving the capacity to record and playback digital TV programming (Amel, 2002). In 2008, PVRs were available to more than 10 million pay-TV households in Western Europe, and their development has been led (if not pushed) by the satellite operators (*Screen Digest*, 2008e). The real competition, however, is in the next generation of DVDs. As HDTV is more suitable for digital television, there is also a need for high-definition DVDs. But as the new generation of DVDs started to make their entrance, a new 'formats war' started among the manufacturers, reminiscent of the VCR format war of the late 1970s and early 1980s, in which Sony's Betamax ultimately lost out to JVC's VHS technology. In this case it was Blu-ray against HD DVD format. Both deliver high-definition graphics and sound, while the film industry has high hopes that the next generation of players will make it easier to protect their content from piracy. TV manufacturers, meanwhile, believe the availability of content such as natural history programming and movies in the new HD standard will provide a reason for consumers to upgrade to the latest in HD TV sets. The winner is expected to inherit a multibillion-euro industry, although consumers so far have been confused by the standards war. Some analysts say that potential buyers have also failed to see the attraction of high-definition video.

Radio: the analogue medium?

Radio was the means of communication that was born, developed and declined in the last century. When people are asked about the media in the last decades of the twentieth century, they think first of television, then newspapers. In the first decade of the twenty-first century, when they are asked about the media, they think first of television and then the internet. In both cases, radio comes third, regardless of the fact that the average European owns multiple radios and lives with this most portable medium in every room in the house, in offices, in cars, etc. Radio is the oldest medium and it is trying to find its place in the new century (see also O'Neil, 2009).

The deregulation of the 1980s resulted in the rapid growth of private local and commercial radio networks. Between 1980 and 1994, the number of radio stations in the EU increased dramatically, though the numbers fell between 1994 and 2000, from 7,600 to 5,500 (Deiss, 2002). This picture has remained unchanged since then, with the radio sector being much more fragmented than the TV sector. On the other hand, European radio is dominated by its 350 public service stations, which account for 56 per cent of revenue and 38 per cent of listening. The EU's 5,050 commercial radio stations account for 44 per cent of revenue, whereas 4,500 of them are affiliated to networks, with the remainder often being part of multi-station owning groups, since they are mostly small and/or medium.

As with television, the advent of new digital technologies has offered challenges and opportunities for radio, which has shown itself quick to evolve and adapt to new markets and technological conditions. The new digital technologies (DAB, DRM, DVB-T, the internet, etc.) will change the way radio is consumed and distributed as digitalization takes hold. Digital radio is accessed in three different ways: digital television through satellite, cable or terrestrial platform; the internet; and stand-alone, portable or in-car DAB sets. As Lax and his colleagues note, in practice all households which receive digital TV are also able to receive a number of radio stations offered by the platform provider. Thus, 'listening to a radio station through the TV is one form of digital radio service' (Lax et al., 2008: 151). But this way of delivery seems to be of limited utility for radio audiences. A second form is listening though the internet. Today, all radio stations, or the overwhelming majority, also transmit simultaneously through the internet. DSL is the main driver for internet radio as well as podcasting. Although low penetration rates in some European countries have decelerated the growth of the internet, nowadays radio is no longer heard only at home and in the car, but also on the PC, as podcasts and on mobile phones. Thus, nowadays any self-respecting radio station has its own online presence, making it difficult to calculate their exact number. It is estimated that, globally, there were in 2007 over 300,000 internet radio stations (comScore, 2007) and every 15 seconds a new one emerges and others disappear. This gives radio a global reach and overcomes local, regional and national boundaries. Interestingly, developments such as Spotify, (www.spotify.com), where it is possible to listen to one's choice of music paid for by advertising (or by subscription), are helping to redefine the function of radio. Once again, the business model for media systems is being revised in ways unimagined only a few years ago.

After years of development, DAB became a Europe-wide technical standard, and the first public transmissions began in the UK, Sweden and Italy in 1995. DAB, considered as the 'real digital radio', was originally designed to replace FM and AM, and has been operating in more than thirty countries around the world (Lax, 2003: 32). Some analysts, however, say that DAB is already outdated and other newer standards, such as DAB+, DRM (+), DMB and DVB-H, are superior in terms of quality and efficiency. This is reminiscent of the case of HDTV in the mid-1980s. In 2007 there were 558 radio stations in Europe, with more than half of those in the UK. Of these, only 127 were DAB only (EBU, 2007).

Simply put, radio in Europe is currently available across a variety of different digital platforms (digital television, mobile phones and the internet), yet its main means of reception is thought to be the traditional analogue FM and AM radio sets. As with much else, digital radio will succeed only if both commercial and public service radio stations are sure that they are going to profit from digitalization.

Newspapers: between the internet and the freesheets

As we noted in chapter 2, the press in Europe, as in other regions, is in decline. Apart from the particular problems associated with the idiosyncrasies of Europe, the internet has had a significant impact on the newspaper industry. On the one hand, search engines have become aggregators of news without people having to pay for the news product. This has impacted on the ability of newspapers to sell to readers at a price; on the other hand, the internet has seen the creation of sites that have swallowed up the advertising that had previously gone to fund local, regional and national newspapers. Given that both these have come at a time when the industry was anyway in long-term decline, their effects are very noticeable and worrying for one of the oldest media sectors. In short, the newspaper industry is in crisis and has been desperately searching for a business model that would combine print and web to shore up its future. To date, none has proved to be a success: investment in the web has not turned newspapers around; their product – news and features – is still freely available, despite often announced plans to charge for content – and so the spiral of decline continues. While they are ready to adapt to the new digital and converged environment, all publishers are well aware that this will be both expensive and risky.

According to the European Commission, newspapers are read by over 180 million people across Europe (CEC, 2005b). But their advertising revenue is falling and their core readership is aged over forty-five and is not being renewed by younger readers, who tend to prefer other media anyway. Digital technologies are fast changing the ways in which content is created, combined, distributed and consumed. For example, younger generations may prefer reading headline news delivered to their mobile phones and surfing their friends' status updates on Facebook or MySpace rather than buying and reading newspapers. The EU publishing sector contributes 0.5 per cent

Table 3.2 Paid-for and free dailies in the USA and Europe (in thousands)

Paid for	2002	2003	2004	2005	2006	(%) change 2002–6
North America	69,499	69,400	68,725	67,171	65,846	–5.26
Europe	98,112	96,190	94,080	93,377	94,069	–4.12
Free						
North America	2,518	3,488	3,833	5,320	6,241	147.86
Europe	8,929	10,023	11,471	16,245	26,720	199.25
Paid for and free						
North America	72,017	72,888	72,558	72,491	72,087	0.10
Europe	107,041	106,213	105,551	109,622	120,789	12.84

Source: Adapted from WAN (2008).

of GDP across the EU-25, with a yearly output valued at €121 billion, and value-added amounting to €43 billion in the EU-15. Publishing provides nearly 750,000 jobs in 64,000 companies across the EU-25. This sector comprises a majority of small and medium-sized enterprises, although firms that employ over 250 people account for over half the sector's total revenue.

Although those over forty-five are expected to sustain newspaper publishing for some years yet, advertising, which commonly contributes over half a newspaper's total revenue, is in slow decline overall, and in some segments, such as recruitment advertising, is fast switching to the internet (CEC, 2005b).

In fact, newspaper websites attract, as in the USA, more visitors than other internet sites, which is also desirable to the advertisers. However, publishers have not yet been able to build the business models necessary to exploit online distribution. Newspaper websites may grow fast, but there is no certainty that online advertising will ever match the rates achieved by newspaper ads in print. Besides, in most of the cases, the websites are cross-subsidized by print revenues. Furthermore, when the publishers try to charge subscriptions for their sites they have met with indifference from the users. All in all, the traditional model of vertically integrated content, production and distribution is already being challenged by new models (see table 3.2).

Although the European Commission has asked for a media policy for the publishing sector in order to strengthen its competitiveness (CEC, 2005b), the fact that publishing industries are still built around country-specific factors is likely to militate against the creation of a single policy. Furthermore, given that companies can move freely across borders, the likelihood of being able to devise a policy – for competitiveness, for pluralism, for journalism – is not that promising.

One other threat to newspapers needs to be mentioned: free newspapers

Table 3.3 Share of newspapers of total advertising spend, selected European countries

Country	1990	1993	1997	2002	2005	2006
France	28.6	25.0	24.4	16.6	18.9	15.0
Germany	51.9	51.7	48.1	41.7	41.7	40.3
Italy	23.8	20.9	21.0	21.1	19.4	19.0
Netherlands	61.0	51.2	49.8	43.5	39.4	39.0
Spain	36.3	30.8	31.5	28.2	25.2	24.6
United Kingdom	43.7	43.3	40.9	40.1	37.3	33.5

Note: The percentages are based on advertising expenditures, which include cinema, posters, etc.

Source: Adapted from Papathanassopoulos (2001), WAN (2008).

or freesheets (for example, *Metro*). Initially, publishers thought that free papers were aimed at people who were more likely to watch television and did not normally read newspapers, so creating a tempting market for advertisers. Gradually, they realized that the advent of freesheets was another major problem. The free daily distributed through public transport was introduced in 1995 in Sweden, and with the successful advent of *Metro* (introduced in 1992 as a commuter paper in Sweden), free dailies sprang up all over Europe. They are now seen as an additional problem for newspapers, already smarting thanks to competition from online and television news providers (see table 3.3).

While some have argued that it is 'very likely that the rapid tabloidization in Europe (UK, Ireland, Sweden, Belgium, and the Netherlands) has something to do with the success of the free tabloids', others believe that these are read by people not usually reached by newspapers and are therefore expanding the industry (Povoledo, 2007). The fact is that free dailies in 2007 accounted for nearly 7 per cent of all global newspaper circulation and for 23 per cent of circulation in Europe alone. Moreover, in the EU, paid daily newspapers saw a drop of –0.74 per cent in 2006 and –4.12 per cent in 2002 and 2006. But, combined with free dailies, circulation in the EU rose by 2 per cent over one year and by 12.84 per cent over five years (WAN, 2008).

In spite of differing interpretations of the impact of freesheets (and of the internet), the obvious point to make is that newspapers will have to change in some way and adapt to a new environment. As John Lloyd argues:

> In the next decade, more titles will die and many more will be cut back. The trend is likely to continue to be that newspapers that cannot establish themselves securely in a 'virtual community' of people prepared to pay, by historical

standards highly, for their daily read, together with advertisers who believe that text and design on paper still commands attention from prospective buyers, will go out of business. Those that remain may become more like magazines, with analysis, essays and reportage at length – ceding the ground of spot news to the screen, which is increasingly likely to be hand held. In the end, the desire to learn and the delight in reading – assuming that these urges remain – may save something of the newspaper culture. The internet may, if a business model can be found, preserve something of newspapers in digital form. (2005: 45)

Summary

Everybody agrees that communications-related media industries are positioned at the centre of a massive global growth. They also agree that the convergence of different communication technologies – television, telecommunications and radio, fixed-line and mobile telephony and the internet – eventually became a reality in the first decade of the twenty-first century. This is the result of the technological progress that made high-bandwidth connections available to most citizens in the developed world, and, at least in Europe, using different mobile- and fixed-connection methods. Convergence and digitalization are expected to change completely the way people access the media and what they consume. Consequently, this new situation will result in many new business models and new job opportunities. The fact is that Europe has witnessed an impressive array of new media developments in the last years in terms of both supply (launch of online and mobile content services, new media deals) and demand (usage and technology adoption) (*Screen Digest* et al., 2006: 263).

The long-awaited digital convergence is becoming an economic reality, creating great opportunities for Europe's consumers, content providers and technology industries. But, in practice, economic considerations seem often to be ignored when making projections regarding the transition to digital. The huge capital costs associated with launching digital services bring higher prices for programmes and make investors 'think twice' before entering into digital commitments. The EU may have announced the switchover from analogue to digital by 2012, but it is uncertain whether the member states will meet their deadlines. Even in the most developed cases, such as the UK, the situation is far from clear. For example, the company which runs DAB radio stations, GCapMedia, announced in mid-2008 that it would cease the operation of two digital radio stations and channels and that it will not go ahead with the planned digital channel One World for the Freeview platform. In Germany, the TV company ProSieben Sat announced that it will cease operating some of its digital channels. Some suggest that digital TV is more risky than the sudden rush to launch free TV in the 1980s. The European media industry is not as it used to be in the 1970s and the 1980s, when each sector was more or less distinct from the others. The main victim of the new environment seems to be the press. European newspapers, like their counterparts all over the world, are struggling to cope with declining circulation, shrinking advertising revenues, rising costs and competition from the internet and freesheets. But Europe must not be left behind. In effect, it has entered a new phase in its competition in the world markets, especially with the USA and Japan. As in the 1980s and 1990s, the convergence and digitalization of the field highlights the industrial imperative of the sector. The European industry is in some areas at the forefront of digital distribution of content and in others is lagging behind more advanced markets. But, most importantly, digital services have to offer tangibly different content to stimulate and retain consumer interest, and this requires large investments in content, since, as usual, 'content is the king' in the development of new media services.

The slow growth, for instance, of digital television and radio in Europe demonstrated that at the early stage viewers were not willing to subscribe, for example, to pay-TV services. Further, it appears that companies and their executives often ignored the realities of household economics. First of all, potential customers (households) appear not to have been persuaded to pay for both new reception equipment and subscription fees. It could be said that the cost of digital services has become too high for many households. There are already industry forecasts warning that fixed telecommunications operators will experience a revenue shortfall between 2007 and 2013 as a result of a fall in fixed narrowband retail revenue and a slowdown in broadband retail revenue growth. IPTV was once talked about as a significant source of income that could help operators address the shortfall in other areas of their businesses. However, while it has an important role to play in operators' strategies, it is now clear that IPTV will contribute little to revenue. This is also related to problems to do with convergence. For example, IPTV services are run predominantly by operators who are telecommunications companies and have no real experience of how to attract TV customers.

Moreover, as we will discuss in chapter 7, the patterns in the consumption of audiovisual and multimedia products may be changing, but some others stay the same. For instance, as we have noted, radio is the archetypal mobile communication system and does not necessarily require to be listened to online though a PC. Moreover, the notion of a combined TV/PC is still some years from mass consumer acceptance. Consumers are in principle indifferent as to how they receive their TV signals – provided the content they want is available. Some claim that more people are watching TV on their mobiles than originally anticipated. But for how long can anyone watch a programme on a mobile TV? Everybody knows and understands that people prefer to watch television on screens that are, if not regular in size, at least larger than those on a mobile, and most adults do not have the time or the need to watch it on a phone. The whole issue is again a marketing one. Mobile operators and manufactures need first to keep and then, if they can, increase their customer base and sell new mobile gadgets. To do that, they periodically add a new feature, a new service (from mobile telephony, to photo, video, mp3, 3G and now TV). The fact is that modern mobiles are used for various things, but it is questionable whether they will be used for broadcast or mobile TV services. Others may argue that this is a pessimistic approach, since millions of consumers in other countries like Japan and South Korea watch broadcast mobile TV. One could equally argue that this is a matter of culture. And mobile TV in these countries does not involve paying a subscription fee. This is not exactly what the major mobile operators had in mind, but, even so, TV experience is different, and industry surveys show that customers prefer to access music rather than TV on their mobile phones.

Europe is, as we know, a fragmented region. Operators in small markets cannot afford the development, while the customers in these countries have to pay double prices for, generally, fewer services. This was evident in the case of digital TV (Papathanassopoulos, 2002), and it seems to be reconfirmed in the case of mobile TV. For example, the Danish carrier TDC Mobil has said that there is not enough demand for mobile TV in a country the size of Denmark to justify investing in a DVB-H broadcast network (*Mobile Media*, 2008). Fragmented media markets and thus small media operators hinder large investments. The traditional media business model, being based almost entirely on national, local and regional advertising revenues, does not fit with new platforms that, due to convergence and digitalization, are not dedicated to a certain region. Yet the television business, traditionally static and conservative, is undergoing a deep transitional process and altering the former boundaries (Rangone and Turconi, 2003).

At the moment it is difficult to predict how digital media will evolve at the European level over the next decade. The development of old and new media confirms that 'all forms of communication media coexist and co-evolve within an expanding, complex adaptive system' (Fidler, 1999: 29). In other words, although we live in the digital and multimedia age, the traditional media are still there: we still read books and newspapers, we still watch TV on the mainstream analogue TV channels, and we still listen to our analogue radio stations, mostly in our cars during the traffic jam going to and from work. Besides, this is Europe: the old and the new always try to find ways of coexisting, and the 'old media survive by adjusting to the new media' (Tunstall, 2008: 24). The new media are growing much faster than the traditional media: daily consumers turn to the videos of YouTube and make contacts through Facebook, and content owners are becoming more interested in new open distribution channels (Berman et al., 2007). Advertising expenditure follows these trends. According to IDATE (2008), online advertising spending has shown a spectacular increase (up by 32.4 per cent in 2007 compared with 2006), but advertising spending on print media (up only 0.8 per cent) is stagnating. In effect, print media and TV are losing ground in the most competitive markets, namely North America and Western Europe. To this, one must add the advertising spend directed to mobile phones and later TV, which is in the early stages of development.

The present economic crisis requires governments to implement a comprehensive policy for the development of new media in Europe. Europe needs to accelerate the ongoing switchover from analogue to digital TV, since this will free valuable radio spectrum, currently used by terrestrial analogue TV, for use by new communications and content services. The Commission estimates that the incremental value of this spectrum for wireless broadband across the EU is between €150 and €200 billion. As noted, the days of a limited analogue media landscape are about to end. Digital media and convergence change the communications landscape as well as the rules of the game. What it doesn't change is the need of the industry for new investment.

Part II

The Europeanization of the European Media

4   Europeanizing the Media of Europe

If the aim of those who founded the European Community, now the European Union, was to create a union of European countries, it is legitimate to ask now whether this aim has been achieved. Later chapters will explore the ways in which the EU is treated and constructed in the media by journalists and others and how the meaning of the Union is itself under discussion. This chapter has a more specific and immediate objective, namely, to explore the extent to which the EU has been able to construct or give rise to a set of media policies that have a European character. Has the EU, in other words, created a media landscape that has a European character and what does this mean in practice? In seeking to examine this question, the first section will summarize the discussion of Europeanization; later sections will discuss the new revised version of the 'Television without Frontiers Directive' of 1989, now renamed the 'Audiovisual Media Services Directive', and various interventions of the European Union in areas of media policy, such as media ownership, and measures to protect the European audiovisual landscape through the Media Programme.

As discussed in chapter 1, the processes of globalization, the integration of member states and the rapid development of the new technologies form the background to the EU's interventions in all aspects of the communications field. In spite of many who question its competence (see Harrison and Woods, 2007: 78–80), the European Commission considers itself the watchdog of the harmonized European communication landscape. However, this may be a bit of an exaggeration, as sometimes its proposals are rejected – as was the case with a proposal in mid-2008 to create an EU Telecoms Authority with broad regulatory powers.[1]

The aim of the then European Community to harmonize and eventually to 'Europeanize' the audiovisual sector began in 1983 with the publication of the report *Realities and Tendencies in European Television* (CEC, 1983), which led to a much discussed Green Paper (CEC, 1984) and then to the well-known directive (CEC, 1989, 1997a) for a 'Television without Frontiers', which became the 'Audiovisual Media Services Directive' in 2007. The effort to 'Europeanize' the communication sector now incorporates a much broader remit than simply television, as seen in the publication of another Green Paper, *The Convergence of the Telecommunications, Media and Information Technology Sectors and the Implications for Regulation* (CEC, 1997c). The breadth of its claimed competence can also be seen in the EU's initiatives in the late 1990s and early 2000s – the public service broadcasting protocol in the 1997 Amsterdam Treaty, the *Communication on the State Aid Rules to Public Service Broadcasting* in 2001, the Chapter of Fundamental Rights of the EU in 2000, and the new *Regulatory Framework For Electronic Communications* in 2002 (Harcourt, 2008: 18–19).

One way or another, the EU has attempted since the mid-1980s to initiate a policy that will 'Europeanize' the whole communication sector of its member states. This policy has sought, on the one hand, to harmonize and protect the media sector (e.g. 'Television without Frontiers'), and, on the other, to make it competitive in both the internal European market and the global market (liberalization of the telecommunications market, the MEDIA programmes, *e*Europe, Info Action Plan). At another level, perhaps, it has also tried to protect European cultural identity (see Schlesinger, 1987) from the 'American challenge'. In the Green Paper of 1997, the Commission explored ways of harmonizing the regulation of broadcasting, the internet and telecommunications (Humphreys and Simpson, 2008: 860). In other words, as in other sectors of the economy and society, the EU has incrementally extended its reach to most aspects of the communication landscape (discussed in chapter 5), even the protection of minors,[2] and from telecommunications to the convergence of the media and digital television (Füg, 2008). As Maria Michalis (2007: 290–3) has pointed out, the EU's communications policy has been more about regulating markets and competition than about technology. This 'EU-ization' of the communication field is also a two-way process, as indicated in our discussion above (see also chapter 1) – one 'from above', orchestrated from Brussels, and one from below, where organizations or citizens of the member states complain and object to the European Commission, and particularly to the European Court of Justice (ECJ), that the member states have not implemented EU policies (Harcourt, 1998, 2002, 2005). In this regard the ECJ has emerged as a key actor in ensuring compliance with European laws and directives among the member states (Glenn, 2004). From above, though the implementation of the 'Television without Frontiers' or telecommunications directives were initially dependent upon how well they 'fitted' in with the widely varying national regulatory structures, the dissatisfaction of the Commission, as well as the ECJ, with the mode of implementation led to substantial pressure for revisions to national media laws. As Alison Harcourt (2002: 738) notes, a range of measures – through competition rules, use of best practice, even overriding national specificities – were used to achieve coherence and implementation.

In short, we can see how the processes of Europeanization/EU-ization are complex, and sometimes contradictory and uneven, since the pace towards this goal is different among the various member states and often creates problems of implementation, so giving rise to discrepancies. In spite of all this, one could argue that this evolution is consistent, if not strong in respect of communications policies, and that European institutions (the Commission, the Parliament and the ECJ) have shown themselves, either directly or indirectly, to be major catalysts of Europeanization (Harcourt, 2002: 749). One should also note, however, that in certain circumstances the Commission has 'offered a good mechanism for national policy makers to shift blame and justify change' (Thatcher, 2004: 772). This is certainly true as regards Central and Eastern European countries that have achieved extensive legislative alignment with the EU, including media activities, in order to become candidates for EU membership (see Smaele, 2007).

Audiovisual policy: from 'Television without Frontiers' to 'Audiovisual Media Services'

On 13 December 2005, the European Commission proposed the revision of the 'Television without Frontiers [TWF] Directive'. A year later, in December 2006, the European Parliament adopted the amendments proposed by the Commission, and months later, in May 2007, the European Council adopted the revision of the new directive, which became known as the 'Audiovisual Media Services [AMS] Directive' (CEC, 2007a). The new AMS Directive was published on 18 December 2007, and the member states were required to incorporate the new provisions into their national legislation by 19 December 2009. As is usual and common with most EU legislation, member states remain free to adopt stricter or more detailed rules (for a synoptic view of the AMS Directive, see the appendix).

As noted earlier, the original TWF Directive was adopted in 1989 and revised in 1997. Since its inception, it has sought to harmonize the European audiovisual landscape by setting up a series of minimal regulations (television advertising, audiovisual production) and to create common rules for a level playing field for pan-European TV channels. After almost five years, extensive consultations and public hearings, the European Commission decided to 'modernize' the TWF Directive by taking into account the sweeping changes in the media field brought about by the convergence of the media and the onset of new technologies (internet broadband, etc.) by adopting a policy based on self- and co-regulatory techniques. Rules on advertising, national production quotas, the protection of minors, and so on, could potentially apply to all kinds of video streams, including video blogs, online games and mobile video services. But many felt that such rules could have a 'chilling effect' on innovation and risk stifling nascent technologies with rules designed for another age (*The Economist*, 2008). As usual, there was reluctance by some member states to relax the 'old' quantitative rules, while there were calls from others to introduce additional rules and restrictions. Moreover, the European Parliament wanted to make clear that the Directive would not cover the internet, while consumers' organizations wanted stricter rules on advertising and independent producers more regulation for the promotion of their productions. Some broadcasters argued that the proposals would continue to shackle them with analogue-era restrictions. Internet media companies, which might face the unwelcome prospect of new regulations, pointed out that the proposals went too far and were too restrictive. But such debates about too much or too little legislation were reminiscent of an earlier era when there were arguments about the desirability of imposing quotas on domestic or foreign programmes. As in most EU matters, considerable discussion and debate produced a series of compromises that were somewhat remote from the ambitions of the AMS Directive.

Country of origin

The country of origin principle is regarded as the cornerstone of EU television policy and, in effect, was an attempt by the Commission to protect the free movement and the continuity of the single market in services across the Union. It has often been criticized as being insensitive to the legitimate national public interest to protect viewers (Herold, 2008: 5; see also Subiotto and Graf, 2003) and to allow them to make choices between what is being offered. As Herold notes, this principle is 'nothing more than a natural consequence of the internal market, stemming from the very commitment by the founders of the European Economic Community back in 1957' (2008: 6). In the consultation phase, several countries, including France, were said to want to change the country of origin principle because it is easier to send programming across borders via the internet than it is over the broadcast airwaves. Members of the European Parliament also wished to amend the basis of regulation from the country of origin to the country of destination, meaning that media companies could get around one country's regulations by basing themselves in another EU member state. In effect, the principle was maintained to ensure the fundamental freedom of trade within the EU, but the AMS Directive will enable a member state to take action against a broadcaster that, they suspect, abuses the fundamental freedom of establishment and settles in another member state just in order to bypass a local, stricter regulation (Article 2).

The new Directive sets out a streamlined infringement procedure with tight deadlines under the supervision of the European Commission. For example, the country of origin principle made it possible for some Nordic channels (such as TV3, based in London) and some French-speaking channels (such as RTL9, based in Luxembourg) to avoid the demanding regulations of Sweden and France (*Screen Digest*, 2007a). As Herold concludes:

> The country of origin principle, coupled with minimum harmonization, is advantageous for consumers and compatible with their interest: It gives them a wide choice of audiovisual media services, which know no borders anymore, but also the security that all services they receive will comply with a fundamental set of principles established at the EU level. It fosters not only free flow of information but also freedom of expression of Europeans. Dilemmas between the internal market and national broadcasting or audiovisual media orders admittedly exist. Even there, the Directive's ingenious legal construct and the general principles of EU law, developed by the ECJ in its jurisprudence, provide a series of remedies. (2008: 23)

Linear and non-linear audiovisual services

The new Directive applies to all audiovisual media services, both linear (or television broadcast service) and non-linear (on-demand) services. However, while both will be subject to some basic rules – such as consumer protection and encouraging European production –they will not be implemented in the same way. The AMS Directive provides definitions in order to distinguish the services (see box 4.1). As Burri-Nenova notes: the broader definition of audiovisual media service and the delineation of the two categories have three important effects:

- all content services are within the reach of the AMS Directive;
- 'most importantly, the "country of origin" principle, as the core to the Community audiovisual media regime, is extended to all content services, including non-linear services. This minimum level of harmonization guarantees a functioning single market and prevents the emergence of an uneven playing field laden with diverging national rules', since most of the EU member states have adopted similar legislation on linear and non-linear media services;
- some flexibility is preserved. (2007a: 1703–4)

The regulation of non-linear services will be much lighter, and it is likely that providers will be self-regulated. The notion of introducing a 'non-linear' category that would be subject to regulation was one of the most controversial points. Some member states (typically France) and MEPs supported the principle that TV-like regulation should be extended to non-linear services (in order to protect consumers and the creative industries). On the other hand, other member states (typically the UK) and MEPs feared that any regulation of these emerging services might inhibit market development (*Screen Digest*, 2007a). This is reminiscent of the divisions over quotas that were debated furiously in the 1990s during the negotiations over the TWF Directive. As always, a compromise has been sought.

While the regulation of TV (or linear) services remains almost unchanged, some broadcasters desired more flexibility. For example, it has been said that the UK agreed to the inclusion of video on demand in the new directive in return for assurances that programming would continue to be regulated in the European country in which it originates, rather than where it is heard or viewed (Pfanner, 2006). Behind the debate is the question of how best to balance competition and protection. But, in practice, the regulations were not due to come into force until after 2010: such a long and slow process seems incongruous given the pace of technological change.

Advertising

The AMS Directive is simpler and more flexible in the regulation of advertising compared with the TWF Directives. In fact, it removes some of the existing quantitative limits and provides a broad definition of what constitutes commercial communications (advertising, sponsorship, product placement, teleshopping, etc.) in order to ensure that all forms of commercial audiovisual content are covered by the same common set of rules, whatever mode of delivery is used (Article 1). The main time limit of twelve minutes of advertising in any given hour has been maintained, while the limit of three hours per day has been deleted. On the other hand, the rules governing the insertion of advertising breaks during programmes have been made more flexible. Complex rules apply to the frequency of breaks, according to genre – generally one interruption for each period of forty-five minutes. In the new text, commercial breaks can occur 'once for each scheduled 30-minute period' for every category of programme. Nevertheless, Article 11(1) stipulates that 'Member States shall ensure, where television advertising or teleshopping is inserted during programmes, that the integrity of the programmes, taking into account natural breaks in and the duration and the nature of the programme, and the rights of the right holders are not prejudiced.'

The change in the frequency of advertising breaks from forty-five to thirty minutes came about due to pressure from the commercial broadcasters, in their effort to generate some additional revenue. In the AMS Directive 'advertising' is replaced by the phrase 'commercial communications' (see also Woods, 2008). By and large, both the Commission and the European Parliament in the new revision of the Directive followed a rather more liberal approach in respect of advertising, and this has generally been welcomed by associations representing broadcasters.

New forms of television advertising enabled by new technologies, such as typical 'split screen' advertising during sports programmes, had already been addressed in an interpretative communication of the Commission in 2004. These are now authorized under certain conditions

No specific provisions are made on the controversial issue of food advertising aimed at children, but the Parliament asked member states and the Commission to 'encourage audiovisual service providers to develop a code of conduct regarding children's programming containing advertising, sponsorship for unhealthy food and drinks'. As Garde (2008) reminds us, when the TWF Directive was adopted in 1989 there was very little discussion on how food advertising should be regulated at EU level. Since then, things have changed as 'a result of rising levels of obesity in all EU Member States'. Consequently, during the German presidency of the EU, it was suggested that the advertising of unhealthy food to children should be restricted. In Article 3.2 of the AMS Directive it is foreseen that:

> Member States and the Commission shall encourage media service providers to develop codes of conduct regarding inappropriate audiovisual commercial communication, accompanying or included in children's programmes, of foods and beverages containing nutrients and substances with a nutritional or physiological effect, in particular those such as fat, trans-fatty acids, salt/ sodium and sugars, excessive intakes of which in the overall diet are not recommended.

But, as Garde also notes,

> food advertising directed at children is subject to various texts of Community and national law, depending on the factual scenario at stake (medium used, practice at stake, interest to be protected . . .). That situation makes the legal landscape very difficult to understand, despite the Commission's express intention to simplify this landscape, so as to reduce fragmentation and consequently increase legal certainty for consumers and business operators alike. (2008: 43)

Product placement

Product placement within programmes (Article 11) was not covered by the TWF Directive. As Woods has observed, the 'legality of product placement was particularly problematic, especially given the reliance of many broadcasters on American programmes which are notable for containing references to products and brand' (2008: 66). Moreover, because the new technologies have enabled consumers 'to "pull" content individually, the incentives to include product placement will be increased both for the content providers and for the companies whose products/services are advertised. This will naturally lead to an increase in the quantity and quality of product placement' (Burri-Nenova, 2007a: 1715).

This was extremely controversial. After debates in the European Parliament, the AMS Directive defined product placement as 'any form of audiovisual commercial communication consisting of the inclusion of or reference to a product, a service or the trade mark thereof so that it is featured within a programme, in return for payment or for similar consideration', and a blanket ban was incorporated. Countries can opt out from this if they wish, but product placement 'shall be prohibited' in principle (Article 3g) 'unless member states decide otherwise' (Article 3.2). According to Article 3f, it is 'admissible' in film, drama and sports, but programmes have to meet all of the following requirements:

> (a) their content and, in the case of television broadcasting, their scheduling shall in no circumstances be influenced in such a way as to affect the responsibility and editorial independence of the media service provider;
> (b) they shall not directly encourage the purchase or rental of goods or services, in particular by making special promotional references to those goods or services;
> (c) they shall not give undue prominence to the product in question;
> (d) viewers shall be clearly informed of the existence of product placement. Programmes containing product placement shall be appropriately identified at the start and the end of the programme, and when a programme resumes after an advertising break, in order to avoid any confusion on the part of the viewer.

There is a let out, though, and 'By way of exception, Member States may choose to waive the requirements set out in point (d) provided that the programme in question has neither been produced nor commissioned by the media service provider itself or a company affiliated to the media service provider.' Programmes must not contain product placement of tobacco products or 'specific medicinal products or medical treatments available only on prescription in the Member State within whose jurisdiction the media service provider falls'.

Finally, the AMS Directive foresees (Article 26) that every three years the Commission will submit to the European Parliament, the Council and the European Economic and Social Committee a report on the application of the regulations and, 'if necessary, make further proposals to adapt it to developments in the field of audiovisual media services, in particular in the light of recent technological developments, the competitiveness of the sector and levels of media literacy in all Member States'.

Support schemes

Just a year after the introduction of the first TWF Directive, the EC launched the first 'MEDIA I Programme'. The driving force at that time was the advent of satellite television, and it was an intervention of the European Commission to provide financial support for the development and competitiveness of the audiovisual industry. The aim was to enable the latter to benefit from a Europe-wide market. This policy was first implemented through the MEDIA II programme, followed by MEDIA Plus and MEDIA Training (2001–6), and then the MEDIA 2007 programme (2007–13) (Euréval, 2007).

Indeed, the new MEDIA programme, called 'MEDIA Plus', was introduced in 2001 and focused on the transnational circulation of European audiovisual works within and outside the European Union (see box 4.1). It reinforced the link between market performance and support mechanisms (i.e. training and distribution) and was intended to be flexible enough to provide support for new projects arising from the development of digital technologies. It also set out to take greater account of the specific needs of countries with a low audiovisual capacity and/or a limited language

---

Box 4.1 MEDIA Plus and MEDIA Training – key figures

- 9,000 projects, 21 per cent of which are in development and 67 per cent in distribution
- Annual number of projects: 974 in 2001, 1,926 in 2006
- The five Group A countries (Germany, Spain, France, UK, Italy) receive two-thirds of the funds allocated
- Average sum per project: €72,000 in 2001, €44,000 in 2006
- Average rate of joint funding: 37 per cent
- Rate of joint funding in the other Group A countries: 39 per cent

Source: Euréval (2007).

---

market. MEDIA Plus has provided complementary support and is implemented alongside other Community measures such as the Fifth Framework Programme for research (1998–2002) and 'e-Europe' (financing of start-ups in the audiovisual sector through risk capital). The budget for the MEDIA Plus programme was €400 million for the period 2001–5.

On 11 February 2007, the Information Society and Media Commissioner, Mrs Viviane Reding, announced the launch of the new MEDIA programme, 'MEDIA 2007', which the Commission is funding with €755 million over a seven-year period to help Europe's film industry. The programme's priorities include improving production facilities, supporting countries or regions with a low production capacity or a restricted geographic and linguistic area, and promoting digitalization. The Commission has also called on EU filmmakers to embrace the new technology to help overcome the fragmentation of the market and improve access to Europe's film heritage.

There is also the 'i2i Audiovisual' support scheme, which aims to help audiovisual production companies access financing from banks and other financial institutions by supporting some of the costs of guarantees required and/or part of the costs of financing. Some 65 per cent of the MEDIA 2007 budget will help screen European works beyond the EU's borders (see chapter 5).

EU policy on media ownership

At the EU level, the regulation of concentration remains a controversial issue. Whereas the Council of Europe, under Article 10 of the European Convention of Human Rights, has been more active with the issue of media ownership and pluralism, the EU has remained ambivalent. But the Council of Europe's powers are rather weak. On the other hand, the EU does acknowledge and encourage competition and favours large-scale companies competing internationally in a liberal fashion. In effect, large firms in the EU, especially after the Maastricht Treaty, have become integral players in the policy-formation process, participating directly as private actors or collectively through new loose cross-border alliances (Papathanassopoulos, 2002).

Since the mid-1980s the European Parliament has been calling on the Commission to take an initiative in order to control, if not impede, the ongoing concentration of ownership in the European media sector. In 1992, the Commission published the Green Paper *Pluralism and Media Concentration in the Internal Market* (CEC, 1992). This consultative document reviewed existing levels of media concentration in Europe. It was heavily influenced by industrial imperatives and the policy orientations of Directorate General III and argued that the European media industry was hindered by ownership rules that were different in each member state. The Green Paper suggested three possible policy options:

- no action at the pan-European level;
- action to improve levels of transparency;
- positive intervention, probably through a directive, to harmonize media ownership rules throughout the member states.

These proposals were sent to the interested parties for feedback. The European Parliament and the Economic and Social Committee favoured the positive intervention policy option, but were against the main rationale of the Green Paper. Member states, on the other hand, were in favour of no action. Moreover, the media owners were against any EU initiative to harmonize legislation on media ownership, while some larger companies, such as News Corporation and Fininvest, were against any action at all, since it could be regarded as an impediment to investment. In the meantime, within the Commission there was growing debate on the matter. As Alison Harcourt (1998, 2005) points out, DG III was in favour of creating a strong internal market. Directorate General X (culture/audiovisual) rejected the industrial and internal market argument in favour of harmonizing media ownership rules at the EU level. At the same time, it was asking for the cultural dimension (pluralism) of media ownership. By contrast, Directorate General IV (competition) considered that regulation was not possible if the aim was to keep up with technological change.

Finally, as in the case of the previous directive, 'Television without Frontiers', many questioned whether the Commission was competent to pursue policies aimed at safeguarding pluralism (Hitchens, 1994). It was argued then that the whole issue should be dealt with by the Council of Europe, since pluralism is integral to the principle of freedom of speech (Lange and Van Loon, 1991: 26). This was also, to an extent, recognized by the Commission, and this seems to be the reason for justifying its intervention under the broad frame of securing the proper functioning of the internal market rather than the protection of pluralism (CEC, 1992: 99). The two main goals, as well as the combination of media ownership and media pluralism, may need different approaches, since some mergers, which do not threaten competition, might pose a threat to plurality, and vice versa (Doyle, 1997, 2002).

In 1993, the issue of media ownership became the responsibility of Directorate General XV (internal market). DG XV did not take any action on the issue, such as producing a draft directive, which would have been the next reasonable step. Instead, in 1994, it published a follow-up to the 1992 Green Paper, in which it presented and evaluated the outcome of the consultation process. Also surprising was that it called for a second round of consultations among the interested parties, in order to have a final answer on whether Community action was needed. These consultations produced exactly the same result as the previous ones: a lack of consensus concerning any attempt to harmonize media ownership policy at the EU level. After a two-year period of consultation, debate and considerable lobbying from major international and national media groupings, in July 1996 Commissioner Mario Monti presented a first draft of a directive on media pluralism to his colleagues. The main proposals of this draft were as follows.

- A 30 per cent upper limit on 'monomedia' ownership for radio and television broadcasters in their own broadcasting areas. One broadcasting undertaking could not control another (new or existing) if that equalled 30 per cent or more in designated market 'zones'.
- A 'multimedia threshold': an upper limit of 10 per cent for 'multimedia' concentration (i.e. ownership for a combination of different media (television, radio and/or newspapers). A venture already in one media could not own a different media (new or existing) if the total audience share of its media equalled 10 per cent or more in the area concerned.
- All market shares would be based on multiple audience measures within the area in question.
- The proposed regulations would allow member states, if they so wished, to exclude public service broadcasters from these upper limits.

Once again these proposals, reasonable and practical for some, raised new controversies. The main one focused on the level of diversity of ownership appropriate for different market sizes (local, regional or national level). The Commission was in favour of the measure of the market share within the specific region for a television or radio station. Some countries (notably the UK and Germany) disputed it. DG XV's response was to promise a more flexible approach to the upper ceilings suggested in the September 1996 draft, indicating that the 30 per cent threshold could be varied if national circumstances so demanded. But the Commission's negotiating position on upper ceilings was constrained by Parliament's consistent support for robust measures to counteract concentrations. Clearly, the greater the discretionary power left to member states in setting their own upper limits on media and cross-media ownership, the less effective any new directive would be, whatever its objectives (Doyle, 1997). But at the meeting on 4 September 1996 the Commissioners were not convinced by the proposals and turned the project down, asking for alterations.

DG XV put forward a new version in March 1997, the title of the proposed directive having been changed from '*Concentrations and Pluralism*' to

'*Media Ownership*' in the internal market. This signalled a move to deflect the focus away from pluralism (where the Commission's competence would be in question) towards the aim of removing obstacles to the internal market (Doyle, 1997).

In this new version, a 'flexibility clause' was added. This meant that the member states could authorize the overrun of thresholds in certain conditions – for example, if it involved a local media company that would otherwise go out of business or an independent undertaking whose programming was not profit-oriented. This exception would apply under the condition that the broadcaster in question was not simultaneously infringing these upper thresholds in more than one member state.

The proposed directive would oblige some member states to reform their legislative approach. They could not introduce stricter rules under the concentration thresholds. In addition, a ten-year transitional period would make it possible to introduce the concentration thresholds gradually, so as to take account of the situation in certain national markets, notably in small countries. During this period, a venture could exceed thresholds in a single member state, provided that 'appropriate measures' were taken to guarantee pluralism (Doyle, 1997). 'Appropriate measures' might include establishing, within any organization which breaches the limits, 'windows for independent programme suppliers' or a 'representative programming committee' (CEC, 1997b).

It is obvious that the proposals of Directorate General XV in this new version made further compromises in order to reach a consensus. What was important, however, was that with the modification of 'flexibility' it was not securing the issue of pluralism. As Doyle (1997) points out, it was clear that, in practice, the 'flexibility' clause would allow member states to maintain whatever upper restrictions on ownership are affordable – either economically or politically – in their own territories. This point makes it more questionable that the proposed directive was eventually abandoned. The fact is that even this proposal, though it enjoyed the support of a number of commissioners, provoked a storm of protest from media companies, especially the European Publishers Council, which saw it as an obstacle to competition in the information society. Moreover, the EU was already preoccupied with the 1997 *Green Paper on the Convergence of the Telecommunications, Media and Information Technology Sectors*, which deems that the trends towards consolidation and diversification in response to new opportunities opened up by liberalization of EU and world markets and with a view to the opportunities offered by convergence will go on (CEC, 1997c: 6–7).

As Radaelli (2000: 36) points out, 'the EU media concentration policy process has witnessed a persistent attempt of the Commission to finalize a draft proposal', but it has become clear that any attempt to tackle the issue of media ownership and concentration at a European level is unrealistic. The industrial imperatives of the information society and the new opportunities, stakes and interests of convergence make it difficult to tackle this thorny problem. In effect, 'convergence has already revealed the inadequacy of European initiatives to harmonise sectoral ownership regulation' (Iosifidis, 1999: 160). Added to this is the inadequacy of the tools used to measure and evaluate such things as market concentration and market influence.

The European Parliament, in its response to the Green Paper on convergence, insisted that the Commission should submit a proposal for a directive on the subject of media ownership and pluralism which would take account of all forms of electronic communication (CEC, 1999b: 8). But it is unlikely that any such an action or initiative to promote control or transparency of media ownership will take place in the foreseeable future. The same applies to the issue of self-regulation.

In short, the EU seems powerless to regulate the issue of concentration, apart from scrutinizing the mergers and acquisitions under the competition law (see also Doyle, 2007). This has been recognized by the Economic and Social Committee, which addressed those questions in its own initiative. On 29 March 2000, the Committee publicized a statement saying that, in order to prevent the eventual risk of abusive mergers, EU member states should consider extending current national media ownership rules (licence schemes, frequency allocation, audience-based thresholds, investments, etc.) to the new digital broadcasting services (terrestrial, satellite and cable). These rules should also be extended to the new sources of audiovisual and written information available on the internet. Community guidelines could be drawn up to uphold pluralism and national differences and to complement competition law by focusing on the social dimension and cultural diversity of the media. There should be coordination at European level too, particularly in the event of very strong international growth. On the issue of 'portal sites', which tend to funnel and standardize the information available to the detriment of pluralism, the Committee has proposed extending the powers of member state regulators, with Commission-level coordination (CES, 2002).

Future market developments will be dealt with in the same way as before – that is, through competition policy (Papathanassopoulos, 2002; Wheeler, 2004a; Harcourt, 2005; Michalis, 2007). The basic rules of competition for business firms are specified in Article 81 (previously Article 85) of the EC Treaty, which is concerned with agreements that prevent, restrict or distort competition, and Article 86, which prohibits abuse of a dominant position in the market. But, as Goldberg, Prosser and Verhulst observe, 'under certain very specific conditions, the Treaty makes provision for an exception to this principle of prohibition by authorising certain agreements between undertakings' (1998: 89). In general, the rules on competition forbid all restraints on competition or on trade rivalry between enterprises in member states except where certain agreements are not likely to be incompatible with the objective of the internal market. These rules effectively ban restrictive practices, which distort or prevent competition by the misuse of a dominant trade position.

Subsidies, which restrict competition, are also forbidden under Articles 92–4. Mergers are dealt with by the 'Merger Regulation' of 1989 (OJEC, 1990). The Commission (DG XV) has the power to prevent the creation of monopolies and cartels which would stifle competition in a substantial proportion of the trade in the commodities they produce. In order to put this into practice, the Commission has set out a number of criteria which would permit it to pass judgement on the suitability and appropriate mergers. In 2003 it issued a package on merger control guidelines (CEC, 2004). These guidelines provide a general framework on issues related to the 'impact on competition of mergers between competing firms'. In particular, as Iosifidis notes, they 'make it clear that mergers and acquisitions will be challenged only if they enhance the market power of companies in a manner that is likely to have adverse consequences for consumers, notably in the form of higher prices, poorer quality products, or reduced choice' (2007a: 105).

The Commission, on the one hand, favours mergers, acquisitions and the creation of joint ventures to provide new television (notably pay-TV) services and, on the other, examines whether these moves can eliminate competition. This is not an easy task, since the one goal contradicts the other. It is obvious that any merger, acquisition or joint venture aims to eliminate competition and at the same time to strengthen its position in the market. Moreover, the regulation on mergers and acquisitions covers only those which affect competition in the market in question (Iosifidis, 1996: 247). Consequently, it has allowed many others to proceed simply because they did not meet the high thresholds.

DG XV, the directorate responsible for competition in the EU, has been called to consider a number of mergers, acquisitions and joint ventures in the television sector (see also Pons, 1998; Pons and Lucking, 1999), but sometimes seems to have become 'sympathetic to the formation of large corporations and . . . does not follow a consistent competition approach' (Iosifidis, 2007a: 109). As Alison Harcourt explains, the EU Competition Directorate, although has taken an active role in determining the developments of national media markets, has gradually, as a result of its liberalization policy, taken on consideration of media pluralism and the public interest in contrast to the rulings of the European Court of Justice (Harcourt, 2005: 41–65). For instance, in July 2010 the Commission allowed Sky Italia, owned by the tycoon Rupert Murdoch, to compete for a digital terrestrial television frequency in Italy, challenging Prime Minister Silvio Berlusconi's media empire and the public broadcaster RAI. In practice, it seems that the Commission has favoured the growth of larger European groups with media interests in many member states but has prevented concentration in national markets (ibid.: 117–50). At the same time, with regard to the application of competition rules, it has asked for a fresh competition policy to follow up the new developments. This would abandon a narrow approach based on specific rules by category of agreement or by sector of activity and adopt an approach based on apprehension of the economic effects of the vertical restrictions whatever the sector of activity concerned.

It is unlikely that the trends towards concentration in the wider communications environment will cease, since every player will attempt to extend its dominant position into new or neighbouring markets. Though the desire remains on the part of the Commission to ensure that citizens have access to a variety of information sources, allowing them to form opinions without 'undue influence of one dominant opinion-forming player' (CEC, 2007c), it has not necessarily had the powers to ensure that this translates into policies. As with other areas, it is easier to point to the risks and the dangers than actually to create mechanisms to support those aims and objectives. This brings about regulatory uncertainty rather than a coherent competitive environment (Harcourt and Picard, 2009).

Public broadcasting and the EU

In recent years, as noted in chapter 2, European public service broadcasters have faced the erosion of both their viewing share and their revenues. Since around the late 1980s, private broadcasters have accused public broadcasters of being overfunded and under-regulated and complained that this has undermined the competitiveness of the television industry, as well as adversely affecting multi-channel television, television production, radio broadcasting, internet content and the press. They have also accused the European Commission of delays in dealing with these issues, since it had taken years to address some of the complaints against the system of funding public service broadcasters. Originally, the Commission had found it quite difficult to deal with complaints from private broadcasters. Although it refused to consider PSB as an exception to the rules on state aid enshrined in Article 87 of the EU Treaty, it was also under pressure from member states to recognize PSB as a special case. Its first effort to create a legal framework for dealing with this issue was the adoption of the 'Amsterdam Protocol' in 1997. Under this framework, state aid would be prohibited when subsidies, coupled with advertising revenues, exceed the costs of meeting public service obligations (the so-called proportionality test).[3] For example, newspaper publishers and other private content providers fear that state aid may be used exclusively to fund the online activities of public broadcasters.

With the Amsterdam Protocol, the Commission started to play an important role regarding the future of public service broadcasting in Europe. In May 2000 it adopted a decision that granted an exemption from normal antitrust law to the rules of the European Broadcasting Union (EBU) governing the joint acquisition and sharing of broadcasting rights for sports events in the framework of the Eurovision system. However, some of the complaints were left pending, and private channels sued the Commission before the European Court of First Instance (CFI) for failure to act in accordance with its obligations.

In November 2001, the Commission released a broadcasting communication on the application of state aid rules to public service broadcasting. It was, for the time being, a definitive stand on the issue, stating the need for a clear definition of the remit (while declaring that a 'wide' definition, practically encompassing everything that a PSB broadcaster puts on the air, could be acceptable), for formal entrustment of the public service mission to a particular broadcaster or broadcasters, for transparency (including dual accounting, so that public funding cannot be used to finance or cross-subsidize commercial activities) and for independent supervision. It also noted that, while member states are free to define the public service remit, subject only to checks for 'manifest errors', they are nevertheless required to lay down the public service obligations in a clear and precise manner (CEC, 2008d). State aid should not exceed the net cost of the public service mission, taking into account other direct or indirect revenues. The broadcasting communication further stated that the existence of state aid for public broadcasters in a particular country cannot be assumed automatically, but must be established on a case-by-case basis, and that the Commission would examine possible disproportionate effects on competition through overcompensation and cross-subsidization into commercial activities, as well as anti-competitive behaviour. In fact, since the adoption of the 2001 broadcasting communication, the Commission has taken almost twenty relevant decisions in this field (ibid.). In 2005–6 it closed the procedures involving Spanish, Italian, Portuguese and French public broadcasters. As Humphreys and his colleagues point out:

> little evidence [has been found] to suggest that EU state-aid policy has impacted negatively on public service broadcasters, unless encouraging a

> clearer definition of their remit and rendering *their* finance more transparent are counted as 'deregulatory'. All of the rulings that the Commission competition authorities have made thus far regarding the development of new media services by . . . public service broadcasters have been in their favour. (Humphreys et al., 2008: 7)

In January 2008, the Commission published a consultation paper on the future framework which will apply to the state funding of public service broadcasting and called for a review of the broadcasting communication, marking the new policy of the EU with respect to the public service remit in the new media environment (CEC, 2008d).

In general, the Commission seeks to 'modernize' the broadcasting communication and, according to Commissioner Neelie Kroes (2008), to give full value to the Amsterdam Protocol, to strengthen the principle of subsidiarity, to enhance the flexibility of the regulatory framework, and to have more effective control at the national level. As Karen Donders and Caroline Pauwels have commented: 'Whereas Member States fear too much Commission intervention, the European Commission, on the contrary, fears that Member States abuse the margins of the European Treaty in order to expand the digital public service remit in unauthorized ways, such as financing commercial digital activities' (2008: 295).

In 2008, the Commission also decided to clear some other cases regarding the state aid of public funding, including in Irish public broadcasters RTÉ and TG4 (Teilifís na Gaeilge) and the Flemish broadcaster VRT, as well as to close another investigation concerning the financing regime for German public service broadcasters in the light of formal commitments from the German government to amend the current regime. The amendments included a more precise definition of the public service mission in particular as regards new media activities. But in April 2008, the Commission launched an investigation concerning state aid for the British Channel 4 in order to meet the capital costs of the digital switchover. In July 2010, it approved the new tax-based funding system for the Spanish public broadcaster RTVE, on which it had opened a formal investigation under EU state aid rules in December 2009. It also approved the annual funding mechanism for France Télévisions, which is deemed to comply with the EU's state aid rules. In the case of the RTVE, the Commission had doubts concerning the compatibility of the new taxes with EU law, in particular the rules on electronic communications networks and services, but concluded that they were in fact in line with the state aid rules, because they ensured that RTVE would not be over-compensated for providing public broadcasting services. In the case of France Télévisions, the concern of the Commission was that the public broadcaster received an additional subsidy from the national budget. This was based on the new public broadcasting service legislation, under which advertising on public channels would be reduced and ultimately abolished altogether by the end of 2011. The Commission concluded that the measure complied with the rules on state aid, particularly as regards the mechanisms for preventing overcompensation for the costs of the public service mission.

These moves on the part of the European Commission suggest that there 'remains an uncertainty with regard to the future application of the state aid rules to public broadcasters' engagement in the new media' (Humphreys et al., 2008: 7), and that it does not follow a clear approach in its wish to protect the competition in the field. As in most of the cases, and as in the past, the Commission may leave the whole issue to the member states to deal with as they see fit.

Summary

Since the publication of the Green Paper on convergence (CEC, 1997c), the European Commission has come to realize that the then regulatory framework for television broadcasting in Europe no longer corresponds to the realities of the communications sector. In fact, in an era where TV is moving away from the traditional set and into mobile phones and broadband internet, the Commission has been forced to extend its competence to the communications sector as a whole.

The EU has consistently sought to provide a framework favourable to the development and harmonization of the audiovisual sector as well as to support the European programme and cultural industry. Regulation shows the effort of the EU to *Europeanize* the media, either through directives and rulings or through the initiatives of larger member states. The case of the transferring of the BBC's public value test to other member states is indicative. The test is a means by which public value and market impact are taken into account for all major service-related investment proposals. The BBC uses this procedure in order to decide whether an audiovisual service has a public or commercial dimension. The Commission, after using a similar approach by the German authorities, the so-called Three Step Test (*Drei Stufen Test*), seems to have adopted this approach and judges the public broadcasters' new media services accordingly (Humphreys et al., 2008: 7–8).

Moreover, the Commission also aims to make the European media system more competitive and responsive to the needs of the global and regional markets. While in the past some questioned the competence/jurisdiction of the EU to deal with media output, today they ask for its support. The television directives and the new 'Audiovisual Media Services Directive', together with ECJ jurisprudence, 'introduce a balance between the internal audiovisual media market and legitimate public interest objectives, putting the protection of viewers of audiovisual media content always to the fore' (Herold, 2008: 23).

The most significant change in the AMS Directive is the introduction of the concept of 'audiovisual services' and of minimal regulation applying to both linear and non-linear services. The much-hyped product placement issue, though politically sensitive, 'is economically over-rated' (Woods, 2008), while the new directive appears to be more realistic compared with its predecessors, since it aims to cope with the changes, present and future, in the media landscape. However, the diversity that exists among member states cannot easily be regulated by rules which aim to harmonize the European audiovisual or communication sectors. Extending the regulations to linear media does mean that the EU can tackle the issue. Since the AMS Directive represents only a minimal regulatory framework and the member states may adopt rules that are stricter or more lax, new and perhaps more flexible rules and, probably, a new directive that will cover the whole communications sector may be needed in the near future. It is yet to be seen whether and to what extent the AMS Directive would apply.

At the time of writing, only a few countries have partly implemented the AMS Directive. According to the Commission, in December 2009 only Belgium, Romania and Slovakia had implemented it in full. Denmark, France, Luxembourg and the UK notified the Commission of some measures taken. Hungary's legislative process came to a complete halt after the draft law did not pass in Parliament. It has been partly put in place by Austria, Germany, Ireland, Malta and the Netherlands without the Commission being notified. In other countries, the draft law is still being discussed, has just been published or is still in public consultation (Europa 2009c). By and large, in most EU countries, regulators and governments have tried to incorporate the new directive, but it should also be noted that the old directive had not been implemented by some of the larger countries, notably Italy and Spain. There may be other problems to contend with, since providers of non-linear audiovisual services are to be regulated for the first time and questions still remain over whether the directive applies in the case of platforms which deliver user-generated content, such as YouTube.

These issues reflect the peculiar mix of liberalism and protectionism that coexists within the EU and the fact that that liberalism, deregulation and market forces mean 'different things in different issue areas and for different groups' (Jabko, 2006: 37). Alison Harcourt (2005) considers this dimension within the frame of 'negative' and 'positive' integration. In the former, the

EU, though the Commission, the Parliament and the aid of the ECJ, removes the barriers to trade, while, in the case of the latter, the same bodies, especially the Commission and the Parliament, have tried to protect pluralism and the public interest. For Harcourt (2005) and Humphreys (2007), the EU audio-visual policy is biased towards 'negative integration'. In one way or another, the Commission has served as an agent of change and now has the experience to frame the market in terms that would produce a broad-based coalition of supporters. Remarkably, even though some governments and vested interests wanted more liberalization and deregulation, they all ended up seeing the intervention of the Commission as a means of accomplishing their own ends. Regardless of the convergence in communications policy (Harcourt, 2003), the European communication field remains fragmented and complex, and 'the absence of strong enforcement tools make non-observance high likely' (Michalis, 2007: 292).

The EU's policy model appears to confirm Castells's (2000) conception of the Union as a 'network state' characterized by a complex network of national and sub-national institutions that give rise to a *Europe à la carte* – i.e. different levels of integration depending upon countries and issues. In the case of media policy, the Commission has shown 'how it has operated as a "network state" in which the principles of global capitalism have shaped its marketization of the European television industries' (Wheeler, 2007: 245).

5   The Question of Content: Quality, Availability and Production

With the deregulation of broadcasting systems, most countries gradually adopted a market-led philosophy of broadcasting similar to the American one – a philosophy which attempts to interpret the possibility of expansion in television outlets, driven by private capital, as something which is in the public interest. The sleight of hand is contained in the manner in which political and commercial objectives are passed off as being made on behalf of and for the public. But, as new channels develop, there has been an increase in both competition and demand for programmes. In fact, many channels, principally commercial ones, appear to be following a similar strategy: a reliance initially on (usually American) imports, a dependence on certain types of entertainment programmes (television games, reality shows, talk shows, soaps and series) and a move away from informational and educational content. Although it has been claimed that viewers prefer local national programmes – and there has been an increase in domestic productions, at least in the prime-time hours – the fact that many such programmes are based on international, mainly American, formats is often overlooked (Keane and Moran, 2008).

Content, then, is an important part of the media sector and in itself part of a significant industry. The content sector alone – media, publishing, marketing and advertising – contributes around 5 per cent to Europe's GDP (about €433 billion), putting it ahead of the telecommunications industry (€254 billion). Online content is still a relatively immature sector, representing less than 10 per cent of total revenues from music, video and games, but according to an Information Society Policy Link report (CEC, 2007d) it is experiencing double-digit growth.

The first part of this chapter will explore developments in the new media content sector brought about principally through the processes of convergence and digitalization. The second part will focus mainly on television programming and the more traditional concerns across Europe with regard to the threats from imports and the challenges of exports.

New media, new content

The proliferation of media and thus of the availability of media content enables consumers to exercise more control than ever before over when and what they access and how they access it. This new situation also throws up challenges for established media and telecommunications companies as technological convergence and digitalization blurs the distinctions between distribution channels and producers of content. 'Content creators', or 'aggregators', have roles that are not confined to a particular platform (Deloitte, 2007), just as the traditional 'television network' is becoming available online. YouTube, for example, has no fewer than seventeen public service media partners distributing their material, and it also now shows full-length television programmes in addition to its shorter video offerings in order to generate advertising revenue. It has also forged similar alliances with news organizations, which have been invited to upload their video content for distribution via its Google News service. In this way, convergence and digitalization not only change the way people access and consume content but they also create a range of different business models. New entrants in the media industry, such as Google and YouTube, have exploited increasing demand for user-generated content, whereas the established, traditional media companies have taken longer to exploit these kinds of opportunities (CEC, 2009c).

A study commissioned by the European Commission which sought both to assess the potential growth of digital content, including TV, movies, games, radio, music and publishing, across new distribution platforms and technologies and to identify the current and potential economic, technical and legal obstacles that might hinder the exploitation of digital content in Europe found that the spread of broadband, the roll-out of advanced mobile networks, and the massive adoption of digital devices mean that online content is on the verge of becoming mass market, especially in the sector of music and games, where the proportion of revenues made already represents a significant percentage of overall income. Although the European market is growing steadily, technological, economic and legal challenges need to be addressed to ensure that the creative industries are able to maximize the potential economic and social benefits (*Screen Digest* et al., 2006). There are, for example, obstacles to the spread of digital content in Europe: 'European markets are not always at the forefront of digital distribution of content and are lagging behind more advanced markets in some aspects. By some measures, Europe is second behind Japan and Korea (but before North America) for mobile content distribution and mobile TV and second behind the US for broadband content distribution' (ibid.: 12). Nevertheless, the report was

Table 5.1 Uptake of digital distribution/exploitation of content in Europe – key figures

Sector	2005		2010	
	€ million*	%**	€ million	%
Music (online and mobile)	196.3	2.0	1,794	20.4
Films (VoD)	30	0	1,269	7
Games (online, mobile)	699	11.2	2,302	33.4
TV programmes (VoD and digital advertising)	4.5	n/a	689	n/a
Publishing	849	2	2,001	5.4
Radio	15	0.3	250	4.8
Total	1,793		8,305	

Notes: * Market size in terms of revenues.
** Percentage of the total sector revenues.

Source: Screen Digest et al./European Commission, 2007: 9

able to identify the key sectors in which developments in production and distribution are emerging (see also table 5.1).

- *Textual content* This generated, in 2005, the most important revenues on the internet (around €850 million per year), which was, however, equivalent to no more than 2 per cent of the publishing industry's total annual revenues. By 2010, this percentage was predicted to have risen to 5.4 per cent, or €2 billion, coming in second after games. According to the study, online publishing essentially covers newspapers, scientific publications and e-books. For example, newspapers have developed business models based on online advertising (generating 1 to 4 per cent of European newspapers' advertising revenue), subscription-based access and pay-per-download. On the other hand, print advertising revenues have declined gradually. Search engines have around 30 to 50 per cent of the market, depending on the particular country, and there is no immediate reason to suppose that this will fall.
- *Video and movies* This is projected to become the fastest-growing market in the near future, with an expected increase in revenues from €30 million in 2005 to €1.2 billion in 2010. The lion's share, researchers say, will come from membership-based video-on-demand services, since the European online TV market (distribution of television programmes over the open internet) is foreseen to generate €689 million. At that time, digital exploitation will account for 7 per cent of all film revenues in Europe. The UK is and will probably remain the largest European market for VoD.
- *Music* Music is the foremost market for online distribution in Europe, with Apple's iTunes still in the lead. In 2005, the online music market

generated €120 million from *à la carte* sales (that is, the sale of music tracks over the internet, either individually or in an album bundle) and subscription platforms, generating €67 million in profit. These figures are expected to increase by a factor of ten. The USA, Japan, the UK, Germany and France are the top five digital music markets worldwide. In general, countries with a high percentage of digital sales are the strongest markets for music sales overall. Online music subscriptions accounted for only 10 per cent of this total. The fundamental value chain of the music business can be segmented into three sectors – production (creation of content), distribution to outlets, and sale/transmission to the end user. The main stakeholder categories therefore fall within one or a combination of these responsibilities. According to the study, companies that are considered the traditional power base of the industry – the four major record labels Universal, Sony BMG, EMI and Warner Music – are involved primarily in the business of creation and distribution.

- *Radio* Fifteen million Europeans listen to streaming radio broadcasts every week. By 2010, that figure is expected to more than double, and 11 million Europeans are expected to listen to podcasts regularly. Radio, however, will remain first and foremost an on-the-air medium, with €250 million, or 5 per cent, of all advertising revenues coming from the online market. There are four different business models for digital radio services: broadcast digital radio, online radio, podcasting and mobile handheld radio. This last is expected to be the fastest-growing radio segment in the near future.
- *Online and mobile games* Games generated almost €700 million in revenues in 2005 and are predicted to become the single biggest source of revenue on the internet, generating €2.3 billion in 2010. This is considered to be the most advanced content market in terms of digital distribution/exploitation. There are a number of different digital 'channels' and business models, including the distribution of games via mobile phone networks, interactive TV systems, and the internet (comprising both digital distribution and the playing of games over the network).

For the European Union and the larger member states, digital convergence is becoming an economic reality which creates great opportunities for content providers and technology industries. At the same time, it represents a major challenge to European companies, which will need to develop strategies and structures that help them exploit content across a variety of platforms and so prevent other countries, principally the USA, from cornering the market. They will therefore need to develop profitable and sustainable business models that are robust enough to thrive in the market of today yet flexible enough to capitalize on the market of tomorrow.

However, this is not an easy task. The transition from analogue to digital content is anticipated to affect every aspect of the communication environment and the relevant market, from technology and marketing to content generation and global distribution. Platform owners (for example, television/radio network operators, and broadband providers) are already losing their monopoly on reaching the public, and media companies are losing their monopoly on creating content (Deloitte, 2007). Moreover, advances in technologies lead to new and improved media experiences, which in turn lead to new forms of content, which in turn create spaces for new providers and distributors. For example, Web 2.0 applications such as blogs, podcasts, wiki, or video sharing enable users easily to create and share text, videos or pictures and to play a more active and collaborative role in content creation, while user-generated content services such as Google Video, YouTube, DailyMotion, MySpace or Flickr give people the opportunity to upload and share video clips, etc. User-generated content has gained momentum in recent years owing to a transformation of the media environment, with major implications for traditional media and new media companies alike. This situation will also cause new investments that drive continued technology advances and the creation of new jobs (CEC, 2009a).

The EU and the new media 'content'

Since the mid-1990s, the EU has emphasized the potential of digital media and their content on account, as noted above, of their economic as well as their societal dimensions (Cawley and Preston, 2007). In 2005 it initiated a four-year programme called 'eContent Plus' to make content more accessible, usable and exploitable in a number of areas – geographic, educational, cultural, scientific, and scholarly. This programme expired in December 2008, and it is currently being continued within other programmes such as that for digital libraries. As is the case with most EU initiatives, such programmes and policies start with big ambitions, but the relevant markets are too fragmented to enable them to be fully exploited (CEC, 2008e). Moreover, policy approaches to content innovation vary at the national level. Finland and Austria have well-structured strategies and support a rich layer of projects to digitalize cultural content, while Ireland framed technological developments as the key driver of innovation (Cawley and Preston, 2007: 262). By and large, the European Commission has undertaken a number of initiatives over the past few years, with a view to promoting the development of creative content online.

- The *i2010 – A European Information Society for Growth and Employment* initiative was launched on 1 June 2005 as a framework for addressing the main challenges and developments in the information society and media sectors up to 2010. Its main objective was the creation of a Single European Information Space, offering increased legal and economic certainty for rich and diverse content to develop and circulate in Europe. Ultimately, this will create a sound market basis for distribution on a European and global scale.
- The *High Level Group on Digital Rights Management Systems* aims to develop a common understanding towards improving cooperation to address challenges such as DRM and interoperability, private copying levies and DRM, and migration to legitimate services.
- The development of a *Film Online Charter*, which was agreed by business leaders in May 2006, represents the joint accomplishment of representatives of three groups of key players – film and content industry, internet service providers and telecom operators. The charter is based on three main principles: working together to improve the availability of film online services on a mutually profitable basis; education and awareness increasing respect for copyright in order to secure the sustainable availability of content; and co-operation to fight piracy.
- The *Digital Libraries Initiative* aims to make Europe's cultural and scientific heritage easier and more attractive to use online. One important objective of the initiative is to facilitate the creation of the European Digital Library, a multilingual access point to cultural collections from all member states. In 2008, the European Commission launched the 'Europeana' project, and within a few months it offered over 7 million digitalized books, maps, photographs, film clips, paintings and musical extracts.
- The revision of the 'Television without Frontiers Directive', which led to the 'Audiovisual Media Services Directive', included regulations which also apply to online media (see chapter 4).

The EU has thus sought to develop a coherent and coordinated policy related to the content and creative industries in order for them to take advantage of convergence and digitalization and realize their full potential for growth and employment. This has been a common theme of the EU since about 2005. In setting out this agenda, the Commission also seeks to draw attention to the four main horizontal challenges which it believes need action at the EU level (CEC, 2008e).

- *Availability of creative content* Lack of both creative content for online distribution and active licensing of rights on new platforms remains a major obstacle for the development of online services. Since online content is a nascent market, the value of new forms of distribution is sometimes still unknown. This results in major difficulties in settling terms of trade. Most of the difficulties associated with availability of content are considered as inherent to emerging markets, and stakeholders are expected to find innovative and collaborative solutions to exploit content online and prevent or remedy bundling, exclusivity or non-use of media rights.

- *Multi-territory licensing for creative content* The online environment allows content services to be made available across the internal market. However, the lack of multi-territory copyright licences makes it difficult for online services to benefit fully from this potential. It seems that rights holders have first priority to take advantage of the potential benefits of multi-territory licensing, and also that there is a need to improve the existing mechanisms to allow for the development of the latter.

- *Interoperability and transparency of digital rights management systems (DRMs)* Digital technologies change the prerequisites of rights management in the new online and digitalized communication environment. This can be seen as a key opportunity which will lead the content sector to the development of innovative business models. As lengthy discussions among stakeholders have not yet led to the deployment of interoperable DRM solutions, there is a need to set a framework for transparency by ensuring proper consumer information. It has also been said that a policy by the EU on this issue may lead to a restriction on the freedom of citizens.

- *Legal offers and piracy* Piracy and unauthorized up- and downloading of copyrighted content remain central concerns. It would seem appropriate to instigate cooperation procedures (a code of conduct) among access/service providers, rights holders and consumers in order to ensure a wide offering of attractive content, consumer-friendly services, adequate protection of copyrighted works, awareness raising/education on the importance of copyright, and close cooperation to fight piracy/unauthorized file-sharing. It should be noted that there is no consensus on the remedies in view of the different visions of stakeholders regarding the future management of intellectual property rights in the digital age (CEC, 2009c).

Within this context and policy environment, actions at the EU level have been requested by telecommunications operators, publishers and commercial broadcasters, while others have asked the Commission not to intervene in a market which is still young and dynamic as the consequences are unforeseeable. For example, although subscription content has mostly failed as a mechanism for the online news business in the past, changes in technology and consumer culture may mean that it is once more becoming an option.

Moreover, media companies, which traditionally have been on the creative side of the value chain, are constantly looking for new ways to reach and sell to audiences. But in order to accomplish this, they must respond to consumers' emerging preferences for pulling content on demand, receiving personalized 'push' content, and contributing content of their own. Telecommunications companies, which conventionally have been on the access side of the value chain, are currently making the lion's share of capital investments to build the infrastructure and networks for the digital turn-on. These companies – despite their heavy financial commitment – will also have to analyse their position and strengths to determine the most profitable places to be in the new communication system – a system that requires companies to be in a constant state of alarm, searching the best position in the converged value chain.

To capitalize may require a new approach at both the technical and the legal level. This may present a new opportunity for European content production. The EU aims, on the one hand, to enable Europeans to access their favourite works wherever and whenever they want and on whatever platform (TV, mobile phone, internet) they want and, on the other hand, to motivate relevant companies and business to react in the digital convergence environment by forming new alliances or mergers. This is not an easy task, since alliances and mergers or acquisitions increase the complexity of the business, making it harder and riskier to manage, as the recent experience suggests. By and large, a significant horizontal integration is expected, according to media pundits, as companies find their new role in the value chain and structure themselves accordingly. This will be a combination of both operational and technical convergence and traditional merger and acquisition-led integration. In this new value chain, traditional labels such as 'movie studio', 'record company' and 'television network' will give way to new roles such as 'content creator', 'aggregator' and 'platform provider' (Deloitte, 2007: 5; 2010).

Traditional content providers are increasingly looking for new business models, although they will have to work within an unstable economic environment. In the past, many of the models have been focused on payment methods, or ease of payment from the consumer's perspective (Cawley and Preston, 2007: 265). Advertisers are increasingly likely to embed advertising into content throughout the chain, at times becoming content commissioners and creators themselves. The future media landscape is therefore likely to become more interactive and the relationships among the players to become more complex (Deloitte, 2010).

But is Europe ready for the new era? The challenges are, to a certain extent, similar to the ones faced in the analogue era. The European Union is fragmented in terms of market and culture. This makes the creation of content a high-risk investment sector, whereas development and production of quality creative content is often very costly. The mix of cultural traditions, languages and practices within the EU makes it difficult to provide content that will achieve success across all the member states. Given the costs of production, risks are inevitable. As Cawley and Preston note:

> local content in local languages, attuned to the cultural specificities of the region, can act as a driver of broadband. So far, much of this has been user generated. There is scope for greater input from professionally generated content. Much may depend on the extent to which state subsidies shift from supporting broadband networks and tools towards favouring innovative content applications. (2007: 266)

Television content

The race to develop content is by no means a new or recent one. It is reminiscent of the race to produce content during the analogue era, although there are some important differences. In the last two decades there has been a significant change in European TV programme production in terms of both distribution and format. In fact, the proliferation of channels has resulted in a sharp increase in the total volume of broadcast hours and consequently an increase in demand for programmes. That said, European TV producers' income is still dominated by commissions and recommissions from the three to six main traditional networks in each market. Public broadcasters still account for half of all commission spend, excluding news, across Europe and about 40 per cent of all produced output (O&O, 2007). But since the audiovisual landscape has become very competitive, TV channels are in a constant race to fill their programming schedules much faster than they used to do and, more importantly, to be more innovative. This means that TV channels, at least in Europe, are always searching for new genres, which in turn has led to a continuous evolution, and adaptation, of traditional TV genres, such as infotainment, edutainment, docushows, reality and reality quiz shows. Moreover, the cost of content rights has increased because of the greater competition and especially on account of the aggressive competition policy of pay-TV channels dealing in films and sport.

The increase in the volume of programming

The demand for new programming comes from increased competition and from the advent of new channels, especially the thematic ones. According to the European Audiovisual Observatory's estimates (EAO, 2008d), of the

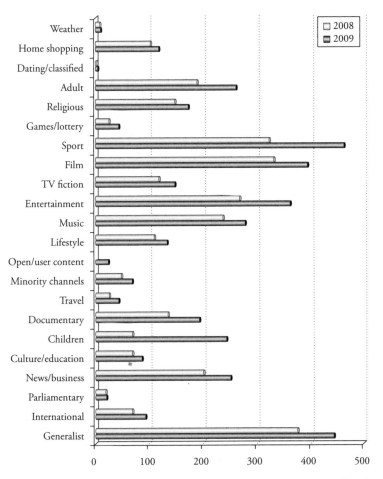

Figure 5.1 Nationwide TV channels available in the EU-27, plus Croatia and Turkey, by genre

Source: Based on EAO (2008d: 111; 2009: 111).

5,068 active channels which were available to EU audiences in 2008, 4,663 were established in one of the twenty-seven EU countries or the two candidate countries (Croatia and Turkey), and 405 originate from other countries. Of the 4,663 European channels, 381 were nationwide terrestrial channels (with an analogue and/or digital national licence); 2,473 nationwide channels were accessible through cable, satellite or IPTV, and there were 1,809 regional and local channels. Of these, 376 were of generalist content and the rest thematic, the majority providing entertainment (films, sports and music) and a few other genres, such as home shopping or adult content (EAO, 2008d, 2009) (see figure 5.1).

The most successful thematic channels are those covering news, sports, music, and children's programmes. According to IDATE (2003), the market for thematic channels will gradually evolve, resulting in:

- a small number of powerful thematic channels with strong brand names which can be marketed either as part of the basic package or as options;
- smaller thematic channels with an annual budget of €6 to 8 million, whose programmes are aimed at a limited audience. These channels will be marketed as options and not as part of the basic package;
- medium-sized thematic channels, in between the two noted above, with budgets ranging from €8 to 15 million. Given that their position has yet to be firmly established, the future of these channels remains uncertain, unless a major corporation backs them.

The UK and the English language continue to drive channel growth. The UK has by far the widest number: 416 channels aimed specifically at British viewers. In Europe, the next largest country in terms of thematic channels is France, with 246, followed by Italy with 206, Spain with 108 and Germany with 93 (*Screen Digest*, 2005c).

A new 'défi américain'

More channels mean more content to fill the TV schedules, but the problem for Europe is that it is difficult to compete with the USA. Although the circulation of European works outside their national markets has improved in the last decade, US productions are still dominant (see figure 5.2). For instance, only 20 per cent of DVDs sold in Europe have European content and over 70 per cent of the films shown are American or are co-produced with the USA (CEC, 2007d). The annual EU trade deficit with the USA in this sector is estimated to be €7 billion. US productions accounted for between 60 and 70 per cent of member states' receipts from cinema ticket sales in 2007, while the respective European share of the American market is in the order of 1 or 2 per cent and in the rest of the world between 2 and 5 per cent. The concern over American imports in light of the deregulation of broadcasting after 1980 has been expressed in the context of the 1993 negotiations in the Uruguay Round of the GATT (General Agreement on Trade and Services), especially on the trade in cultural goods and programmes, as well its successor GATS (General Agreement of Trade in Services), started in 2000 under the general liberalization of online services (Wheeler, 2000; Puppis, 2008) and the Trade Related Intellectual Property Rights (TRIPS) agreement (Young, 2007). The EU, though concerned with the

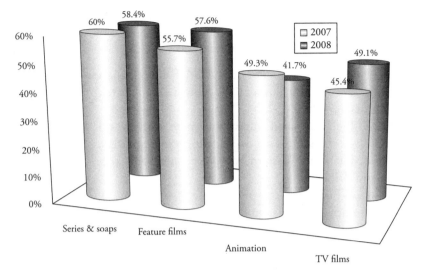

Figure 5.2 US programming in European television, 2007–8

Source: Based on EAO (2008d: 166; 2009: 166).

défi américain (the American challenge), could not take any further steps as it was not able to impose stricter TV programming quotas in the 1997 revision of the 'Television without Frontiers Directive'. Thus, in terms of policy direction, the EU has in practice failed to support its initiative on *exemption culturelle* in spite of the fact it 'is much the most lucrative export market for US media' (Tunstall and Machin, 1999: 3). One might also note that the programming sector has been 'protected' because it was seen as serving functions other than regulating competition (such as maintaining cultural diversity and integrity), taking the 'characteristics of social trade politics' (Young, 2007: 802).

While the US industry remains distribution led and the European one production led and fragmented, there is a convergence between the European and the US media. According to Jeremy Tunstall (2008: 247), 'the European and American media are becoming a single Euro-American media industry'. The other industries are those on the Indian subcontinent and in East Asia (China, Hong Kong, South Korea and Taiwan) plus the Arabic-language media (from Morocco to the Persian Gulf) (ibid.: 8–9). Although this suggests that there is no longer any dominating or controlling centre and that the USA is nowadays 'only one among many media production centres in different world regions that exchange their products more or less reciprocally with one another, with none of them so much larger than the others that it could be said to dominate them' (Corcoran, 2007: 91), for Tunstall, the US media 'play a much lesser role than national media'. 'Euro-American media is a more accurate description than the global media' (Tunstall, 2008: xiv), and this can be identified in the following ways.

- In terms of media technology the USA has been the traditional leader. While it developed the internet, the growth of mobile telephony was led by European companies.
- Although the Hollywood studios dominate in the world market, US production is at the same time dependent on its importers, principal among which are the bigger Western European countries: France, Germany, Italy, Spain and Britain.
- Hollywood–European 'co-productions' of various kinds have been common since the 1920s (with the exception of the 1940s).
- While the USA has advantages in the provision of entertainment (movies, TV programming), Europe has advantages in news, since its 'big collection of big news agencies outpoints America's lone Associated press'.
- Many US media companies seek to establish production subsidiaries in Europe by looking for local partners in order to invest in projects.
- Increasingly since the 1980s European and American media policies have been coordinated. The EU in practice follows similar policies to the USA in the media sector, for example, in antitrust, fair competition and copyright.
- The European media started lobbying in Brussels in order to promote or defend their interests long before the establishment of an EU competition commissioner, while the Hollywood majors began to do so in the 1920s and 'lobbied aggressively in Europe'. (Ibid.: 3)

The Euro-American media, according to Tunstall, is the 'the leading media force', but perhaps not for long. India, China and Japan, the big population countries, now export at least as much as they import. In effect, at least 85 per cent of the US population consumes media which is not made in the USA. Moreover, the big population countries have media exports of their own that equal or outstrip any imports. China, with 1.3 billion people, relies overwhelmingly on home production in local languages. So, with Bollywood, does India. Egypt looks after the Middle East. Moreover, the bigger Latin American countries now make most of their own popular media – and export lurid soaps to Spanish-speaking channels everywhere, including the USA. Despite the decline in Euro-American, in particular US, content in global media, the US media are still hugely dominant economically. In Europe, American firms still held a 'commanding position' (Tunstall, 2008: 278), while US media formats (e.g. American Idol TV) are widely copied around the world (ibid.: 382).

The increase in the volume of European productions

In spite of US dominance, European works have had a greater impact on the programme schedules of European TV channels, with broadcasters preferring EU films and fiction to those produced by Hollywood or other countries. The input of the EU should be recognized here, since both the TWF and AMS directives encourage the broadcasters of member states to transmit as much European content as they can. The AMS Directive requires (Article 3i) member states to ensure that on-demand audiovisual media services providers promote, where practicable and by appropriate means, the production of and access to European works. They also have to report to the Commission on the application of this provision within two years of the transposition date of the Directive and every four years thereafter. A recent Commission report examining the implementation of the provisions, published on 23 September 2010, confirmed that, by and large, the rules have been observed, with more than 63.2 per cent of EU programming time devoted to European films and fictions in 2008 (CEC, 2010), with almost three-quarters of prime-time TV viewing devoted to European programmes. In addition, the average share of independent producers' works broadcast by all European channels in all member states declined from 35.3 per cent in 2007 to 34.1 per cent in 2008. However, the decline was greater if one looks at the data for 2006 (37 per cent) (CEC, 2010).

Another recent study published by the European Commission measures for the first time how long viewers spend watching European programmes and shows that these are very popular. In 2007, *74 per cent of viewing time* – and 75.5 per cent between the hours of 18:00 and 23:00 – was devoted to European programmes and films; 33.4 per cent was devoted to independent European productions (see figure 5.3). The majority of VoD services provided by television channels offer almost exclusively European content: more than 90 per cent of the television channels approached stated that European content represented over 75 per cent of their on-demand listings. By contrast, independent VoD services promote European productions far less: 25 per cent stated that they offer less than 25 per cent of European programmes in their listings. It is therefore important to monitor the development of VoD available in the EU in order to support the promotion of culturally diversified content (Attentional et al., 2009)

The TWF Directive has also called upon member states to guarantee at least a 10 per cent share of transmission time to independent works. This target was reached in both 2005 and 2006 in all the EU countries apart from Cyprus, where in 2006 the average was around 6 per cent. On the other hand, that same year independent works represented 65 per cent of the

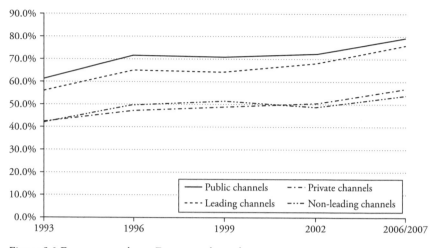

Figure 5.3 European works on European channels

Source: Attentional et al. (2009) /European Commission

programmes aired in Germany, 55% per cent in Luxembourg, 54 per cent in Hungary and 53 per cent in Sweden and Belgium. It should be noted, however, that policy on supporting independent television producers varies significantly around the world (see table 5.2).

According to *Screen Digest* (2006), only France and the UK have specific measures in place to ensure independent producers are able to retain rights to exploit their content through international marketing, DVDs, sales to cable and satellite channels, and new media platforms. In contrast, independent producers in Germany and Sweden are routinely expected to hand over all their internet protocol (IP) rights to the commissioning broadcaster. Elsewhere, producers have to negotiate on a commission-by-commission basis, which leads to costly legal bills and puts less experienced producers at a disadvantage. The figures reveal that the newer member states have applied the Directive just as well as the old members, despite the shorter transitional period. As noted in chapter 4, the EU also extended the rules promoting European TV works to video-on-demand services, although it set no specific target.

The MEDIA programme

In seeking to increase the number of domestic productions, the Commission decided to continue its audiovisual support programme, MEDIA. MEDIA has been developing and strengthening Europe's film industry since 1991. Through MEDIA I, MEDIA II, MEDIA Plus and MEDIA Training, it has

Table 5.2 EU programming in European television, 2007–8 (EU-27)

Country	% European works		% European works by independent producers	
	2007	2008	2007	2008
Austria	81.0	79.1	49.0	48.7
Belgium	74.9	69.1	54.0	46.0
Bulgaria	55.6	55.6	25.2	25.2
Cyprus	27.9	30.0	39.6	41.9
Czech Republic	64.3	65.9	32.2	34.7
Denmark	84.9	84.8	28.1	25.5
Estonia	61.6	64.6	50.3	47.8
Finland	64.0	56.8	40.1	35.7
France	72.6	71.7	47.5	45.6
Germany	64.2	63.9	61.7	62.3
Greece	54.1	61.7	14.5	15.1
Hungary	68.5	75.3	39.7	41.8
Ireland	55.0	56.4	21.9	23.0
Italy	62.9	52.7	22.6	17.0
Latvia	62.2	62.2	18.4	19.7
Lithuania	59.3	59.1	39.0	41.5
Luxembourg	69.6	70.7	56.2	56.9
Malta	55.9	69.0	41.4	45.2
Netherlands	80.8	80.3	40.2	31.2
Poland	85.0	83.1	25.0	26.3
Portugal	72.5	63.8	39.5	24.1
Romania	63.0	67.2	28.2	25.9
Slovak Republic	66.5	67.3	24.0	23.8
Slovenia	34.1	44.6	10.9	15.9
Spain	54.2	55.7	31.3	29.6
Sweden	45.1	45.5	41.6	42.9
United Kingdom	51.7	50.7	29.8	28.3

Source: CEC (2010).

supported the development and distribution of thousands of films, as well as training activities, festivals and promotion projects throughout the continent. Under MEDIA Plus and MEDIA Training (2001–6) alone, the sum of more than €0.5 billion was distributed among 8,000 projects. Every year 300 new European films are funded by the Commission, and half of the European films watched in cinemas are shown with its support. Several MEDIA-funded films have proven this investment worthwhile, as they have won the Palme d'Or (*Entre les murs*, France) and the Grand Prix (*Gomorra*, Italy) at the Cannes Film Festival, as well as Oscars (*The Counterfeiters* [*Die Fälscher*], Austria; *La Vie en rose* [*La Môme*], France; and *Slumdog Millionaire*, UK). The MEDIA 2007 programme is providing a €755 million boost to Europe's film industry and is intended to cover the period 2007–13. Almost 65 per cent of the total budget aims to help the broader circulation of European works. MEDIA 2007 provides easier access to finance and increases the use of digital technologies, making Europe's audiovisual sector more competitive. It is focused on the phases before and after film production, with a budget spread across five action lines:

- training (scriptwriting techniques, financial management, digital technologies): 7 per cent;
- development (single projects, catalogues, new talent, co-productions, other financing): 20 per cent;
- distribution (distributors, sales agents, broadcasters, cinema exhibitors, digitalizing works): 55 per cent;
- promotion (market access, festivals, common events, heritage): 9 per cent;
- horizontal actions (to make it easier for small and medium-sized enterprises to access funding, and to encourage the presence of European films on digital platforms): 5 per cent; and pilot projects (embracing new technologies for film development, production and distribution): 4 per cent.

By making the distribution of European works a clear priority in the new programme, MEDIA is seeking to improve the market share of European films shown in member states. The programme will also significantly raise the visibility of the diverse cultures of Europe on the world stage and help to increase the competitiveness of the audiovisual industry. This financial support has had a strong knock-on effect in terms of investment in the sector. During the earlier MEDIA programmes, each €1 of Community funding generated about €6 in private investment. Around 300 European films annually receive MEDIA backing, as well as more than fifty distributed outside their countries of origin, including the Oscar-winning documentary *March of the Penguins*, *Amélie*, *Volver*, *La vita è bella*, *Mondovino* and the Cannes Palme d'Or-winner of 2006, *The Wind that Shakes the Barley*. Like its forerunners, MEDIA 2007 is focusing on preproduction and post-production activities (distribution and promotion). However, in contrast to MEDIA II (1996–2000) and MEDIA Plus/MEDIA Training (2001–6), EU funding is now being channelled through a single programme, MEDIA 2007.

The Commission is exploring ways of launching a new programme to increase the share of European movies in markets outside the EU, which is currently very marginal. The project MEDIA Mundus foresees expenditure of €60 million from 2011 onwards to promote cooperation with third countries, particularly Canada, Australia, Japan, India and China, to improve the penetration of EU movies into their markets, and vice versa. Although in principle the project will be open to anyone, it is clear that it is meant to counter US dominance in the global cinema market. A desirable outcome for the Commission would be to increase the presence of Canadian or Japanese movies in the EU market to counter American over-representation, and conversely to increase EU cinema shares in these markets. However, the following needs to be taken into account.

1 Since 1997, the European film market has entered a period of constant growth, mainly due to the DVD retail sector. In 2005, it generated €13 billion in consumer spending (excluding revenues from the sale of lucrative pay TV and free TV rights to pay-TV operators and broadcasters), of which almost 60 per cent was generated by DVD retail. However, there was a downward dip, as revenues dropped from a high of €14 billion in 2004 (CEC, 2008a), primarily because of a levelling out of DVD sales and a poor year at the European box office, with only the UK bucking the trend. The drop in revenues reveals an important fact. With the threat of piracy looming, and the DVD market no longer a growth business (at least not in terms of revenues), the film industry, and the Hollywood studios in particular, has turned its attention to exploring new business models, such as video-on-demand (VoD) and digital retail. These ventures are still in their infancy, and it is not yet clear whether or not they will be able to generate revenues to compensate for declining receipts elsewhere.

2 According to the European Audiovisual Observatory (EAO, 2008a) a total of 1,041 feature films were produced in the twenty-seven member states of the EU in 2007. Since 2003, European production levels for entirely national and majority co-productions have increased by 1.1 per cent year on year and by an annual average of 5.1 per cent (754 feature films). Overall growth was due primarily to a rise in the number of entirely national productions, increasing from 543 in 2003 to 711 in 2007 – and ten films up on 2006. Increased production activity in France, Spain and Italy contributed significantly to overall growth.

3 European co-productions travel better than their 100 per cent national counterparts to the extent that, on average, they are released in more than twice as many markets (EAO, 2008b). But, with programme budgets under pressure, 77 per cent of all co-productions get released in at least one non-national market, compared with 33 per cent for entirely national films. European co-productions earn on average 2.7 times more admissions than national films.

Nevertheless, the main concern of filmmakers, broadcasters and producers has been less to do with the trade balance and more to do with the new ways of providing their content for as many different distribution platforms as possible.

In general, the MEDIA Programme has been adapted continuously to support the European audiovisual industry since 1991. But the Commission has gone further: within the Maastricht Treaty, it has exploited an additional discretionary exemption for 'aid to promote culture and heritage conservation where such aid does not affect trading conditions and competition in the Community to an extent that is contrary to the common interest' (Bellucci, 2010: 212). In effect, the Commission has called for support for the film industry, which has been suffering from structural weaknesses, including the under-capitalization of companies, the fragmentation of national markets, which are dominated by non-European productions, and poor transnational circulation of European works. National aid enables the member states to develop their capacity to define and implement policies for the purpose of preserving cultural diversity in Europe, while the Commission has aimed to encourage cooperation between member states, or even to support and supplement their action. It has, in effect, taken the view that small amounts of aid (*de minimis* aid) – in general €200,000 over any three-year fiscal period[1] – do not have any effect on competition and trade between member states. The *de mimimis* rule sets a threshold figure for aid below which Article 87(1) of the Treaty can be said not to apply, so that the measure no longer needs to be notified to the Commission in advance. Moreover, the Commission has also considered the imposition of a fee on movie distributors to help fund the shift to digital cinema, which is expected to increase the EU's share of the global film market but is deemed to be too expensive for small cinema operators.

The importance of programme rights

Technological developments and more effective marketing though new services such as VoD and, generally, pay-TV services have ensured that the acquisition of rights to content has grown in importance. Thus, the cost of acquiring such rights, especially for sports and films, continues to spiral as the need to launch more channels grows. The largest five European countries – France, Germany, Italy, Spain and the UK – generated more than €49.5 billion in television industry revenues in 2008, almost half of which (€24.7 billion) was spent on TV programming (*Screen Digest*, 2008f).

Sports are one of the main forms of content driving the launch of mobile TV, and most of the major athletic and football associations have sold rights to mobile TV platforms. The market for sports on the internet is also developing quickly as broadband connections increase. However, rights holders for major events are cautious, afraid of cannibalizing pay-TV deals. On free TV, major sports events such as international football and the Olympic Games continue to attract millions of viewers, despite audience fragmentation. The cost of rights to events like the Olympics and the FIFA World Cup finals has increased massively (Papathanassopoulos, 2002). In fact, the costs of sports rights have spiralled in the last twenty years: European TV rights to the summer Olympics increased by 1,200 per cent between the 1998 Seoul games and those in 2004 in Athens, and the value of the rights for the World Cup finals grew from €57 million to €1.63 billion for the 2010 finals in South Africa (Westcott, 2005; Pfanner, 2010). At the same time, the market for sports rights on mobile telephones and the internet is developing rapidly. Of the two, mobile telephony is closest to developing into a genuine business offering incremental revenues to rights holders. The internet, despite the rapid growth of broadband, is still a secondary medium for most major sports, though it has emerged as an ideal distribution mechanism for niche sports.

For some broadcasters, major sports are too expensive to be viable acquisitions and are less reliable in ratings terms than other forms of programming. Most countries in Europe have introduced rules preventing the sale of exclusive rights to major sports events to subscription TV operators. These rules have had a significant impact on the rights market and have benefited mainly public service broadcasters. But after the crisis of 2002–3, when digital platforms faced bankruptcy or even collapse, TV sports rights, especially for football, rose once again in value. For example, UEFA saw the income from TV and commercial contracts increase from €556 million in 2003/4 to about €819 million in 2007/8. In many countries, the rights holders (soccer associations, etc.) have sought deals with free-to-air broadcasters and pay-TV channels. In Italy, rights are split between RAI and Sky Italia; Antena 3 TV and Sogecable share network has the first choice of matches on one evening while a pay broadcaster has exclusivity on another. As the free-to-air window keeps sponsors and advertisers happy, UEFA is also able to dip into the deep pockets of subscription TV operators, offering them a measure of exclusivity (Westcott, 2008). Besides, the European Commission favours the break-up of rights into smaller TV packages (Westcott, 2007).

Copyright

The issue of copyright and related rights is becoming a central concern in the operation of the convergent media industries, mostly related to the difficulties in accessing content on account of the definition of new media exploitation rights, terms of trade and collective management of rights. Content management, copyright regulation and intellectual property have become major issues within Europe as well as in other regions.

The conflict between copyright holders and internet users has been raised and various protection models have been discussed (see Blàzquez, 2008), among them the so-called creative commons – i.e. a system that aims to facilitate the widest possible dissemination of protected works. It is questionable whether this can replace traditional property systems, and there have been attempts to propose principles and guidelines that might govern the contemporary legal system of protection of authors and works. The fact is, however, that in Europe, as elsewhere, there is the problem of piracy through illegal downloads from the internet. Internet service providers (ISPs), for example, have long resisted any attempt to take responsibility for unauthorized downloading.

The European Commission initiated a proposal in 2005 urging the adoption of a new directive on copyright infringements (CEC, 2005a). This proposal was heavily criticized: almost all position papers characterized it as disproportionate and noted that it fails to make adequate distinction between commercial piracy enterprises, legitimate/lawful activities undertaken by business competitors, and even the common activities of ordinary Europeans. It should not be forgotten that, in almost all cases, civil enforcement (rapid injunctions and damages) works better to protect intellectual property rights. In many countries the IP criminal law – although well developed –in practice plays only a subordinate role, and this is mainly because some member states are reluctant to accede further to European rules meant to harmonize areas traditionally reserved for national authorities.

Copyright and related issues, such as piracy and unauthorized up- and downloading of copyrighted content, remain an ongoing concern. As the European Commission has observed, the fight against online piracy involves a number of complementary elements: '(1) developing legal offers; (2) educational initiatives; (3) enforcement of legal rights; (4) seeking improved cooperation from Internet Service Providers (ISPs) in stopping dissemination of infringing content. The idea of education and awareness-raising on the importance of copyright for the availability of content is widely supported as a tool in the fight against piracy' (CEC, 2008a: 7).

Efforts to combat piracy against conditional access systems have varied, and there is a lack of uniformity and enforcement. The Commission believes that many new and thriving types of service are protected by the Conditional Access Directive – video on demand, mobile TV and online streaming all use conditional access systems to restrict access to paying customers (CEC, 2008c) – but that more information is required as to possibilities for extending protection.

On the other hand, in July 2010 the Commission took a strict stance over allegations of anti-competitive behaviour in internet search services amid concerns that the dominant players might be abusing their position.

By the end of 2009, the EU had ratified the WIPO (World International Property Organization) Copyright Treaty and the WIPO Performances and Phonograms Treaty – the so-called internet treaties concluded to make the world's copyright laws 'fit for the internet'. By ratifying these treaties, the EU and its member states aim to protect the European creators and creative industries.

Summary

It is generally accepted that commercialization and increased competition have affected the content of the offline media in general and of TV programmes in particular. Initially there was a reliance on the 'tried and tested', on entertainment and on imports, but the real question was whether that pattern will change as the new broadcasting systems 'mature'. In practice, the pressure on commercial media, particularly broadcast media, has increased, more so given the squeeze on advertisers, the fragmentation of the audience and the competitive elements brought about through the emergence of newer means of delivering and accessing content.

The prevailing wisdom among media pundits is that 'content is the king', but as content today moves from one medium to another it can increase in value (and sometimes decrease in value – e.g. downloads and piracy). The case of the newspaper industry is illustrative: the content of newspapers feeds websites and blogs, and is read by many, though few directly contribute to its collection and distribution. And it is doubtful whether advertisers or purchasers of media, on their own, can support this plethora of new and old media outlets.

In this rapidly changing context, the question one must continue to ask is whether the European Commission has the means, the resources, the will or the capacity to enable European producers to begin to exploit the new media environment, especially in a period of financial crisis in the eurozone. It has shown some signs of being able to encourage developments and innovations, but the fragmentation of the EU, the diversity of media and corporate interests, and the difficulty of managing twenty-seven entities may prove to be major obstacles to greater integration. In the meantime, audiences continue to enjoy domestic/national programmes – as before – and to access what is new via newer digital technologies.

6   Audiences and Consumption

Europe is moving towards a new media revolution, amplified by unprecedented connectivity. In this new era, convergence and digitalization are the major drivers of the demand for new media services. Europeans have media choices like never before. On any given day, the average citizen can choose from dozens of TV channels delivered terrestrially by cable or satellite, several FM or internet radio stations, newspapers in both paper and online form, and of course access to the web and other alternative media and related devices. Although TV and its programmes remain popular, the way audiences, especially young people, access and consume media content in most European countries has changed dramatically. The current media landscape is characterized by an explosion of widely distributed digital products, a growing share of user-generated content (produced both by professionals and by members of the public) and a move towards a new use of media services. This is compounded by new consumption patterns and users' demands – particularly for access on demand, social and community media and content personalization. There is thus a move from a traditional press-broadcasting environment to more personalized and on-demand universe. This chapter identifies the changing patterns of media consumption and the variations in those patterns that are evident across Europe.

A media-rich society

European citizens today live in a media-rich society. Thirty years ago, a 'typical' household would have had access to a handful of public and private television services, three to four radio stations and a number of print outlets (magazines, newspapers and books). Today, that same household has access to hundreds of media outlets, and in most cases either via their television sets or through personal computers. Hand in hand with the growth in the choice of media available has been a change in the nature of the content. Today, a substantial part of the media industry is devoted to creating and distributing content specifically aimed at particular audience segments, from children and adolescents to executives and the elderly. Television, in particular, has moved from merely offering family programming to providing thematic channels aimed at segments, large or niche, of the total audience.

The European media universe is changing not only in content but also in the ways in which audiences discover, use, consume and interact with that content. Nowhere is this more evident than in Northern Europe, where one can witness the transition from the old to the new media, from traditional to advanced media societies, and from analogue to digital media. While these trends are global, Europe remains an interesting case study because of the differences that exist within it.

Changing media, changing patterns of consumption

Although TV programming remains fashionable, the way that the new generation of audiences accesses and consumes content in Europe has changed dramatically. Based on existing research, we can identify a number of new patterns.

The impact of the internet

First, the internet is becoming a primary means of information and entertainment, and more and more Europeans have started using it for a range of activities. Shopping online, for instance, has increased steadily, from 20 per cent of individuals engaging in the activity in 2004 and 26 per cent in 2006 to 30 per cent in 2007 (Eurostat, 2009). According to research by the European Interactive Advertising Association (EIAA, 2009), within five years the use of the internet has increased by 32 per cent. These data suggest that Europeans are using the internet not only increasingly for leisure pursuits but also for actively enhancing and managing their lifestyles. Over half (55 per cent) of European internet users are now online every single day, while 75 per cent are using the internet during their evenings and 51 per cent (up 13 per cent from 2007) are on the web at weekends. Freedom and flexibility are key watchwords for today's consumers too, with almost half (49 per cent) of broadband users using wireless. Almost three-quarters (73 per cent) state that, as a result of the internet, they are staying in touch with friends and relatives more; 54 per cent have booked more holidays or made travel arrangements and almost half (46 per cent) are better able to manage their finances. In addition they claim that the internet has provided them with a greater choice of products and services and access to important information resources (see figure 6.1).

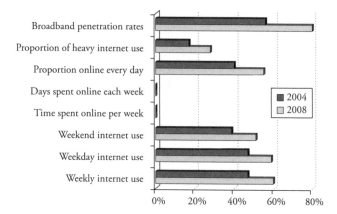

Figure 6.1 Changes of internet use in Europe

Source: Based on EIAA (2005, 2009).

If current growth trends continue, the internet may overtake broadcast TV as Europe's most popular form of media in the near future. Furthermore, according to a Microsoft report (2009), internet use in 2010 will average 14.2 hours per week, or over 2.5 days a month, compared with 11.5 hours a week, or 2 days a month, for TV. The report, which covers mainly EU countries, also observes that, while the internet will become the most popular medium, this does not signify a decline in TV but simply reflects the changing ways people experience audiovisual content. For example, figures for 2008/9 suggest that about 9 per cent of Europeans watch live TV on their PCs and 4 per cent record TV programmes onto a hard drive (ibid.). Television is thus becoming a two-way connected experience delivered via broadband to multiple screens, including TV, PC and mobile.

Internet use in Europe is driven primarily by content and communication services (i.e. news sites, online video, social networking sites and email). This represents 65 per cent of all online time. Usage is expected to grow on account of the variety of internet-enabled devices that are becoming available. For example, while traditional newspaper readership is falling, digital versions add extra functionality: 58 per cent of newspaper websites feature some form of user-generated content, and 75 per cent of sites allow users to comment on their articles and other content (more than doubled since 2007). In these ways, users' involvement helps to shape output.

The Microsoft research also shows that, for some eighteen- to 24-year-olds, the PC is often the only screen used to watch television, while for others it can be a second or third screen. For this generation, TV frequently means video delivered on demand, with one in seven in this particular age group now watching no live TV at all. This suggests that over the next five years the PC could move from being the dominant internet access device (today accounting for 95 per cent) to representing just 50 per cent, as other web-enabled or web-connected devices grow in popularity. For example, 48 per cent of Europeans are expected to use a Smartphone by 2013, making internet connectivity effective nearly everywhere.

Second, the internet is becoming a primary source of entertainment. According a European Commission Eurobarometer survey at the end of 2009, almost 57 per cent of Europeans in the twenty-seven EU member states had an internet connection – with 48 per cent of them using broadband and 7 per cent narrowband (Special Eurobarometer, 2010). Another survey, by Microsoft (2009), reveals that, in 2008, people spent almost nine hours per week using the web, up 27 per cent from 2004. Both pieces of research, as well as others, indicate that Europeans are spending more and more time on the internet; most importantly, this is more time than they spend reading print media, watching movies offline or playing video games. The main reason for this is that high-end internet-enabled devices (e.g. interactive TV sets, game consoles, 3G devices, etc.) are flooding the market – confirming, in other words, the view that content is indeed important for the end user.

As with other aspects of the media discussed in this book, there is a clear North–South divide in respect of the internet: citizens/consumers in Northern Europe have an internet penetration rate of 76 per cent on average compared with 45 per cent in Southern Europe. For example, although 35 per cent of EU citizens were using a social networking site in 2009, there is a different consumption pattern among Northern and Southern Europeans, with the Netherlands, the Scandinavian countries and Latvia presenting the highest rates (more than 48 per cent) and countries in the South – Spain, Portugal and Italy – with low rates (less than 30 per cent) (Special Eurobarometer, 2010). In the same way, preferences and viewing habits appear to depend not only on taste and culture but also, not surprisingly, on the status of the available infrastructure. Among the EU countries, the communications universe reveals a region that is separate, unequal and less well prepared for the new challenges: the proportion of those with high-speed internet access is the highest in the Northern countries. In the Southern countries of the EU-15, together with Cyprus and Malta, people have less access to high-speed internet, while the Eastern European countries generally lack high-speed access altogether. The proportion of citizens in Northern Europe with high-speed access at home and/or in the workplace is even higher than in the USA. This picture reveals not only the fragmentation of the European communications landscape but also the vast 'digital divide' among the North, South and East of the region.

TV versus internet

Patterns of media consumption are changing (see figure 6.2) as a result of the advent of multiple distribution channels and the emergence of new media and assorted devices. Consumers increasingly want to obtain their entertainment content at any time, anywhere and with relative ease (Datamonitor, 2006). Accessibility of the web as well as of digital TV has dramatically expanded the range of content and its distribution. Media consumption habits are changing as a result of the emergence of multiple distribution platforms and the ever-growing number of media outlets. The access to high-bandwidth broadband services, spurred by Web 2.0, social networking, podcasts and user-generated content, supplemented by camera phones, MP3 players and mobile data services, has stimulated further change.

Analysis of internet usage indicates that time spent online is not a displacement of TV viewing but rather can operate as an add-on to TV viewing. Given that most people use the internet for communication or socializing activities, it is not surprising that television has, so far, remained strong. In several European countries, traditional ways of watching television have seen a steep decline, especially among the young (OSI, 2008: 17). To make things more complicated, consumers are becoming accustomed to accessing video content through new devices. The internet is helping people watch more TV, whether streamed or downloaded, not less. On-demand entertainment is one of the most revolutionary trends for both online content and digital television, creating new challenges. The trends show that audiences will continue to migrate to multiple content platforms and, since the delivery of media content has changed, traditional TV programming may lose its value. The emphasis is now on release dates and on-demand content, either paid or free. For example, according to JupiterResearch (2008), 28 per cent of Europeans in 2008 regularly watched online video, more than double the rate in 2006.

On the other hand, there are numerous signs that TV still has a future. Watching television remains the most popular free-time activity among Europeans, and increasing broadband penetration has driven overall media consumption without cannibalizing traditional forms of media (Banerjee et al., 2008). Research from the USA also indicates that adults are exposed to screens – TVs, mobile phones, even GPS devices – for about 8.5 hours on any given day, and, most importantly, TV remains the dominant medium for both consumption and advertising (Council for Research Excellence/Media Consumption and Engagement Committee, 2009). In Europe, according to JupiterResearch (2008), the time spent watching online videos expanded by 50 per cent in 2007/8, but not at the expense of TV: European internet users still spend more time watching TV than going online.

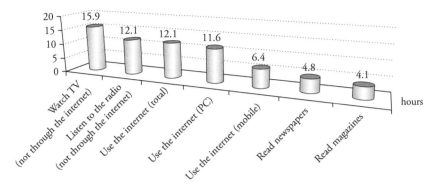

Figure 6.2 Media use in the EU-15, 2010

Source: EIAA (2010).

Moreover, the growth in broadband video doesn't signify the end for television viewing. Although the number of European consumers watching online video has risen in recent years, home TV ratings have not been affected significantly. This is probably because, as analysts point out, the net is largely an incremental new way of viewing rather than a substitute. It is also argued that audiences will demonstrate a preference for watching video on the television set over the PC, because of the better quality. One way or another, the screen will continue to be at the centre of the new multichannel universe of Europe, as in the USA.

In the near future there will be a simultaneous use of TV and the internet. In the above mentioned Microsoft study, it is predicted, however, that the traditional TV will convert into an internet-enabled device that will offer consumers the ability to watch on-demand videos and connect them to their social networks and other online activities. If this is the case, European broadcasters must develop strategies to distribute content across online and TV to engage an increasingly fragmented audience.

In Europe, as in the USA, TV has managed to defend its leading position in terms of media consumption (OSI, 2008: 22), although the internet and related technologies have affected the media environment. Nevertheless, TV in Europe remains 'anchored in national-cultural contexts . . . although programme content and story formats will draw on a wider variety of experiences and images' (Wenger, 2008: 56).

There are no major differences in the spread of people watching television over the internet: it is slightly more common in the new member states (7 per cent viewing rates) than in the old (5 per cent), while, in the USA, 9 per cent of people with internet access watch TV (Eurobarometer, 2007). Although

TV viewing remains the third main activity in Europe after working and sleeping, one has to consider, as noted, the trends among the younger generation. As is well known, TV is of declining interest to young people aged sixteen to twenty-four, as they on average watch one hour less than the general viewer – although the largest drop is among persons under forty. For this group at least, the internet has, to a certain extent, replaced the old television medium.

Cable and satellite TV

A similar picture emerges when we look at access to cable and satellite TV in Europe. Almost one-third of Northern countries among the EU-15 generally have not only good availability of high-speed internet but also of cable and satellite TV. In countries that have good coverage of cable, the use of satellite tends not to be widespread, and where broadcasts are characteristically received by satellite there is a lower dependency on cable networks. For example, in Belgium, where cable coverage is almost complete (94 per cent), only 10 per cent of the population have satellite access. In addition, there are many European countries with a high proportion of citizens lacking either option to access international TV channels.

By contrast, those in the Southern EU countries have less access to either high-speed internet or cable and satellite TV and consequently turn less to international news channels. The vast majority of people in Greece (83 per cent) and two-thirds in France and Cyprus have neither cable nor satellite access. The same is true for the majority of the population in Spain (59 per cent), Italy (59 per cent), the Czech Republic (56 per cent) and Finland (56 per cent).

In general, with the advent of cable and satellite, most Europeans have adopted a multi-channel viewing habit. In France, Italy and Spain, multi-channel viewing increased from between 7 and 8 per cent in 2000 to between 13 and 15 per cent in 2006; in Britain the figure jumped from 16 per cent in 2000 to 33 per cent in 2006. Moreover, the BBC's iPlayer, which offers BBC radio and TV programmes on the internet, has become a popular service. BBC TV programmes are limited to users from the United Kingdom only, while the radio programmes can be accessed by a worldwide audience. BBC iPlayer is in this regard like many of the other TV channels on internet services that restrict the ability to view based on IP addresses. Users from the UK can watch the TV programmes of the past seven days on the website, download and stream HD programmes, access iPlayer from supported mobile phones and download programmes to their computer systems with the help of BBC iPlayer Desktop. In 2008, the total number of requests stood at 271 million, and the fact that BBC1 delivered most of its popular programmes on BBC iPlayer is an indication both that the broadcaster's brands remain strong and that good TV content is popular across all delivery platforms (Khan, 2009).

Different patterns of media consumption

There are significant differences in viewing habits within the EU between East and West, North and South. Daily viewing time varies considerably from one country to another: from 4 hours 31 minutes in Hungary and more than four hours in Italy, Cyprus and Greece, to less than three hours in Ireland, Slovenia and Finland and around two and a half hours in Denmark, Austria and Sweden. Nevertheless, individual characteristics (age, educational level, etc.) still play an important role in media consumption (Elvestad and Blekesaune, 2008: 442; Médiamétrie, 2010). Although on average Europeans watch more television (see figure 6.3), the proliferation of new channels signifies less time per channel. With the advance of new media (internet and mobile TV), TV audiences are going to be divided into even smaller segments (Dawson, 2008).

Another obvious distinction between the media in the various European states is the different levels of newspaper consumption. Southern and Eastern Europe present a strikingly low level of newspaper circulation compared with Central and Western Europe (and a corresponding importance of electronic media). Mass-circulation newspapers did not develop in any of the Eastern

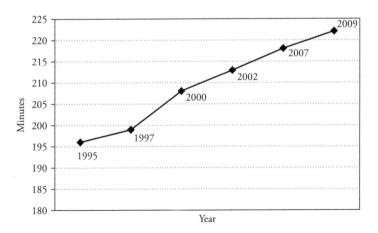

Figure 6.3 Average time spent viewing TV in Europe, 1995–2009

Source: Médiamétrie (2010), EAO (2009).

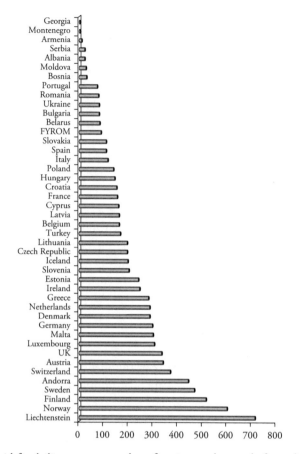

Figure 6.4 Paid-for dailies: average number of copies per thousand of population

Source: WAN (2008).

European countries for obvious reasons (see figure 6.4). Georgia has the lowest circulation and Bulgaria the highest (82 per thousand of population in 2007). A similar picture is evident in the Southern European countries. Malta had the highest circulation rate of the four, at 111 per thousand in 2007, and Portugal the lowest, at 75 per thousand. The rest of Western Europe ranged from 155 (France) to 601 per thousand (Norway).

Preferences in TV programmes

The European TV market is characterized by its diversity and by changing patterns in consumer taste and demand (Vissol, 2005: 17). Interest in TV news has increased in the last decade, but there are dramatic differences across the member states of the EU. The biggest news fans are the Italians, the Portuguese, the Romanians, the Bulgarians and the Dutch, while Estonians and Latvians are not so keen (23 and 27 per cent, respectively). Also with low rates of interest are the British (31 per cent), the Germans (30 per cent) and the Maltese (33 per cent). A similar picture is presented in France and the Czech Republic. However, Germans do watch an above average number of documentaries (14 per cent vs. 11 per cent EU average), as do the British (17 per cent). In terms of second and third preferences, EU citizens opt for movies (43 per cent) and documentaries (30 per cent).

Younger people are generally not attracted by news programmes. Only one-third (36 per cent) selected the news as one of their first three preferred options. While those who are more highly educated or self-employed consume more news overall, the elderly and those with lowest levels of education watch more TV news. Half of the elderly (47 per cent) watch several TV news programmes on a daily basis, while only one-fifth of the youth (in the fifteen to twenty-four age group) do so (18 per cent). As a rule, people in both the USA and the EU tend to be informed by TV rather than the press or the internet: 68 per cent of the US population never watches TV news over the internet, although 15 per cent do so several times per week, while 80 per cent of EU citizens do not watch news programmes online and only 12 per cent access the internet to watch such programmes at least once per week (Eurobarometer, 2007: 35).

According to TV ratings, fictional programmes still lead the way in most European markets, with 46 per cent of programmes classified in this genre compared with 36 per cent in entertainment and 18 per cent in factual. Series are the driving force, since they represent more than 50 per cent of the best audiences. By and large, entertainment represents more than a third of the favourite TV programmes (Médiamétrie, 2010). Moreover, programmes covering special events and live broadcast shows are usually a safe bet, and the Eurovision Song Contest or the finals of competitive shows such as 'Britain's Got Talent' remain as popular as ever in Europe (IP Network, 2008). The same applies for sports programmes, especially football (EAO, 2008d).

The plethora of channels in Europe, as noted in chapter 2, has increased audience fragmentation and created niche markets serving particular audiences (Vissol, 2005: 17). Perhaps surprisingly, according to Eurobarometer research (2007: 20), the most popular specialized channels are those reporting local or regional news. The least popular are channels dealing exclusively with political and parliamentary matters (see figure 6.5).

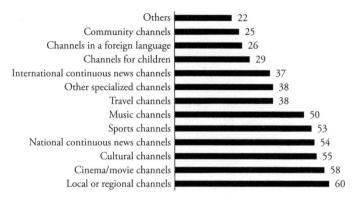

Figure 6.5 Numbers and types of specialist channels viewed in the EU

Source: Eurobarometer (2007).

Media consumption at home

Although the EU countries continue to experience a 'digital divide' and varying access to certain media, most Europeans, especially in the West and North, have access to most media most of the time. As we have seen, television has penetrated 96 per cent of all EU-27 households, while the main means of reception are via aerial (41 per cent) and cable TV networks (34 per cent); more than 95 per cent of those same households have DVD/video players, radios, and compact disc and tape audio players. Overall, 56 per cent of European households have personal computers – though in the Netherlands and Denmark this figure rises to 90 per cent and 85 per cent respectively – and about 46 per cent with internet access have a Wi-Fi modem/router (Special Eurobarometer, 2008). Moreover, the typical European lives in a household equipped with two to three TV sets, VCR and/or DVD players, three radios, DMPs (for example, an iPod or other MP3 device), two video game consoles, and a personal computer. By and large, Europeans have entered the age of the digital home, which is characterized by an increasing consumption of content from a variety of different consumer electronic devices.

The numbers of television and radio sets have reached near-saturation levels in most European households, and thus only the new digital media devices seem most likely to find their way into households with children. For example, according to the European Interactive Advertising Association, adults who live with children are more engaged online than those without, indicating that family needs and wants are shaping web behaviour. The study demonstrates that people living with children are more technologically aware and advanced on account of their heightened experience of, and exposure to,

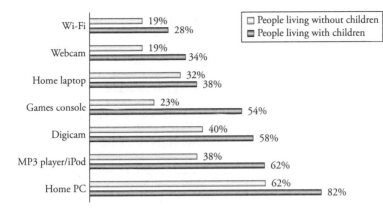

Figure 6.6 Technology at home

Source: EIAA (2009).

gadgets and devices. Their 'Digital Families' Report (EIAA, 2008), reveals that 73 per cent of people living with children are logging on to the internet each week, compared with only 52 per cent of those without. They are also engaging in a wider range of digital activities, ever extending the depth and complexity of their experience. Almost a third (30 per cent) of these digital parents are watching film, TV or video clips online, demonstrating how entertainment is becoming integral to the family internet experience. It is an activity which is growing enormously in popularity (up 150 per cent since 2006), and, with 22 per cent intending to upgrade to broadband within the next six months, this trend is set to accelerate: 32 per cent are listening to the radio online and 66 per cent now regularly use the internet as a source of news – showing how broadcast and other traditional media are increasingly being consumed online (see figure 6.6).

In addition, digital parents use the internet to express themselves more and to interact with others. Web activities such as offering ratings and reviews and creating and sharing content have experienced a significant boost since 2006 (up 40 per cent and 27 per cent respectively). People living with very young children (up to the age of four) are increasingly visiting health and film websites (up 24 per cent since 2006), while those with children between five and nine are going to games sites (up 32 per cent). Price comparison sites are seeing a boost among those living with children between ten and fifteen (up 31 per cent), and those with older children (between sixteen and eighteen) are enjoying more TV sites (up 77 per cent). Users living with older children also seem to be more technically advanced – almost half (47 per cent) of those living with teenagers between sixteen and eighteen use instant messaging services, compared with 37 per cent of people living with children up to the age of four. A similar trend is seen when comparing film, TV or video clip downloads (30 per cent vs. 22 per cent) and music downloads (36 per cent vs. 32 per cent).

People living with children are also more likely than those without to use a mobile phone, PDA or BlackBerry (91 per cent vs. 83 per cent) and to engage actively in a wide range of mobile phone functions – further indicating the influence of youth on technical skill and openness to adapt. More than half (53 per cent) have taken a photo or video clip (vs. 37 per cent of those without children), 12 per cent have surfed internet sites (vs. 9 per cent) and 8 per cent have watched video or film clips on their mobiles (vs. 5 per cent).

Overall, digital parents are ramping up their web time, spending 11.6 hours online each week (up 36 per cent since 2004), and over a quarter are heavy users of the internet (27 per cent). Digital families are also more likely than those households without children to use the internet at the weekends (58 per cent vs. 40 per cent).

This online activity has meant that families are consuming other media less – 44 per cent of digital parents are watching less TV, almost a third read fewer magazines and newspapers (31 and 30 per cent respectively) and almost a quarter (24 per cent) listen to the radio less. This can be attributed in part to the fact that time-pressured adults living with children find the web provides what they want quickly and saves them time (76 per cent vs. 68 per cent of people without children), while almost half (47 per cent) believe it puts them in control (vs. 42 per cent).

Summary: the multimedia environment and multitasking

Today's media consumers use a wide range of equipment. There are a good number of new devices (such as hard disk drives and digital cameras) at the disposal of the average European consumer, while newspaper and magazine readership and TV viewership is declining. As analysts observe, there is going to be increased competition as providers compete to offer ever more complex devices, and packages, for accessing material (O&O, 2007).

Newer forms of media (such as blogs or social networks) and changes in behaviour (such as downloading TV programmes) are indicators of shifting patterns of communication, production and consumption. The TV viewer experience is no longer defined simply by the signal reception quality and the size of the TV set, but extends to recording, programme planning and VoD options. Time and place shifting will become increasingly commonplace as enabling devices and platforms penetrate the market. As Derek Johnson argues: 'today, the consumption of television takes place within the hyperdiegetic worlds of television. So while multi-platforming has been embraced by the industry as a strategy for marketing content streams, it has transcended economic exigency, significantly altering the cultural and spatial character of television' (2007: 78).

Recent developments in the communications landscape, as we have seen, have had a profound impact on consumption modes and users' demands for new services. The traditional broadcasting approach is thus giving way to more personalized and on-demand solutions, with an impact also on the infrastructure and the access technologies required – for example, content awareness and advanced tools and systems for intuitive content creation and for multimedia-based search. In these respects, as Sonia Livingstone has observed, the history of audiences 'suggests that relations between reception and consumption are themselves historically contingent' (2004: 84).

The emergence of digital media, and the portability and convergence of devices, has accelerated the fragmentation of media in Europe, with a whole new generation of consumers bypassing newspapers and television to source their news on the internet. Among younger audiences, there are some clear indicators that the web is affecting media usage. The data show that sixteen- to 25-year-olds watch the smallest amount of live TV of any age group, spend the most time text messaging and watch the most online video. In the UK, for example, this segment of the audience watches one hour less than the average viewer. Instead, the internet plays the major role in their viewing lives. But, while past reports have highlighted peaks of growing popularity among this age group and the older generation, we are now seeing a wider spectrum of Europeans using the internet for sustained periods of time to deepen and diversify their online experiences. However, it is those aged twenty-five to thirty-four, the first generation to grow up in the technology era, who seem to be collectively driving recent growth; they spend the most time of any group watching DVD or VCR videos. Those aged thirty-five to forty-four spend more time on the web than other group, while those between forty-five and fifty-four spend the most time on email. Consumers over the age of sixty-five watch the most live TV.

The ways people use the new media, especially the internet, are many and varied: for work, for study, to access websites and blogs, and to shop. The use of the internet in the field of education has become widespread, and an environment conducive to its use is becoming increasingly well established. But the changed pattern of media use, particularly among young people, presents a challenge for the old media, especially the TV stations and the press: private-sector media companies have not found a sustainable business model to refinance their offerings.

In one way or another, people in Europe consume more media content, have greater access to media and content, and consume multiple media (linear and non-linear) at the same time. This doesn't mean, however, that we pay more attention to media and the relevant content, but that the media surround us and have turned up their volume. At the same time, the increase in the number of media outlets has increased the fragmentation of the markets. Each generation creates new consumption patterns, and the media are forced to follow this path; gradually, generational change results in dramatically different profiles for media consumption. In many ways, contemporary patterns of consumption – and these are related to both production and technologies – are being led by a younger generation of consumers/producers.

Part III

Europe as a Cultural and Political Project

7 Public Communication in Europe: Constructing Europe and the European Public Sphere

While previous chapters have paid particular attention to the organizational and regulatory dimensions of the media in the European Union, the aim of this chapter is to explore the journalistic dimension. It focuses not on Europe as a continent-wide collection of nation-states, but on the EU as a specific arrangement of countries that are bound together by a series of agreements and expansions that have taken place in stages since the mid-1950s.

As seen here, then, the EU is much more than a collection of (currently) twenty-seven separate member states: it is partly an intergovernmental organization and partly a supranational one that has increasingly sought to create an integrated union of countries that is much bigger and more significant than the sum of its parts. As Dunkerley has pointed out, 'since the early 1970s there has been growing support within the EU institutions to give "Europe" a larger presence in the hearts and minds of the citizens of the member states' (2002:116–17) and, to an extent, 'to promote a sense of common identity among member states nationals' (see also Bruter, 2005; Kaina and Karolewski, 2009).

Such aims, however, are controversial, since they make many assumptions about the aims and objectives of the EU (e.g. What is it? What it is trying to become?), the attitudes and aspirations of the citizens of member states (e.g. How do they see themselves? Do they want to be Europeans? What does it mean to be European?), and the possible future forms that the EU could take. Part of the underlying problem here is the common criticism that 'the wider goal', as identified by Dunkerley (2002), has been very much a top-down approach to the creation of a union of member states and not a 'natural', organic growth that would have perhaps created a common identity or, at the very least, identification with the EU. The integration 'project' has thus often come across as one that has been imposed on both member states and citizens, from afar and from above.

There are, then, marked divisions of opinion, not only as to what the EU is but also as to how it should develop. For example, critics often portray the moves towards greater integration as threats 'to national cultures and identities' (Dunkerley, 2002: 119) and even as attempts to bully citizens into agreement.[1] By contrast, those who support the overall direction that the EU is taking would argue that it needs a large measure of support, integration and consensus if it is to be able to present a united front on international affairs and to play a global role. As we shall see in chapter 8, these divisions were replayed during the Irish referendum on the Lisbon Treaty (June 2008) and reveal the many ways in which the nature and progress of the EU remain thorny subjects.

While these controversies are significant in themselves, since they identify the many obstacles that lie in the path of the creation of new forms of governance beyond nation-states, they take on an extra quality when one considers that they are played out and replayed in the media. The media then become not only a means of communication between elites and between elites and citizens but also part of the process through which the EU governs itself, develops and seeks to create that element of Europeanness that underpins the bigger project of integration.

As numerous studies have shown, and as we shall see below, the media do play a significant role in creating the context for the development of perceptions about things European: whether it be the Euro-sceptic British press sounding out about the EU for insisting on some inane – and possibly misinterpreted – policy or the French or Greek press being critical of moves to bring Turkey into the fold, or even the critique of the Northern media against the Southern Euro-countries in the case of the financial crisis. In one way or another, the media continue to play a part in the debates that surround the EU. More than this, the media are the means through which we can become part of the EU as an 'imagined community', to use Benedict Anderson's (1991) phrase, or part of what Charles Taylor has called 'a social imaginary' – that is:

> something much broader and deeper than the intellectual schemes people may entertain when they think about social reality in a disengaged mode. I am thinking, rather, of the ways people imagine their social existence, how they fit together with others, how things go on between them and their fellows, the expectations that are normally met, and the deeper normative notions and images that underlie these expectations. (Taylor, 2004: 23)

The media thus play a dual role. While the EU's mechanisms can operate fully at a bureaucratic and policy level with minimal citizen engagement, the media can help it explain itself and so overcome problems that may derive from the alleged lack of accountability and representativeness – i.e. the so-called democratic deficit whereby it is said to be insufficiently representative and accountable to the member states and citizens. On the other hand, the media can also play a role in creating the environment – Taylor's 'images, stories and legends' (2004: 23) – that will make citizens *in* Europe become citizens *of* Europe or, at the very least, provide the lens through which those citizens come to understand Europe. For these reasons, how the media cover or represent the EU and its work becomes a central concern for those who are interested in the construction of a European political entity. More so when there are no *European media* available across all member states: there is no European newspaper, for example, and only one very minority interest European-wide TV news channel, Euronews. If the press helped to shape 'imagined communities' (Anderson, 1991), the absence of a European press (or television) is undoubtedly a significant consideration in the construction of an all-inclusive, familiar, common Europe.

Yet there are other numerous obstacles that lie in the way of creating a fully functioning and integrated Europe of nation-states that exists beyond our immediate concern with the media. For this to happen, citizens of distinct European states would have to:

- accept the political legitimacy of something that exists as an institutional and political formation beyond the nation-state, the more common taken-for-granted primary object of legitimacy for most citizens;
- align themselves to a body that is physically distant from the nation-state and to which there is rarely a common, immediate, affective link. The European Commission and the Parliament are 'over there' somewhere (hence the importance of 'explaining' them);
- overcome differences between citizens – differences in language and in social and cultural mores – to the extent that similarities and a unity of like-minded publics can be presupposed. Is the EU really just too diverse to become a single unity? Will it always remain so?
- accept the existence of a singular agenda or framework for the development – in the present and in the future – of an EU whose actual make-up is open to different visions and scenarios. There are, in other words, many ways forward.

When discussing the media in the EU we are therefore faced with a multitude of complex issues and problems that intersect:

- historical – How did the construct of 'Europe' emerge?
- political – Is the EU a 'patchwork'? Are citizens aligned with nation-states? What is the way forward? Is further expansion desirable?
- and social and cultural – Is diversity important? Is unity critical? Are we all 'European' now?

Significantly, all of these issues and problems are mediated, mediatized and colonized by the media (see also Gavin, 2007: 149–62). To put the matter differently, all aspects of the EU, as of politics at national levels, are reflected and refracted by the media and consequently open to different constructions by them. At all levels, the media are central for both elites and publics for their understanding and perception of what the EU is, how it operates and how it seeks to entrench itself in the lives of citizens. The media can enhance the status of the EU or can traduce it: when the President of the Council and the Foreign Minister were appointed in November 2009, for example, the British media took some delight in highlighting the secretive, smoke-filled-room nature of the deal that led to these two appointments, and there are countless other examples in the British media of a quizzical-cum-negative take on matters European which may well be a factor in the way the British see the EU and its work. In general, then, so long as the media remain separate from the EU – and that independence is a central feature of all democratic societies – it is likely that the EU will have to work hard to ensure that its preferred profile is enhanced (Kaitatzi-Whitlock, 2008). As will be discussed more fully later on in this chapter, the communication dimension of the EU's activities has long troubled it and continues to do so.

But if the media are as central for elite and citizen perceptions as suggested above, they have also become something of a preoccupation for academics and EU commissioners. Academics have certainly relished the opportunity to deal with the whole gamut of questions identified above, and EU media studies – separate from EU studies – have generated a veritable plethora of research – research often funded by the EU itself! EU media studies, paradoxically, by pulling European academics together, led to the creation of better European academic networks – networks, one should add, whose purpose may be to continue to examine the media–EU agenda. The *European Journal of Communication* (2007), for example, devoted a special issue to 'The Media and European Public Space', with papers on such topics as the nature of the European public sphere/space (Is there one? Where is it? What is it? Will there ever be one? Will there be many?), the nature and role of journalists working in Europe (Are they educators, partisans, proselytizers or just hacks? Should they work with/develop a European, in contrast to, a domestic/national perspective?) and, finally, Can the media be used to create a European space/sphere/identity? Two years later, *Journalism Studies* (2009) published a special issue entitled 'Questioning European Journalism'.

The continuing relevance of these sorts of questions is abundantly simple: with so many differences – cultural, political, social, etc. – can the European Union establish what Nicholas Garnham considers a fundamental question in Habermas's work on the public sphere, namely, 'solidarity among strangers' (2007: 202)? And, if so, how would this be achieved? Garnham summarizes some of the positions that follow on from the emphasis on the means of communication:

> The formation of European public opinion should come in the first instance through the mechanism of national media reporting for their national audiences on debates in other European polities. And, in the first instance, at any rate, the European public opinions formed on this basis will influence political will formation through the political systems of their respective states. Since Habermas sees democracy not as an ideal normative form to be imposed, but as an historical learning process within which common norms are fashioned and refashioned, the creation of a cosmopolitan polity will always be a long-term evolutionary process. (Ibid.: 210)

Alongside academics, EU officers have spent some time considering the media–EU agenda, since many have taken the view that the way the media have mediated the EU partly accounts for the lack of interest in EU affairs, low turnout at elections, and so on. If the media are at fault, so the argument goes, then there must be a strategy to deal with them better so as to get better coverage. The problem with this approach is that it lays the blame for the problems the EU is facing in creating an integrated system and a European citizen at the feet of the media. This may be a mistake. As Slaatta, has argued, one should not simply blame the messenger:

> When politicians and bureaucrats feel betrayed by the media and the public, media researchers all too often take the same perspective. They easily fall prey to a general critique of journalistic performance and to the way in which the news media institutions are producing negative effects when compared with the ideals of the public sphere model. However, another line of argument is probably more important. It must be stated firmly, that a natural consensus on what Europe is, and how the EU is representing European interests and societies does not exist. Thus, the media should not be expected to be this neutral, mediating platform for information and debate. (Slaatta, 2006: 22)

Obviously, 'the news media continues to be a precondition for modern politics' (ibid.: 23), but how they treat EU affairs, and why they treat them in the way they do, is a far more complex set of questions than simplistic analysis and recommendations suggest. While focusing on the media allows us to consider some of the complex questions out there, we should not expect all the answers to come from the creation of more favourable media representations of the European Union or a cadre of European journalists. In fact, quite the opposite may happen: the adversarial, professional and investigative strain of British political journalism forensically dissected the workings of the British Parliament and MPs during the 2009 'expenses scandal', yet few would argue that this has enhanced the reputation of the political class. If there is a lesson to be drawn from this, it is that more professional journalism is just as likely to expose shortcomings as it is to paper over cracks. The question for those working in and for the EU is whether, in wishing to improve representation, they are also ready to face scrutiny. To date, the absence of extensive coverage reflects both the facelessness of those who run the institution and their ability to hide behind it. More active media might thus be a challenge too far.

Although this chapter focuses mainly on the EU–media couplet, it should ideally be read in conjunction with chapter 8, where there is a fuller discussion of the range of 'identity' issues with which researchers constantly grapple.

EU media studies

In his review essay for the special issue of *Journalism Studies*, Henrik Örnebring (2009) organized his analysis around three areas that feature prominently in discussions about the nature and content of European journalism and media. These are:

- *representation* – the nature of media coverage of Europe;
- *production* – the nature of European journalism or journalisms;
- *participation* – the question of the European public sphere.

Although he framed his argument in terms of 'the perceived failures of journalism *vis-à-vis* Europe' (2009: 5) – that is, what the media and journalism have not (quite) achieved in respect of coverage of the EU – his classification is essentially a framework for looking at studies of the EU and the media. As he observes towards the end of his paper, the failures overlook signs of positive developments. In other words, the research in this area provides us with mixed results; judgements about failures (or successes) often make sense only in the context of original expectations, and we must take these into account when exploring how the media work in the EU arena.

The three-way classification offered by Örnebring (2009) provides a useful structure in which to explore the themes of this chapter, and the following sections deal with these – though in a different order.

The European public sphere – what is it, is there one and do we need it?

The public sphere is that communicative space within which conversations and discussions ('democratic deliberations') take place. As Thompson observes in his discussion of the public sphere, 'between the realm of public authority or the state . . . and the private realm of civil society and personal relations . . . there emerged a new sphere of "the public": a bourgeois public sphere which consisted of private individuals who came together to debate among themselves the regulation of civil society and the conduct of the state' (1995: 70). However, and by way of contrast, the European Union is not a single nation-state but a union of many and different member states. And so there is not the physical and socio-cultural and political proximity that is more typical of the nation-state, nor is there the singular communicative space within which communication – national, regional and local – takes place. The EU is therefore a different sort of union, a supranational union, and one where the more common understanding of a public sphere does not easily apply. As Schlesinger has observed:

> Customarily, in the international system of states, *politico-communicative* space is taken to be co-extensive with *national* space. . . . By introducing a new, 'higher' political level above that of the nation-state, the shift to a supranational formation begins to transform the established communicative relations between national publics and state-centered systems of power. . . .
>
> . . .
>
> Both national and European discourses coexist. 'Europe' is *inside* the nation state as part of the domestic political agenda and as part of the broader politico-economic framework; at the same time, it is also still another place, a different political level and locus of decision making that may be represented as outside. (Schlesinger , 1999: 264, 266)

But given that, as Risse has pointed out, the European public sphere, like other public spheres, 'emerge[s] through social and discursive practices' (Risse, 2003: 5), it does beg the question of how we get from where we may have been – a national public sphere – to where we may want to be – a European public sphere. We must therefore identify those elements that would help us to determine whether, or when, the European public sphere has been formed.

The European public sphere

One of the earliest and most helpful elaborations of the European public sphere was offered by Philip Schlesinger in 1999:

> If we think beyond elites to a putative network that knits together a range of European publics, typically these would be composed of *transnational citizens* who have (a) an equal and widespread level of communicative competence, (b) relatively easy access to the full range of the means of communication, and (c) a generalized communicative competence that embodies sufficient background

knowledge, interest, and interpretative skills to make sense of the EU and its policy options and debates. A hypothetical *European sphere of publics* would, among other things, (a) involve the dissemination of a European news agenda, (b) need to become a significant part of the everyday news-consuming habits of European audiences, and (c) entail that those living within the EU have begun to think of their citizenship, in part at least, as transcending the level of the member nation-states. Moreover, these rational attributes would need to be accompanied by an affective dimension. (Schlesinger, 1999: 277–8)

Without going into every single statement, we can easily imagine the transition that Schlesinger is seeking to articulate – namely, a transition from individual citizens imagining themselves as part and parcel of one particular, geographically delimited nation-state towards a moment when those same citizens can imagine themselves to be transnational European citizens. Within that transition, though, is an implicit recognition that media content and the media practices engaged in have *a European* dimension or have become *Europeanized* in some way, be it in terms of the topics discussed, how they are discussed or considered, and/or how they are consumed.

On the one hand, then, citizens need to feel, and become, part of a larger European political and cultural entity; on the other, they must be able to consume media content that is, to some extent, European and that reflects a European agenda. The former becomes an issue of building an affinity across member states and integrating national citizens into a new political and cultural formation, while the latter involves interrogating the channels of communication that enable not only institution-building but political and cultural participation and communication across the citizenry of the European Union. The latter strand of work, according to Christoph Meyer, has produced a veritable torrent of research, including research on 'the Europeanization of public discourses and public discourses': whether there has been 'an increasing interpenetration, synchronization and possibly convergence of national public discourses towards a European sphere of publics . . . or a common communicative space' and numerous quantitative and qualitative studies of media content drawn from across member states (Meyer, 2007: 2–3).

Since Philip Schlesinger's intervention in 1999, many other authors have sought to develop a more sophisticated understanding of what such a European public sphere might entail and, more critically, whether such a sphere has developed. Schlesinger had postulated that it would involve media systems disseminating 'a European news agenda' and a public that would both consume European news content and begin to consider itself as being European (Schlesinger, 1999: 277–8). These elements are fairly general and fairly basic in a foundational sort of way, but they point to those things that could be examined. So, for example, is there a European news agenda and, if so, what does it look like? Can it be found in the media of Europe? Is it similar across Europe? Can these elements be found in a range of media – the elite press, say, but not in the tabloid media?

Some, like Trenz (2004), have argued that we can now trace, and identify, the existence of a European public sphere. When we look at 'the political landscape of Europe', according to Trenz, we can already begin to see the emergence and actual working of a European public sphere. The reasoning behind this is that the 'political landscape' shows the interconnections not only between national public spheres but also at other different levels of communication: political actors will be speaking to one another, business people to one another, civil society actors, and so on. In other words, there is a flow of communication at many levels that incorporates European concerns. Hence, the European public sphere is as much about the flows of communication as about the form it takes. Similar points can be found in Calhoun's work, where he distinguishes three forms of the visibility of a European public sphere in the media:

> First, there is the official Europe of the EU and the common affairs of its members. . . . Second, there is an elite discursive community that is much more active in public communication, is often multilingual (on the continent, at least), reads more and more internationally, and consists of leaders in business, higher education, the media themselves and to some extent government. . . . Third, there are networks of activists committed to many different causes, from whole foods to human and indeed animal rights. (Calhoun, 2003: 266–7)

This is largely in tune with Schlesinger's analysis of the European public sphere and its constituent elements and, as with Trenz, illustrates how the research agenda has sought to identify those elements – of practice, content, etc. – that can be used to determine the nature and shape of the European public sphere.

However, there are questions as to whether the elements that they identify extend to all citizens rather than just a select few. This is one point that Christoph Meyer has raised: while a European agenda might emerge from the communication flows that currently exist (or may develop in the future), there remains the issue of whether this will lead to the 'transcendence . . . of exclusively national identities' – as put forward by Schlesinger in 1999 (see above) – since, 'for the world to be seen from a European perspective, transcending purely national perspectives is not enough' (Koenig et al., 2006: 151). For many, the discussions surrounding Turkey's accession in 2004 showed how there was 'a predominant tendency within national public spheres to talk in civilizational ways, whether arguing in favour or against Turkish accession rather than in liberal individualist ways. This does not encourage the development of a European public of individuals, of a European public sphere, but something at odds with the idea of a European public sphere' – i.e. a Europe of different cultures and peoples who may or may not be in conflict with one another (ibid.: 166). In other words, there was no evidence of those elements that would make the EU a truly liberal European public sphere wherein individuals are encouraged 'to see others as individuals with rights and responsibilities and imagine them as at least potential partners in critical rational dialogue' (ibid.: 152). The national, domestic and separate nature of member states' agendas still dominated rather than being transcended by a European vision of the question of accession. (See chapter 8 for a fuller discussion of Turkey.)

It may be possible to argue that, although they are well put, Meyer's comments set the hurdles of the European public sphere too high, and that the objectives of the European public sphere are well beyond what can be achieved even within the public sphere of individual member states. Moreover, that if there were to be some elements of a European-inflected conversation in our media and in public discourse, that, in itself, would be a positive step towards the desired goal. The danger, and it is ever present in many discussions of the *European* public sphere, is that one can become obsessed about the merest hint or sign of this or that type of discourse rather than perhaps celebrating the fact that a discourse that incorporates the European Union ideals may in itself be a positive step forward. The evidence that would permit us to lend support to any of the above claims is discussed below when we begin to explore how the media in different member states deal with EU affairs.

EU journalism and the European public sphere

It is dangerous to assume that all member states have similar media systems or that the journalism that is practised within them is similar. There are different models of and different levels of professionalism in journalism in the EU, and that is part of the backdrop to our understanding of what is currently taking place in the development of a European news agenda. As we can see from table 7.1, derived from Hallin and Mancini (2004), there is no common media structure across the twenty-seven member states and there are important differences in journalistic traditions, ranging from the critical/sceptical approach of the British through to the more 'expert' commentary tradition of French journalism.

Missing from the model are East-Central European states such as Romania, Bulgaria and Lithuania. These would, in turn, illustrate other, and different, media arrangements and journalistic traditions or, most likely, be

Table 7.1 Hallin and Mancini's classification of media and political systems

	Mediterranean/ plural model France, Greece, Italy, Portugal, Spain	*Northern European/ corporatist* Austria, Denmark, Finland, Germany, Belgium, Sweden Netherlands, Norway	*North Atlantic/ liberal* Britain, Ireland, Luxembourg (?)
Newspaper industry	Low circulation	High circulation	Medium circulation
Political parallelism	High	External pluralism	Neutral commercial press
Professionalization	Weak	Strong	Strong
Role of the state in media	Strong	Strong	Market domination (except BBC)

Source: Hallin and Mancini (2004: 67).

incorporated within the Mediterranean/plural model. Recent monitoring reports on television systems in some of these countries relay stories of 'editorial independence, in both public and private media', continuing to 'deteriorate' (OSI, 2008: 21). While these conditions may be more significant for the coverage of domestic politics and less relevant for issues that may be deemed somewhat distant and not as important for national politics, they nevertheless highlight the ways that domestic pressures can impact on media work. Thus, the questions that need to be asked include whether the different media systems found across the EU lend support to, and frame, different journalistic practices and forms of EU coverage or whether there is a convergence of practices, so that one can talk of a European form of journalism that is distinct from specific national forms.

In seeking to examine these sorts of questions, research has tended to confront three broad areas of investigation:

- What is the nature of the journalism practised? Is there a form of European journalism?
- How extensive is EU coverage in the media?
- What drives EU news coverage? What are the news values adopted?

What drives EU news coverage? What are the news values adopted? How do journalists work?

Media coverage of the EU or EU-related matters is produced in a number of different locations (Brussels and Strasbourg – the fashionable 'news media beats'), in member states' capitals, principally of the larger and financially

Table 7.2 Interest in what is going on in the European Parliament

	% great deal /quite a lot	% not very much/ none at all
United Kingdom	19	52
Germany	25	45
Sweden	20	49
Italy	20	50
Spain	20	54
Latvia	13	63
Poland	14	55
Republic of Ireland	14	62

Source: Curtice (2005: 19, table 4.1.3).

Table 7.3 Turnout in European parliamentary elections, selected countries (percentages rounded up or down)

Member state	1979	1989	1999	2004	2009
Germany	66	62	45	43	43
France	61	49	47	43	41
Netherlands	58	47	30	39	37
United Kingdom	32	36	24	39	35
Greece		80	75	63	53
Poland				20	25
Hungary				38	36

Source: www.europarl.europa.eu/parliament/archive/elections2009/en/turnout_en.html.

stronger states, and in the home offices of media organizations. According to Basnee (2003: 80), there were 813 accredited journalists in 1999, mostly based in Brussels, compared with 645 in 1992. Published research suggests – as we shall see below – that the relationship between reporters and the news organizations' home office is important for generating, developing and mediating EU stories. All this, though, is against a background of a notable lack of interest in EU affairs, and in European Parliamentary affairs in particular (see table 7.2), as well as low turnouts in European parliamentary elections (see table 7.3).

Two studies of British journalists illustrate the significance of the relationship between the 'home' office and their 'overseas' location. David Morgan picked up the tensions very quickly when he noted that 'it was abundantly clear that most reporters are conscious of having to report with a highly developed sense of the domestically acceptable as far as EU news is concerned. For British reporters, particularly, this is highly significant because they know that the Euro-sceptics in the House of Commons cultivate London editors' (Morgan, 1995: 327–8). A more recent study carried out by Julie Firmstone

(2008) placed the work of individual reporters within the broader context of their organizational setting. She argued that those who wrote 'leaders' (i.e. opinion pieces expounding the newspaper's position) could express their own opinions but that freedom was mitigated by the overall position of their paper – that is, it was unlikely that a journalist who was pro-EU could work for an anti-EU outlet (and vice versa):

> Individual leader-writing journalists occupy a position of influence within newspapers that imparts them with the opportunity to make a significant contribution to editorial opinions towards Europe in three key ways: determining the level and qualitative nature of opinion by providing resources for producing editorials; shaping coverage through their personal attitudes and values towards Europe; and fulfilling specialist leader writing roles. (Firmstone, 2008: 225)

What journalists write – especially if they are journalists rather than leader-writers – is very much domestically inflected. This comes out of the work of Morgan (2004) and of others (see Dougal, 2003), but it is not just a British media phenomenon. Research on Romanian journalists covering the EU came up with very similar conclusions. As Lazar and Paun conclude: 'Reporting on the EU is first and foremost conditioned by the national political context, related to Romania's EU accession. EU issues are at the cross-point between political agendas, public agendas, and media agendas' (2006: 19).

Heikkila and Kunelius's study of journalists 'based on 149 semi-structured qualitative journalist interviews conducted in the home offices [i.e. not Brussels] of mainstream news organisations in ten European countries', also emphasizes the domestic/national inflection of much EU coverage. They identify three main ways ('discourses') in which journalists see themselves and the ways in which such positions impact on their practices and thinking: a 'classical professionalism discourse', a 'secular discourse' and 'the cosmopolitan discourse wherein the locus of news is shaped by emerging supranational trends in international politics and business' (Heikkila and Kunelius, 2006: 72). Yet, and despite these different discourses, they point out that

> the classical professionalism and secular news discourse are the two main discourses of the professional culture of mainstream EU journalists situated at their home offices. It is hardly surprising, but still impressive, how strong and naturalized a position the category of national identity still holds in journalism. It is only slightly provocative to conclude that mainstream journalism is a nationally fundamentalist profession. (Ibid.: 77)

As Gerd Kopper concluded from his extensive review on journalism in Europe:

Table 7.4 Different types of advocacy: attributing intentional ideological bias over Europe (pro-European/Euro-sceptic)

		Partisan dimension	
		–	+
Raising awareness	+	'Educational'	'Ideological campaign'
Informative-educative dimension	–	'Business as usual'	'Biased'

Source: Statham, "Journalists as commentators on European politics," *European Journal of Communication*, 22 (4): 467–77. Reprinted by permission of SAGE.

> each activity within this core sphere of 'European journalism', be it in Brussels or within the home offices, is from the start determined by the *national jour-nalism culture* existing and by the particularities of the channel, the medium and the service that an individual or a group is working for. . . . [The] major determining elements are those of the national media systems and of particular media organisation. (Kopper, 2007: 9; emphasis added)

But is it possible for journalists to transcend this domestically inflected coverage and to inject the sorts of input that would help bring about a transformation in the ways that citizens view the EU? As Statham asks:

> how do journalists see their role and 'act' in response to their perceived oppor-tunities and constraints for entering the mass-mediated public debate by mobilizing opinions over Europe? Do they see themselves as 'educators' raising public awareness, or as 'partisans' pushing specific European viewpoints? Are they able to write 'independently' from influence of proprietors or political parties? (Statham, 2007: 463)

Although, as he points out, there are possibilities for a range of behaviours – from using 'normal' news values to deal with EU stories ['business-as-usual'] to 'biased' reporting (see table 7.4) – there was 'little evidence for journalists using commentaries for partisan purposes over Europe' (ibid.: 473). As with other studies, journalists worked within the constraints set by their organi-zational settings, although the 'mainly perceived public knowledge deficits . . . motivate journalists, and the emergent and relatively undefined nature of European politics . . . allows them the freedom to express opinions, not that they see themselves as advocates with a political axe to grind' (ibid.).

To return to Heikkila and Kunelius (2004), the 'classical professionalism' discourse, wherein 'the national interest' inflects coverage, and the 'secular discourse', wherein the market helps mediate output, dominate the proc-esses of news production vis-à-vis the EU. This leaves little room for a more active educational role and, at the same time, underpins the importance of a professional – i.e. detached, adversarial – approach to news production.

Too much or too little coverage of the EU?

Although there is no real, objective or agreed measure of what could be considered adequate coverage of the EU, numerous studies have grappled with this question. It is, after all, a question that links back to the discussion of the European public sphere, since coverage can be used as an indicator of the existence of such a sphere. As Schlesinger (1999) pointed out, the European public sphere presupposes the existence and dissemination of a European news agenda and that European news should become a staple diet of media consumers.

In seeking to determine its extent and nature, most researchers (see Gavin, 2007, for an extensive discussion) acknowledge that it has now become part of an accepted and recognized domestically inflected agenda. Morgan notes, for example, that even in Britain, which has an ambiguous relationship with the EU institutions, 'Union news is no longer foreign news within member countries but has been nationalized and treated accordingly' (Morgan, 1995: 338). Or, as in the words of Trenz, the 'spreading rhetorics about Europe in different political contexts can be identified as a form of "banal Europeanism". Europe becomes a taken-for-granted reality. To make rhetorical references to Europe is no longer exceptional but enters the routine way of making sense of the world in everyday political talk' (Trenz, 2004: 310).

Whether that 'taken-for-granted reality' is *every* citizen's 'taken-for-granted reality' is a matter of controversy. As research shows, EU coverage tends to be extensive – although even here variably so – within the 'quality/serious' media, but this does not extend to the 'popular' press – hence, the restricted nature of the European public sphere. To quote Meyer: 'we have seen over the last ten years the emergence of a geographically and socially restricted public discourse in Brussels, revolving around particular elites, including Brussels based journalists, who read similar publications and can and do engage in transnational debates, not always, but frequently enough to call it cohesive' (Meyer, 2007: 4).

Though there are European-inflected conversations, these are not as inclusive and as extensive as one would presume should take place within a Europeanized public sphere. To give an illustration of this point (of which more later): during the 2004 Turkey accession debates, the 'serious' British press gave some coverage to this story, yet significantly less than either the French or the Greek press (Negrine et al., 2008; see also chapter 8). Recent research on the coverage of the European parliament election of 2009 reveals variations across countries and across media (Maier et al., 2011). An analysis by Trenz of a sample of serious newspapers in 2004 indicated that there were variations but sufficient reporting to argue against those who claim that there is insufficient coverage of the EU:

> The sample that results from our key word research indicates that European political communication forms a part of approximately 35.2 percent (in the German *FAZ* up to 55 percent) of all the political news articles in the individual newspapers. . . . In detail, we find an average of 7.8 European articles, 2.8 Europeanized articles and 7.3 articles with a European referential frame in each edition of a European quality paper. By simply adding these figures we must concede an astonishingly high level of Europeanization of national newspapers, which contradicts all previous findings on the scarce visibility of Europe in the media. (Trenz, 2004: 297)

There is no comparable study of television coverage although work by Neil Gavin on reporting of economic activity in the British media led him to conclude that 'news about Europe is a persistent and significant aspect of coverage, and in a quantity sufficient to suggest that it should be taken seriously in an assessment of European identity formation. The amount of European reporting rarely dips below 10 per cent of all economic coverage in the 1996–1997 period and a similar picture emerges in 1998–1999' (Gavin, 2000: 361). As elsewhere, one can argue over the significance and adequacy of this – or similar – figures, but its occurrence is itself of importance, and it does mean that the EU is not absent from television screens, at least in Britain.

More politically charged moments in the life and times of the EU, such as European parliamentary elections, referenda, debates about the appointment of the President of the Commission, etc., will obviously generate more news. How it is mediated is another matter, as we have shown, but it does nonetheless confirm the general view that the EU is not absent from the media of member states.

Does the nature and extent of coverage lead us to conclude that this is evidence of a transnational discourse in that the media of all member states cover a similar range of stories at the same time and feed off one another? Does it permit us to describe this as a European agenda or a Europeanized news agenda? Is this akin to a conversation about Europe by Europeans? The fact that *The Guardian* reported German and French opinions and newspaper comment on Turkey's accession and that Turkish newspaper coverage included comment from the media of EU countries could be seen as a coming together of a Europe-wide discussion, and possibly represents the Europeanization of 'national quality papers' that Trenz identified:

> Europeanization is promoted by several intervening factors that explain a certain degree of convergence of national news agendas: the socializing effects of European journalists, the standardization of the modes of operation of the quality press, the cultural alignment of the underlying news values, the impact

of European actors and institutions and the structuring effects of the public resonance of common events as well as of the processes of policy change at the European level. (Trenz, 2004: 311–12; see also Risse, 2003: 3)

Whether these conversations were widespread or in-depth may be a related concern, but it is perhaps no different from concerns about the coverage of domestic politics and parliamentary institutions within each member state (see Negrine, 1999). If there is a valid concern here it may be that the processes of commercialization have, over many years, gradually eroded – though not eliminated – the space given to 'serious' news in general and to political news in particular.

In summary, then, research has confirmed that the EU is not absent from the serious media. While there may be further questions to ask about the ways in which national lenses mediate EU news, the existence of that news is itself welcome and a step towards acknowledging the embedding of the EU in the politics of the member states. For those in charge of the Commission, there is an explicit desire for more and more positive coverage, but this may have less to do with the nature of EU news – bureaucratic, unexciting, etc. – and more to do with questionable practices – e.g. in selecting a president, not having the accounts audited, etc. – that lead to 'negative' news. As Slaatta (2006) reminded us, it is too easy to blame the media for the shortcomings of the EU political process. Yet, and unfortunately, that is often what the Commission has done and often what it seeks to redress through its many communication plans, the latest being its *Plan D*.

The EU communicating the EU: Plan D for Democracy, Dialogue and Debate

Neil Gavin (2007: 155), like Slaatta (2006), has made the point that the various institutions and their members cannot avoid taking some of the blame for the EU's low profile. In making this point, he draws on a range of work that emphasizes the importance of strategic communication and of various ways in which the content of the media can be managed (in both a 'positive' and a 'negative' way) in order to achieve good coverage. While a more proactive communication strategy is, in theory, always desirable, the EU does not perhaps contain the sorts of elements that would make it, or its members, immediately newsworthy: MEPs are largely unknown in comparison with their domestic counterparts, the EU is geographically distant and shrouded in mystery, the deliberations of the EP are complex, and some of the ways in which it operates are less commendable than they ought to be. To return to an example used above: in an age when transparency in politics is highly desirable, not auditing the accounts is problematic and not establishing open and democratic procedures for the appointment of the President of the Commission is clearly undesirable. So, as the substance of the work of the institution is rarely the stuff that would make journalists wild with excitement, it does leave itself open to critical attack.

It would nevertheless be unusual for the EU's many parts not to try and engage with the media so as to generate publicity. This is what all modern institutions do, and this is precisely what the EU has done in the past and continues to seek to do. When Roy Perry looked at the work of the EU in 2004, he noted that the 'latest report adopted by the Culture Committee in February 2003 on information and communication policy for the European Union is that of . . . de Perogordo. In his report he cites no fewer than *nineteen* similar reports, going back as far as a resolution of 15 Feb. 1957 on "informing public opinion about the activity of the Community"' (2003: 65; original emphasis).

The existence of so many reports has not deterred the EU from producing yet more. Its most recent White Paper on communication policy was seen as an essential part of communicating Europe and its activities to the citizens of the EU and as part of the process of gaining legitimacy and support. In part, this new plan was a consequence of setbacks – lack of interest in the EU and its work, rejection of the constitution, low turnouts (table 7.3) – and a determined effort to change the situation and to deal with the key issues:

> There are many reasons behind the EU's communication challenge:
> - there is a general *lack of trust in politicians and governments* in all modern western democracies;
> - the EU has a unique and *complex system of decision-making* which is hard to understand and there is a lack of attention paid to it in national education systems;
> - *linguistic barriers* add to the complexity of EU policies;
> - national decision-makers have a tendency to *blame the EU* when unpopular measures need to be introduced and to take the sole credit for popular EU decisions;
> - there are *no genuine EU-wide political parties* and therefore any referenda or election with a European dimension will always be seen through a national filter;
> - there are *no big EU-wide media* and national media will look at EU policies only within the context of their national political system;
> - the EU's information and communication strategy has always had more of an institutional and *centralised PR dimension* (with 'streamlined' information) than a real citizen-centred 'public sphere' dimension, and

- the role of member states in communicating Europe at *national level* has always been underestimated.[2]

In order to begin to deal with these, in October 2005, Commissioner Wallström launched a *Plan D for Democracy, Dialogue and Debate* (CEC, 2006), urging member states to start a debate with citizens on the future of the EU.[3] The plan sets out five 'areas for action in partnership with other institutions, governments and civil society' that would allow for a better means of communication between citizens and the EU, as well as a more efficient way for the EU to get a better sense of what citizens think. At the same time, and of importance to the discussion in this chapter, one area of action involves working 'better with the media' by creating special networks of communication – for example, via satellite links and other means (youtube.com/eutube, ec.europa.eu, www.euranet.eu) to make better connections with the public, journalists and the media in general.

Many, however, will continue to argue that the 'failure' to communicate the EU in its many guises cannot simply be reduced to a technical question relating to the provision of better or more efficient facilities. The issues that ought to be addressed go beyond the media, as Slaatta (2006) pointed out. If those in the EU seek to raise their profile, they may need to think differently about the need for transparency and openness in decision-making processes. Thus, 'the efforts to encourage democratic debate by means of public relations efforts are hampered by a policy to maintain "the one voice" in representing the EC to its publics . . . The EU Commission and European Council try to avoid public interference in their debates; they conduct these behind closed doors, while at the same time presenting themselves as the ultimate guardians of the European public good' (Lauristin, 2007: 405).

Media and politics in a European context

Public communication in Europe comprises activities both at the EU institutional level (as discussed above) and at the national level. Some of those activities are obviously related to the need to deal with the 'democratic deficit', but much revolves around the need to explain the EU to citizens in member states. At this level, though, the interaction between politics and media often involves no more than the traditional pattern of relations and activities; the 'new' media introduces some significant new elements. In important respects, the countries of Europe have all entered the 'third age' of political communication. With a fragmented media landscape and with the internet in place, many of the traditional elements of the relationships between politicians, the media and the public have necessarily changed. Politicians in Europe still need to reach, persuade and mobilize the public – and in increasingly professional ways – but they now do this using both the 'old' and the 'new' media. In turn, the 'old' and the 'new' media have developed new ways of reaching the audience, with the added factor that (a section of) the public ceases to act as an audience and becomes both citizens and communicators (bloggers, tweeters, etc.), consuming as well as creating content. As Helms notes:

> While both governments and the media have a natural interest in reaching the public and influence the public agenda, they consider and address the public from different angles, as voters or customers. But citizens are bound to combine these roles and may not always be able, or even willing, to distinguish strictly between the different worlds they are living in. This creates a huge challenge for all actors involved in political communication, yet the implications are particularly serious for governments seeking to strike a balance between democratic responsiveness and leadership. (Helms, 2008: 30)

In practice, it is still too early to offer a definitive account of the ways in which the 'third age' will transform processes in politics and communication, in part because the technologies are themselves evolving. For example, it is only within the last three years that the iPhone has been available and become part of the communication landscape, and Twitter has only been in existence for a year or so. Similar points can be made about Facebook, MySpace and a host of other networking sites that are increasingly entering the spaces for political communication and contributing to a growing set of conversations.

Yet we are becoming aware of certain common factors across Europe in the ways in which politics and media interact, if only for the purpose of ensuring the continuity of political systems via election practices. As each country displays individual characteristics and arrangements, the comments below are intended as general and indicative guides to the shifting terrain. This discussion will be organized under two headings: change at the level of *media and media practice* and change at the level of the *political party*.

Change at the level of media and media practice

This refers to changes *in* media (e.g. newspapers to television) but also to changes in the ways in which media work. Thus, one must include here the processes of commercialization that privilege 'media logic' over 'political logic' (Mazzoleni, 1987) with the effect of forcing those in politics to become aware of the needs of the media and of personalization, whereby the boundaries between the private and the public lives of politicians disappear.

The latter trend is obvious in Italy with Silvio Berlusconi, who has become the country's longest-serving prime minister after the Second World War and who features prominently in the tabloid press. In France, President Nicolas Sarkozy appears to be the 'master' of the TV image; in Germany, Gerhard Schröder was known as the 'media chancellor'; and in the Netherlands, the late populist politician Pim Fortuyn, with his adversarial tone, style and culture, increased his popularity through the magnifying-glass effect of television. By and large, all the main actors in the European political communication system nowadays have to adjust to new conditions and use marketing logic and professional consultants (Papathanassopoulos et al., 2007) to deal with generally highly volatile public opinion. In other words, a range of intermediaries – consultants, spin doctors, advisers – has been placed at the political end of the spectrum to deal with – i.e. manage and control – political communication on the part of actors. For its part, the media have pulled in other participants from a spectrum of non-governmental but interested bodies (e.g. the blogging community) to help shape discussions and agendas. This means that the objective of total media control is increasingly problematic, as more and more members of different publics enter conversations through blogs and interactive media opportunities.

Changes at the level of the political party

There have also been vast changes *at the level of the political party*, and their transformation into electoral professional political parties is an example of this. The consequences contribute to a different approach to the practice of political communication, political advocacy and political engagement. Much of this is common across Europe, where political parties have witnessed a decline in membership (see also Mair and Biezen, 2001) and a changed relationship between voters and parties. Voters are no longer making political decisions on the basis of traditional allegiances (e.g. class, religion) and are more prepared to switch votes, and hence are more open to persuasion. This has major implications for the political process. In Italy, the political system underwent dramatic changes following numerous scandals and judicial inquiries which led, in turn, to the demise of most of the traditional parties and to the arrest of many important political leaders. The political subcultures in which Italy was divided between the socialists-communists and the Catholics have progressively lost their importance and have almost disappeared (Mancini, 2007). In Sweden, traditional political stability has to a certain extent been challenged by a more volatile public opinion (Nord, 2007). In the Netherlands, ideology and religion are less of a dominant factor in voter choices, and party membership has fallen to one of the lowest in Europe (Brants and van Praag, 2007). Moreover, the number of floating voters has grown at every election and the numbers who have been 'turned off' politics has increased. Just as in Italy, the traditional pillars of Dutch society (Catholic, Protestant and socialist) have almost disappeared. In Germany, where three parties dominated the political process for decades, the establishment of new parties, and of the Greens in particular, has changed the landscape and brought about new competition (Holtz-Bacha, 2007). In France, the Greens from the Europe Ecologie party made significant gains in the 2009 European elections, aiming to alter the political map of the country as the Greens did in Germany. In Sweden, the Pirate Party – created after the Pirate Bay web portal and campaigning on reformation of copyright and patent law – secured 7.1 per cent of the Swedish vote in the 2009 European Parliament elections. In Greece, the leading political parties, since they have become increasingly similar, have faced considerable difficulties in getting their agendas placed before the public, and Greek citizens have become less supportive of them. In Eastern Europe, although the political systems have changed completely over the last dozen or so years, the new parties are characterized by their lack of embeddedness in society, their lack of formal structure and the small number of members.

In general, trust in the political system has declined in European countries: only about a third of the population trust their national political institutions (Eurobarometer, 2008). More precisely, 32 per cent trust their government and 34 per cent their parliament, compared with 62 and 58 per cent, respectively, who do not trust them; 76 per cent do not trust their national political parties and only 18 per cent trust them. Denmark is the only member state where a majority of respondents (50 per cent) trust their political parties. Levels of trust are higher in Spain and the Netherlands (40 per cent in both cases) and in Malta (35 per cent) and Cyprus (33 per cent).

The decline of the pre-eminence of the traditional party within the political process (and in the media!) is leading to a greater questioning of how parties should operate in competitive elections in the future. By and large, in a situation where citizens have become less supportive of parties, less trusting of the system and more likely to abstain, there is likely to be a greater incentive to employ those skilled in the arts of communication and marketing – the 'professional' consultants, communicators and organizers – to help parties position themselves in the minds of the voters (figure 7.1). Similarly, it is likely that greater resources will be devoted to reaching smaller groups of potential voters via non-traditional communication outlets such as Facebook, Twitter and websites. In general, as the media landscape fragments, more attention needs to be devoted to reaching smaller groups of differentiated voters.

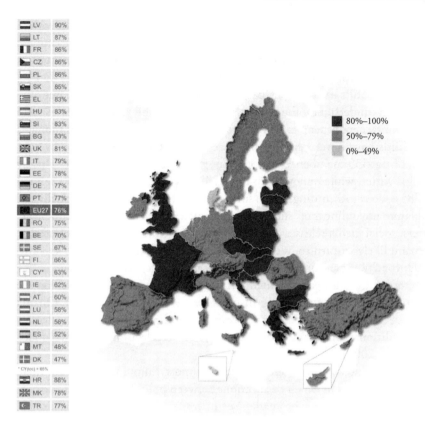

LV	90%	
LT	87%	
FR	86%	
CZ	86%	
PL	86%	
SK	85%	
EL	83%	
HU	83%	
SI	83%	
BG	83%	
UK	81%	
IT	79%	
EE	78%	
DE	77%	
PT	77%	
EU27	76%	
RO	75%	
BE	70%	
SE	67%	
FI	66%	
CY*	63%	
IE	62%	
AT	60%	
LU	58%	
NL	56%	
ES	52%	
MT	48%	
DK	47%	
* CY(tcc) = 65%		
HR	88%	
MK	78%	
TR	77%	

Legend:
- 80%–100%
- 50%–79%
- 0%–49%

Figure 7.1 Lack of trust in political parties in the European Union

Source: Eurobarometer (2008).

Media and politics in the era of the internet

The changing landscapes discussed above have already had an impact on the way the media and politics interact and on the conduct and nature of political communication. Leaders such as Nicolas Sarkozy and David Cameron make considerable use of both old and new media. Cameron – one of many – has made a point of using a regular videoblog (webcameron.com) as one way of presenting a more modern look to the Conservative Party but also as a way of bypassing the traditional media gatekeepers. While European countries still lag behind the USA in terms of internet campaigning, there are indications that they are catching up. For example, all the modern tools were used, including blogs and Twitter, in the 2010 British general election.

There is also a change taking place in terms of the activity of individual politicians on the web, though here again European parliamentarians are still making scant use of the internet and fail fully to grasp the potential of digital politics to engage with voters. A recent (2009) survey found that 75 per cent of MEPs use their personal websites to reach the electorate, but only a minority understands the potential of using online technologies to help them interact with people. Only half visit blogs once a week or more, and two-thirds have never heard of the social networking tool Twitter. In contrast, of the 535 members of the US Congress, 116 (22 per cent) are already using Twitter, while only twenty-seven MEPs – just 3.5 per cent of the total of 785 – do so. According to the survey, a number said they occasionally use or plan to use online tools such as social networks, personal blogs, html newsletters, social media releases or online videos. Over half of all MEPs said that they are likely to turn to Web 2.0 in the coming years (Fleishman-Hillard, 2009; for 2009 data on Britain, see Hansard Society, 2009). As one of the directors of the study commented: 'The vast majority of MEPs are using the internet and are certainly being inspired by the success that Barack Obama has had, but too many of them still believe that digital tools are less effective than traditional forms of communication, such as television and newspapers' (EurActiv, 2009).

With the internet developing rapidly in most European countries, there are countless ways in which connections between political (and other) organizations and publics can be made. Yet in respect of the communication of politics:

1 mainstream news media are still dominant as sources of news, though this is changing since, as noted in chapter 5, the average European is spending more and more of his/her time online;
2 though elites can create and control their own media spaces (their websites, blogs, etc.), these are of little use unless they are accessed. However, the potential for interactivity exposes elites to interrogation and contradiction in a way that has not happened before;
3 websites compete and link with other websites, so creating a network of information. In the world of politics, this can increase the level of scrutiny and monitoring of political elites, confirming the existence of what John Keane (2009) has called 'monitory democracy'. A good example of such scrutiny is the site www.theyworkforyou.com, where all activities of British MPs can be checked;
4 the existence of a multiplicity of networks of information can open up discussions beyond what is made available through elites or traditional media outlets;

5 with the internet, social movements can bypass traditional media outlets. This gives them a source of power and a way to challenge the traditional forms of political power and order. Following the shooting of a teenager by the police in Athens in December 2008, activists organized their marches using the net and mobile technologies. Such activities challenge traditional forms of action and organization.

As internet penetration increases in Europe, the old mass-audience-centred campaigns are being transformed in order to deal with the fragmentation of European audiences. This transformation makes life in the public arena much more complex than ever before and the process of reaching the various segments even more complicated: old and new media and communication tools will be needed in order to reach potential voters. Will this herald a new era of politics and public engagement or will it, as some believe, lead to a situation in which the 'web will become a tool for "politics as usual"' (Leadbeater, 2008)? It is still too early to tell.

In spite of the enormous changes that have taken place in the media landscape and the declining dominance of political parties, it is still the case that most political action is still organized around them and their activities. The core features of representative democracy remain in place, not only because they have been so completely normalized in Western capitalist societies but also because those who have invested most in such structures are themselves able to adapt and co-opt forces of change – which is why political parties will make use of the internet and why they will modernize themselves.

All in all, the new information and communication technologies create new possibilities and new circumstances which were not possible when other modes of communication were dominant. Movements can be loosely organized, leaderless, flexible and continually regenerating; they can be local or global; they can change their nature and adapt rapidly to different circumstances. The global reach and speed of the new technologies make them useful for rapid, global and easy communication and organization. Internet websites created by such movements become, in effect, sources and resources of information and action. They become those elements that link individuals to one another and to larger groupings so as to advance, protect or challenge authority or centres of power. What all these different ways of connecting peoples and organizations means is that the 'political impact' of the internet can take many forms and be looked at from a number of different perspectives. The discussion thus far has been about how parties communicate and how the internet has been used in recent elections, but the other ways in which the internet can play a part in politics are by no means unimportant.

Summary

Any attempt to summarize such an extensive field of enquiry is likely to be incomplete. In looking at the way in which journalism and politics, broadly defined, overlap, we have been able to identify a varied picture where there are failures but also successes (Örnebring, 2009). There is some media coverage of the EU and its institutions, but perhaps not enough; there are some elements of 'Europeanization', but maybe not many, and so on. Before making any firm judgements on such matters, though, it is important to recognize the recent origin of the EU and the fact that it may take time to create the sorts of circumstances and conditions for a deeper union. On the positive side, European Union affairs are now regularly covered, though not in all media and perhaps not very extensively, but that is no different from the coverage of domestic parliaments or other political affairs! Similarly, at the national level, the changing nature of populations throws up issues of identity and unity, and these will feed into debates about the nature of the European Union. Perhaps so long as these matters keep being discussed, there is some hope that they will continue to matter to people to the extent that they become part of their day-to-day concerns.

What is yet to emerge from all this is a sense that all citizens of Europe address the same issues at the same time. Even when elections to the European Parliament are taking place, there is a tendency for domestic politics and domestic political issues to be seen as more important than European-wide concerns. In most cases, these elections are of lesser importance than domestic ones and attract less attention. As with much else in this book, this reinforces the view that member states continue to operate as units in a complex relationship with the centre. In other words, differences remain amid similarities that emerge out of a process of Europeanization or globalization, Americanization or professionalization (see Negrine, 2008). For instance, each member state has its own characteristics derived, as they inevitably are, from a long historical, political, technological and cultural process. Yet, similarities are emerging: there is a greater personalization of politics, and there are similarities in the ways in which political leaders operate and work with the media, in the way that representatives of both domestic and European parliamentary bodies use the old and new media (see EurActiv, 2009), and in the way in which domestic and parliamentary representatives and political parties are generally distrusted. The task of the EU, the media and representatives is to overcome the growing mistrust of all those in authority and to address the 'democratic deficit'.

This, though, is still a very 'top-down', 'traditional' and 'one-way' process of communication. The internet, as we have indicated, allows for much more and different communication. It permits two-way communication, unmediated communication, and creates spaces for groups to mobilize and overturn older ways of doing things. It also creates opportunities for a greater level of scrutiny of EU institutions and those who help oil the machinery of a large supranational entity. The challenge for the EU institutions and their members is to connect with these new constituencies and to begin to talk to them directly and, perhaps, gain their support.

8   Media and European Identity

> ... a certain degree of collective identification with the European Union is necessary to treat fellow Europeans from other member states as legitimate voices in one's own public sphere. It does not imply a deep sense of loyalty toward each other, but some minimum sense of belonging to the same political community is required. (Risse and Grabowsky, 2008: 7)

The long process through which the European Union has come into existence has given rise to a number of different topics for research and comment. One of these areas, as we have seen in chapter 7, has been the topic of discussion around the development of a European public sphere, a space where all members of the European Union can take part in conversations as equals and as citizens of one political entity. A related topic has been, almost inevitably, the intriguing question of how citizens of different member states – different in cultural, political, social and linguistic terms – can come to see themselves as Europeans and so belonging to the same political entity. As the discussion in the previous chapter has indicated, there is a real issue about how citizens can come to identify with an intergovernmental supranational body that was formed out of a process of negotiation and consensus over six decades or so. And, as the quotation at the top of this chapter implies, a prerequisite for the development of deep bonds and understanding across the member states of the EU is 'some minimum sense of belonging'. How that can be, and whether it has been achieved, is the theme of this chapter.

In a general sense, it is taken for granted that citizens of a nation-state have 'some minimum sense of belonging' to it – a 'sense of belonging' that draws on historical, political and socio-cultural forces which enable an individual to define themselves as British, French, Greek, and so on. The European Union, by contrast, has not grown up – organically and over time, one is tempted to say – out of a long historical or cultural process in which citizens (and their predecessors) have played a part. That it was driven from above is equally noteworthy, and the comparatively short process through which it has emerged may not have created the circumstances for its members – its citizens – to become fully integrated into it. Nonetheless, it is a political, cultural and economic 'project' of immense significance. As the historian Ian Kershaw (2008) has recently observed:

Seventy years on, our present Europe, for all its flaws and fault lines, provides such an attractive contrast that it is hard not to see the European project that arose from the lessons of the Second World War and out of the far-sightedness of, especially, postwar German and French statesmen as a huge success story. The main objective of these postwar visionaries was to prevent circumstances ever again arising in which European nations could go to war with each other. . . . Having come this far, logic suggests that we need to look to a future in which, without any loss of national identity, a European voice can speak more strongly and urgently for the interests of a united continent than can the current prevailing and persistent dissonance. (Kershaw, 2008)

But the worthiness of 'the project' is dented somewhat by the nature of the institutions that are at its heart. The Commission, for example, has enormous powers, but is unelected and appears distant, so giving rise to the 'democratic deficit' that lies at the heart of much commentary regarding the failure of the EU to be sufficiently representative and accountable (Bache and George, 2006: 66–70). It is clearly one of the problems the EU has to tackle if it is going to gain more than superficial and grudging support of the citizens, which is why it invests in its media strategies (see chapter 7). The EU can very obviously function without public support and acceptance, but the bigger 'project' of the creation of a European citizenry cannot reach a satisfactory conclusion until citizens buy into it and become 'stakeholders'.

It follows, therefore, that there are many reasons why the EU would wish the people of Europe to commit themselves to the EU 'project', to the notion of a citizen of Europe, to a level of participation in political processes that at least suggest some acceptance of the reality and legitimacy of the EU. This explains, in part, why European parliamentary election turnout rates are so significant: they can be used as a measure of allegiance, as an indication of how much one cares and feels involved, as a measure of how important the EP (and the EU as a whole?) is to its citizens. As Bruter observes, 'every time a new political community has been created . . . the legitimacy of the contract that links it to its citizens and gives it its fundamental institutional acceptability requires the creation of a new political identity' (2005: 2). Without that identification, the political entity lacks legitimacy and any of those things that would make its citizens accept its claims to competence and its rights to make decisions over them.

Having raised the spectre of identity and identification, we must confront other questions: *What* is identity and what does it mean in a practical, routine, everyday sense? What or whom should one identify *with*: a flag, an idea, members of other nation-states? What does being a member of the European Union mean and does it differ from being or identifying oneself as a European citizen? All these questions require some consideration, since they are not only complex but are based on assumptions that need to be examined critically. Similarly, we need to explore whether the objective of creating a European citizen or a citizen of Europe (which may be different) is absolutely necessary for the smooth functioning of the EU. As we shall note in regard to our discussion of media coverage of Turkey's bid in 2004 to join the EU, British political actors had no qualms about its joining an economic and trading bloc – the EU – but many members of the French political elite had problems with accepting a non-'European' state into a (predominantly) Christian EU (see Negrine et al., 2008) Identity and citizenship was not a fundamental issue for the former, in considering the enlargement of the EU, though it clearly was for the latter.

This chapter begins with a brief analysis of identity before moving on to a discussion of identity in the context of the European Union.

Europe and Europeanness: Where is Europe? What is the European Union?

The significance of this analysis can hardly be overlooked. Not only does it feed into debates about the future of Europe but it also exposes different narratives of Europe's past which inevitably impact on visions of the future. This was (and continues to be) pertinent in the discussions over the future of Turkey – a secular state but a predominantly Muslim country – in ('Christian') Europe and so exposes differences over how the future of the EU is constructed. At the same time, though, one is alerted to differences in narratives about the European past. As Dunkerley has written, '"Europe" and "European" are *ideas*, and as such the manner in which they have been defined has altered since the Middle Ages, when . . . interest began to grow in them' (2002: 110).

Similarly, Delanty has forcefully maintained that the meaning of Europe has shifted considerably over the last five hundred years or more and has never been fixed: in that 'process of invention and reinvention as determined by the pressure of new collective identities' (1995: 2–3), different groups have been variously included and excluded. Delanty has gone further to argue that, from the seventh century onwards, '"Europe" as an idea embodying certain values was increasingly defined in opposition to Islam' (in Dunkerley, 2002: 114). These discussions are part of ever present 'myths' in the historical construction of the idea of Europe, which usually privilege a Christian heritage while ignoring the roles of other religions (Judaism, Islam) in the creation of a sense of a European culture and entity.

Irrespective of the specific reading of the historical record that one adopts, it is clear that the 'European' heritage has drawn on Christian values but, as others also argue, it has also drawn on, or adapted, Judeo-Christian and Islamic values and practices – in language, architecture, art, mathematics, science, etc. – to give rise to a particular construction of what we currently accept as 'European'. One problem, though, is that what we may concede to be European does not always easily or readily map onto any sort of geographic boundary. In this regard, the borders of Europe – in the past as today – are porous: is the descendant of a Greek Orthodox Christian who was displaced from the Ottoman Empire to Thessaloniki in the 1930s 'European' because of an act of nationalism when the Greek state was founded? How did Thessaloniki become Greek, and hence European, after centuries of Ottoman rule (Mazower, 2005)?

In these circumstances, the questions 'What – and where – is Europe?' and 'What does it mean to be a "European"?' (Delanty, 2005) become more than simply idle enquiries. They highlight not only the problem of conceptualizing and identifying something that is continually in a process of change but also the questionable task of attempting to set out real and tangible boundaries of inclusion and exclusion. For, if the idea of Europe has evolved over centuries in particular ways and in opposition to certain groups, what needs to be explored is not only how the idea is being configured but also who has the power to define what the idea of Europe is (see Nicolaidis, 2003). As Stråth notes: 'The meanings of Europe are a discourse of power on how to define and classify Europe, on the frontiers of Europe, and on similarities and differences' (Stråth, 2002: 388). Consequently, particular versions of Europe are likely to be partial and inflected and a favoured portrayal of what, in effect, has been a tortuous and complex process of interactions between a multiplicity of ideas and peoples.

At issue here, then, is the question of how the European Union – and member states within it – has sought to define and characterize Europe so as to construct – or seek to construct – some sort of unifying and distinctive sense of belonging for those living within its boundaries – and, conversely, to construct boundaries that are intended to keep others out. Moreover, in an age where all have multiple local, regional and national identities, it may be almost impossible for there to be a single 'overarching European identity in the sense of a generalized categorical identity that includes all Europeans' (Delanty, 2005: 17). This does not mean that efforts to create such an identity should not be tried or that they are bound to fail – only that the process may be a long one and that the role of the news media (Bruter, 2005), policies ('Europeanization'), and symbols (the flag, the euro) (Shore, 2000) are probably crucial in that process. In this respect, these efforts represent attempts to reshape cultural identities in ways that can lead to the creation of an 'imagined (European) community' (Sassatelli, 2002: 436–7) or 'social imaginary' (Taylor, 2004), in order, perhaps, to overcome what are deep and significant differences coexisting within a singular entity.

The problem – as will emerge below – is one not so much of visualizing such a transnational and cosmopolitan objective but of devising strategies that will bring member states and their citizens closer to it. In a reflective moment, Philip Schlesinger brought together some of the key obstacles that lie in the path of such a 'European' project:

> In fact, states, nations and regions remain crucially important as locales for debate and as sources of identity. Europeanization is itself a profoundly ambiguous process. Who now – and who in the future – will be permitted to be a 'European' is an increasingly intense focus for struggles between inclusion and exclusion both within member states and at the borders of the EU itself. (Schlesinger, 2007: 424)

While there are obvious obstacles to the objective of European integration (Bruter, 2005), there is some evidence to suggest that aspects of 'Europeanness' – in contrast to other forms of identity – do exist in an everyday and 'common' sense. Writing of the Romanian experience of accession to the EU in 2007, Lauristin makes the point that not only were 'the West' and 'Europe' 'understood as virtually synonymous, as a cultural and political entity, different from the "eastern" communist type of civilization . . . [but] Europe was perceived as a "promised land", as an embodiment of common "western" values: freedom, democracy, solidarity, justice, prosperity' (2007: 398). As Lauristin adds, integration into the EU was seen as 'as an ultimate recognition of 'belonging to the European family' (ibid.). That sense of identification both with a common objective and of difference from other bodies and systems comes out very strongly in this instance and illustrates how everyday perceptions are important in guiding people towards, and away from, institutions, ideas and practices.

This should not be taken to mean that simply belonging to the EU makes one automatically and instantly a 'European' or a citizen of Europe, but it clearly is part of the process by which identities may come to be formed. Similarly, just because one uses the euro should not necessarily be deemed to be an active step in the process of constructing a European identity. It can certainly aid the process but it need not necessarily do so. As Mick Billig notes, such things as the currency and the flag may represent 'the forgotten reminders' of the EU (Billig, 1995: 38): 'background noise that is no more than a reminder of something of which one may approve or disapprove, when one is alerted to it!'

Almost at odds with this much larger integration 'project' and the explicit aims of creating a European Union in more than a physical sense are the views of those who continue to emphasize the nature of the EU as no more than a political and economic union of countries – a 'trade bloc'. This emerges quite clearly in moments of crisis, of which there have been several in recent years – for example, in respect of enlargement ('Why should Turkey not join the EU if the EU is no more than a trading bloc?') and ratification of the EU Constitution or Lisbon Treaty ('Does non-ratification lessen your role within the EU?'). Indeed, when Irish voters rejected the EU Treaty in June 2008, it became quite obvious that what was being rejected was the EU project as an all-encompassing, overbearing, supranational body that wished to super-impose its mores over member states. By implication, what the Irish voters wanted – if such a thing could be detected as a singular and rational position – was a large measure of independence within an international framework, as well as greater clarity in regard to the document that they were being asked to ratify. Yet at a deeper level, as an *Economist* leader pointed out, the EU can function perfectly well without the Lisbon Treaty, and its non-ratification – in Ireland and/or elsewhere – need not derail the EU machinery. The position of *The Economist* in this instance was that 'there is no longer a serious appetite for a federal Europe' and that the EU can function well without a new measure of constitutional agreements. In essence, as it also pointed out, 'the EU is an intergovernmental organisation that needs a consensus to proceed'. As that consensus can usually be achieved, constitutional discussions are unnecessary digressions. Put differently, the EU is essentially a group of countries working together; there is no EU 'project', nor, perhaps, should there be one (*The Economist*, 2008).

For the media, the issue is not simply (and perhaps superficially) about how the EU should be reported – something discussed in chapter 7 – but whether they should play a different role, an advocacy role, in representing the EU and a role that goes beyond mere reportage and takes on a distinct (favourable) position. Should they, for instance, play a positive role in reporting the EU to an extent that they become an adjunct to the process of unification and integration of disparate elements? Or should they simply treat it as a news story when it so merits? At the same time, to what extent should the media become part of the communication infrastructure of the EU if it helps create something akin to a *European* public sphere?

Becoming European

The idea of 'Europe' and 'Europeanness' raises important questions about the ways nation-states and larger geographic and socio-political entities come to define or construct themselves and their boundaries. They come to do so by 'imagining' themselves as unitary entities that can somehow be distinctive or distinguished from those others who are excluded, be it on the grounds of ethnicity, religion or some other such factor. As Bruter (2005) usefully reminds us, the state of Israel was formed in 1948 and has had to develop and utilize various means to build itself, to construct itself, as a state for external purposes but, perhaps more significantly, for internal purposes also. This latter dimension cannot be overlooked, since it can serve a double purpose: on the one hand, it can make individuals and groups feel that they 'belong' to the state and give their allegiance to it, while on the other it legitimizes the political processes within the state, since those who feel they belong to the state – and are encouraged to feel they belong by the state – accept as legitimate all that is done on their behalf.

Perhaps surprisingly, the same sets of considerations come into play when we turn to the matter of 'identity' in respect of the EU, a transnational, intergovernmental union of twenty-seven separate member states. As with the brief discussion of the case of Israel – or indeed any other recently formed sovereign state – there are questions that arise: How can peoples of different nation-states be made to feel 'European' or that they belong – in an affective and deep-seated emotional sense – to the European Union (or to Europe?)? How can they be made to feel part of the European Union to the extent that the policy outputs of the EU are seen as legitimate and not something produced elsewhere by policy-makers who lack the legitimacy of those associated with governing member states?

Importantly, and quite unlike the case of the state of Israel, the EU is ill-defined in terms of its geography. It does not have an external threat – which allows for the emergence of bonds internally, if nothing else – and it is made up of member states that have different languages, political systems and cultural values. Not only does it have to construct itself but, and at the same time, it has to devise ways of constructing the European citizen (as well as the European public sphere). But how it does so is problematic: What or where is 'Europe', and is it coterminous with 'the West'? How has 'Europe' crystallized as an idea, as an identity? Furthermore, and critically, as the nature of European populations changes – with, for example, different ethnic and religious mixes within the EU as a whole or within member states themselves – is the idea of 'Europe' anything more than a construct that has been overtaken by migratory and globalizing trends?

We can begin to see the relevance of these points when we look back to an interview that the former French president Valéry Giscard d'Estaing gave to the French newspaper *Le Monde* in 2002, in which he suggested that admitting Turkey to the EU 'would be the end of the European Union' because 'its capital is not in Europe and 95 per cent of its population live outside Europe. It is not a European country' (Giscard d'Estaing, 2002). At stake, at least as far as Giscard d'Estaing was concerned, was a particular political, cultural and geographic vision of Europe that would be significantly altered by admitting into it a country with a predominantly Muslim population that was geographically at the edge of the European continent. As others joined the debate, it quickly emerged that a number of different ways of looking at both the EU and Turkey began to populate media discourse: the EU was a 'Christian club', a 'political and economic union', a 'democratic union', a 'European' (*sic*) union; by contrast, Turkey was a 'Muslim country', a 'secular and democratic country', it had 'European characteristics', it was geographically (and implicitly culturally), as was pointed out, 'in Asia'. If, and following Giscard d'Estaing's pronouncement, the EU was a union of *European* countries, how could it admit a country that was neither geographically in Europe nor culturally European?

These sorts of questions – and the positions that they represented – were by no means new, since the relationship between Turkey and Europe has a long, complex and difficult history. Its complexity arises, in large part, out of the long-drawn-out process through which Europe has sought to define itself as a cultural and political unit by setting itself up as different from others, be it 'the Orient' or, more recently, the USA (see Delanty 2005, 1995; Kushner, 1999; Neumann, 1999; Robins, 1996). As Delanty argues, 'the early history of the idea [of Europe] reveals a tension between its function as a geographical construct and as a cultural-political idea. The principal polarisation with which the idea of Europe was linked, Christendom versus Islam, had in reality very little to do with the idea of Europe, but nevertheless influenced the future of the notion to a great extent' (1995: 29; see also Neumann, 1999). Furthermore, and as Bruter usefully adds, it has a problematic and shifting eastern border, making it the only continent 'not to be a continent at all from the point of view of most geographers' (2005: 81).

Even when this much broader cultural debate about the meaning or location of Europe is layered onto a geographical, political and economic union, the fundamental issues remain unresolved, though they have real and significant consequences. For example, if the EU is seen as no more than a trading bloc – a French jibe at the British perspective – it follows that those who fulfil certain minimum requirements should be able to join. However, if the EU is seen as a 'Christian club', to paraphrase Giscard d'Estaing, it follows that some will never be able to join.

There is also the much bigger question of how the changing population profiles of the European member states impact on what Europe means and, consequently, what being a European also means. Giscard d'Estaing overlooked the 6 million Muslims living in France, yet they too belong to 'Europe'. When controversies arise such as the publication in 2005 of the Danish cartoons depicting Muhammad in an unfavourable light, they highlight the many ethnic and religious divisions that coexist in Europe itself. Similarly, when considering the meaning of 'Europe' from the perspective of someone who lives in an English Midlands city that will, within the next two decades, become the first city in the country to have a non-white majority population, it is inevitable that the nature of belonging and identity generally but specifically to 'Europe' causes so much heart searching.

Such shifts in population cannot be ignored, and writings that overlook the changing profiles of populations and the changing make-up of Europe do so at a cost. According to some, it is asking for a forgetting of past injustices done to those within Europe but also to those who had long suffered at the hands of Europeans. As Elseewi has pointed out:

> Europe had to 'forget' the many injustices of its colonial enterprises, its treatment of immigrant populations, and its violent place in the contemporary world in order to 'remember' what Enlightenment tolerance was. Europe had to forget its history of fascism, intolerance, and social engineering in order to 'remember' its liberal democratic history. Muslim rioters and intellectuals alike, however, have not forgotten the injustices of previous and contemporary forms of the European/Western/American exertions of identity and power and use the very iterations Europe employs about itself as further examples of European hypocrisy. Within Europe, the very need to reiterate a Western identity that is based on secular, humanist ideals serves to remind Europeans of the countless examples of the violation of those ideals or the excesses those ideals have wrought. (Elseewi, 2007)

This resonates with those Turks who looked askance at Europeans holding up Turkey's human rights record as a reminder of longstanding problems. Yet some of these ideals were apparently still worth pursuing. In 2008, President Abdullah Gül of Turkey was quoted as saying: 'I wish to see Turkey as an island where the *European* standard of democracy is being fulfilled and the free market economy is functioning very well' (Kinzer, 2008).

European identity

The bigger obstacle that lies in the path of the creation of a European citizen or a citizen with a European identity is that, in an age in which many of us have multiple local, regional and national identities, it may be almost impossible for there to be a single all-encompassing European identity. While it may be easier to create a common European 'civic identity', it may be more

Table 8.1 Conceptual definition and operationalization of European identity variables

Variable	General identity	Civic identity	Cultural identity
Conceptual summary	Do respondents naturally think of themselves as Europeans?	Do respondents identify with the European Union as a political institution?	Do respondents identify with Europe as a cultural community?
Targeted elements	• Do I feel European?	• Does it mean anything for me to be a 'citizen' of the European super-state?	• Do I identify with Europe as a shared heritage?
	• How strongly do I identify with Europe?	• Do I identify with the symbols of European political integration?	• Do I think of Europe as a concentric identity level, finding Europeans less close than fellow nationals but closer to me than non-Europeans?
		• Do I identify with the civic aspects of European integration?	

Source: Bruter (2005: 109).

difficult to create a 'cultural identity' (Bruter, 2005; see table 8.1). The distinction between civic and cultural identity used by Bruter is useful in that it alerts us to the possibilities of acceptance and action on some grounds but not on others. According to Bruter, 'civic identity' relates to identification with structures and institutions of the EU, while 'cultural identity' has to do with identification with groups and people and the growth of a sense of belonging. When the citizens of Europe vote, they may be identifying with the EU – at least in the sense of acknowledging its legitimacy and importance as an intergovernmental institution – but this is not the same as identifying with its cultural dimensions. It is, by this reasoning, easier to achieve the former than the latter. It may be true that ,'while the EU is "for real" for European elites who have to deal with it in their daily lives, it is more remote for the European citizens' (Risse and Grabowsky, 2008: 3). Indeed, those for whom the EU may be 'for real' may be taking on a cosmopolitan identity that emphasizes certain 'European' ideals that transcend locality and geographic specificity, but this will be the case for a minority only. The rest, perhaps, will continue to navigate the various identities that they can inhabit. The issue, then, is how the rest will acquire that sense of European identity and whether the media – and their coverage of EU matters – create the foundations for the emergence of an EU identity. The case of Turkey presents us with an interesting testing ground because it exposes the many levels at which the EU operates and the many ways in which Turkey and its inhabitants are seen by both politicians and publics.

Being part of Europe

This strand of research has sought to chart the way citizens see themselves in the age of multiple local, regional, national, transnational and global identities. It also touches on the process by which identities come to be formed and, by extension, the extent to which the EU, and its constituent parts (EP, Commission, MEPs, etc.) and activities (monetary union, constitution, legislative activity, funding, research etc.), help bring about a sense of Europeanness. Somewhere within this complex lie the means of communication – the journalists and media – who together provide those things – the content, frames, stories, music – that can help create and give sustenance to the EU or, by negation, call its very own nature and self-image into question.

The evidence, generally collected via public opinion studies by (usually) Eurobarometer, sets out some important differences between citizens of different member states and the task that lies ahead if the EU is to become one imagined and unified entity. So, for example, in a study at the end of the twentieth century, Eurobarometer 'found that nearly 6 in 10 EU citizens feel very or fairly attached to Europe. People in Luxembourg (78%) are most likely to feel very or fairly attached', although people 'in the UK are least likely to feel attached (37%)' (CEC, 2001: 10). Eurobarometer also observed that, 'although at the end of the 20th century one can still not speak of the existence of a truly European identity, the majority of EU citizens feel to some extent European'. There were, as always, variations, with citizens in some countries feeling very European while others identified largely with their own nationality. As Eurobarometer noted: 'Although we find lower levels of agreement among nations where there are more Eurosceptic people, feeling European and believing in the existence of a shared European cultural identity do not go hand in hand' (ibid.: 10–12).

There are numerous problems in trying to make sense of the meaning of Europeanness in general but also in the context of any survey conducted on that matter. What goes through the minds of respondents when they answer such questions, and, perhaps more seriously, what motivates them to vote for or against the Lisbon Treaty, as the Irish did in June 2008? Is it a belief in national independence as against European and foreign incursions? Is it an act of revenge against something that one does not understand ('Don't be bullied' was a common slogan)? Is it a studied preference for national self-determination (despite having gained so much from it)? Furthermore, is one conflating what Michael Bruter describes as the 'civic' as opposed to 'cultural' dimension of European identity and consequently confusing rather than clarifying issues (Bruter, 2005: 101–4)?

To ignore these issues is to underestimate the complexity of what is being investigated, but at the same time it touches on the bigger question of what it is that the citizens are thinking and their affinity with different levels of governance (the 'civic' dimension), as well as their integration into a larger whole (the 'cultural' dimension). (It also touches on the extent to which the media have accurately and fully explained what is at stake.) When all this is taken into account, what we are left with is a sense that people see themselves as citizens of nation-states and possibly also of an ill-defined European entity and relate to these in different ways and to different degrees. In numerous cases, they may have been cajoled (led, invited, enticed, forced) into becoming part of that larger entity without necessarily fully comprehending the significance of the process or the outcome.

With time and much work and expense, different allegiances and alignments to the EU will most probably emerge, but there is the big and ever present issue of how citizens of different member states can be transformed into European citizens when, traditionally, loyalty has been seen in the context of national (linguistic, cultural) boundaries – unless, of course, one bifurcates the topic and accepts political allegiance and continuity and becomes less fixated with the cultural aspects of the EU and cosmopolitanism. The point to stress here is that, as a body, the EU (the Commission, the Parliament, etc.) has taken steps to seek to create an integrated European identity by adopting symbols such as the flag and particular pieces of music (Shore, 2000) that can become identified with it. The associations that these symbols trigger are then important for union-building. In the same way, but at a different level altogether, European researchers and academics (and students) are being encouraged to see themselves as part of Europe and to work through such schemes as framework funding of Erasmus programmes.

How Europe sees itself and others: the coverage of Turkey's accession bid in 2004

As the EU expands further, and beyond its enlargement with Bulgaria and Romania in 2007, the core idea of what Europe is or means may need to be ambiguous and flexible if it is successfully to accommodate different cultures, nations, ethnic groups, etc. One could argue that this is precisely the challenge the EU faced when it took on board the issue of Turkey's accession: not only is Turkey a large and poor country that might destabilize the EU as an economic entity, but it is a largely Muslim country, albeit a secular nation-state, and one that has historically featured as the 'Other' in the formation of Europe.

Even Turkey's efforts to 'modernize and Westernize' from the early twentieth century onwards – efforts which included the adoption of 'a democratic and multi-party political system, crowning the generations-long reforms' (Kushner, 1999: 684) – have done little to disturb the 'memory of earlier representations' (Neumann, 1999: 62). As Robins put it, the Turks may 'have succeeded in establishing their credentials as a westernized and a modernized society . . . Among Europeans, however, there has remained the sense that Turkey is not authentically of the West; the sense that it is alien, an outsider, an interloper in the European community' (1996: 65). In fact, the prolonged nature of talks about their country joining the EU led many Turks to believe that 'European nations . . . simply did not see Turkey as one of them. They did not *want* Turkey to become a full member of the European Community and consequently . . . some of the reasons for non acceptance . . . were just delaying tactics' (Kushner, 1999: 686). More than a decade after that was written, and after continuous stalling on the part of EU negotiators, that sentiment has probably not changed.

Yet many have argued that the desire to 'belong' to Europe has long been prevalent in Turkey. From a Turkish perspective, Europe – and the EU is its actual and symbolic representation – has always been a mysterious object of desire, a space to be part of and a thing 'to catch up' with. 'Westernization', 'modernization' and 'reaching a level of contemporary civilization' are the terms that have long defined this desire and it has become translated into the objective of becoming a member of the EU (Seni, 2001, quoted in Negrine et al., 2008).

For many Turks, then, Europe continues to be seen as something that needs to be emulated and copied, something that one should join. As President Gül observed, its democracy is worth aspiring to. But Europe – and its member states, its media and its citizens – were (and many still are) less sure whether or not they want it to join the Union. Reservations in the past have included such things as the lack of resolution over the Cyprus conflict, the economic consequences of the membership of such a large poor state and, significantly, a host of socio-cultural reasons as to why Turkey should not be part of the EU. In this respect, the study of press coverage of the 2004 accession talks reveals much about how the EU is seen by, for example, its member states and the part the press plays in the generation of a European sense of itself (for full details of the study, see Negrine et al., 2008).

Turkey, the EU and accession talks in 2004: newspaper coverage in some member states

One of the most obvious points to make about the reporting of the talks between September and December 2004 is that the press of different countries (in this case Britain, Greece and France) gave the story differing amounts of coverage. Only 208 items were coded from the French press (in *Libération*, *Le Figaro* and *Le Monde*, out of a much larger sample of over 600 items) and 248 items in the Greek press (*Eleftherotypia*, *Kathimerini* and *Ta Nea*), but only 48 items in the British newspaper sample (drawn from *The Guardian*, the *Daily Telegraph* and the *Daily Mail*). This may reflect the very competitive nature of the British press and the general low level of foreign news coverage, but it also probably has something to do with the prevailing lack of interest in and concern about Turkey, on the one hand, and about the EU, on the other. In France, on the other hand, there is a large Muslim population and hence a concern about Muslim Turkey in a 'Christian' Europe, and Greece has its own concerns over the stalemate in discussions about the future of Cyprus. In other words, the extent of coverage – and its nature – is inextricably linked to the ways in which the press reflects national politics, culture and history and domestic news values.

These observations need to be set against some other obvious ones, including the fact that the popular/tabloid press gives hardly any space to such stories. It is the high-brow/quality press that more often than not engages with these issues. This is part of the 'high and growing degree of differentiation and specialization of the national media landscape' (Trenz, 2004: 312), so that even something as significant as the prospect of Turkey entering the EU can be treated very differently – in respect of depth and type of coverage – across a range of media. At some level there is an effort to inform Europeans about what is going on in member states – for example, the French and British press constantly referred to French and German opinion polls as a signal of those countries' public opposition to the policy towards Turkey as well as to the prospect of a Muslim country joining the EU – but this may be as much a matter of imposing traditional news values ('anti-Turkey' views create conflict) as creating an informed citizenry.

When we begin to explore the nature and content of the coverage during these months in 2004, certain key differences are immediately obvious. The first (and this is confirmed by the data in table 8.2) is that this was not a critical issue for Britain and the British press. Had it been, it would have been covered much more extensively. Second, although there were a large number of common themes identified across the newspapers in the sample – themes that related to the economic, political and cultural consequences of Turkey's membership of the EU – they were not discussed 'with the same . . . structure of meaning' (Koenig et al., 2006: 158). Briefly, the French press referred to the internal domestic dimensions of the question and particularly the way the subject played in French politics (17 per cent of all coded mentions) more than any other theme; the British press mentioned dissent in Europe and the negotiations quite extensively (13 per cent of all themes coded) but the most frequent theme was the need to treat Turkey in a fair and equitable way since it had been seeking to join for many decades (14 per cent). Although the Greek press referred to the negotiations extensively (54 per cent of all themes coded), the issue of Cyprus and of Greek–Turkish relations featured quite prominently (21 per cent). Given the relations between Greece and Turkey, this may not be surprising, yet the significance of the Cyprus issue within the framework of the negotiations might suggest that its prominence should have been higher in the newspapers of other countries. As it happens, it continues to be a significant obstacle to Turkey's future within the EU and, from a Greek point of view, an understandable one. As the Greek upmarket newspaper *Kathimerini* observed in 2004:

> The Europeans are being led to this decision because they do not feel they have the strength to resist the USA's will to impose Turkey as a partner in their union. At the same time, they seem unable to object to Ankara's absurd refusal to recognize the Republic of Cyprus, a country that is already a member of the 25-strong bloc. As a consequence, there seems to be no point in discussing the prospect of an integrated European power functioning as a counterweight to America's global leadership. The mere fact that Turkey, a significant US ally, is to be awarded candidate status while Russia remains outside the European home betrays the blatant failure of the EU to outline its geopolitical shape in the new global order on the basis of a solid analytical model.

One of the most interesting findings from this study was that the *economic* case in support of Turkey joining the EU was hardly ever made: it was mentioned in the British press but rarely elsewhere. This finding is replicated in the study by Koenig and his colleagues in the context of their discussion of the 'economic consequences' frame. As they point out:

> The possible benefits of Turkish entry either to the EU-European or the French economy [*sic*] based on neo-liberal theories of trade and comparative advantage were largely absent (in the French and German press). This is in contrast to the UK where the economic benefits of Turkish accession were mentioned in the context of an overarching argument in favour of accession – neo-liberal economic arguments worked in tandem with liberal multicultural political arguments in favour of accession. (Koenig et al., 2006: 164)

Overall, the case *in support* of Turkey's bid to join the Union rests on the fact that it had been kept waiting a long time (and, by implication, Europe must now do the 'decent' thing) and that it was 'compatible' with the EU and not different from it. The country's strategic importance and its part in helping resolve diplomatic issues with Greece further contributed to seeing Turkey as a suitable candidate for enlargement. Significantly, the arguments *against* its bid emphasized the substantial cultural and religious differences,

Table 8.2 Reasons mentioned why talks should not proceed (up to three reasons were coded)

	French	British	Greek	Total
Turkey is different culturally, geographically, religiously	102 34%	42 47%	103 68%	247 46%
EU structures will not be able to cope with Turkey's accession	40 13%	33 37%		73 14%
Cyprus issue		5 6%	18 2%	23 4%
France must just say 'No'	20 7%			20 4%
Economic and cultural reasons, e.g. migration			20 13%	20 4%
Turkey would become too influential in the EU	12 4%			12 2%
Turkey needs to deal with Armenian/ Kurdish/Cyprus issues	10 3%			10 2%
The EU would become simply a trade zone	10 3%			10 2%
The process is undemocratic on part of the EU and the French government	10 3%			10 2%
Other	94 32%	10 11%	11 7%	115 21%
Total	298	90	152	540 100%

Source: Negrine et al., "Turkey and the European Union," *European Journal of Communication*, 23: 47–77. Reprinted by permission of SAGE.

and this is in spite of the many references made to the compatibility of the EU and Turkey. In fact, the key reason for not supporting the bid was the *difference* between Turkey and the EU, with 46 per cent of all coded reasons stated in the press of Britain, France and Greece (table 8.2). The overwhelming impression given in the coverage is of differences that exist between the EU and Turkey that would make the latter's inclusion problematic.

It was the British press (incidentally reflecting the British government's overall position) that stood out as being most in support of Turkey's bid to join the EU. At the same time it also featured a range of positions that could be taken as being either favourable or unfavourable. In order to understand better how this could be achieved, it is worth looking at how news content deals with controversial views and conflict in the context of representations of Turkey, the EU and the bid for accession. In all cases, as we shall see, media coverage tended to draw on history, culture, memory and politics to explain the significance and implications of Turkey's bid.

The place of history, culture and memory in the French and British press coverage

Of the three British newspapers sampled, *The Guardian* was by far the clearest in its support of Turkey's accession, yet its news items often articulated the chasm between Turkey and Europe. On the one hand, one could find the following:

> Opponents of Turkish membership imply that they want to keep the EU a 'Christian club'. The EU, of course, is no such thing, and membership depends on political and economic criteria, not religious or ethnic identity. Eighty years after Ataturk, Turkey is a secular democracy with a majority Muslim population – and one to be encouraged in a post-September 11 world in which the feared 'clash of civilisations' often looks like a self-fulfilling prophecy. (*The Guardian*, 2004a)

Yet, on the other, one could also find descriptions of a 'traditional' society. Helena Smith, reporting from Van, made the most of Turkey's differences:

> On October 6, the day Turkey was formally recommended by the European Commission to start talks with the EU, Ayse Ozgur woke up in a bank.
>
> For three weeks she had been on the run in eastern Turkey – from the man who raped her, a mother who had starved her and a father who had sold her in exchange for money and guns.
>
> . . . In recent years Turkey has made huge strides in stamping out human rights abuses. . . . Yet human rights violations continue. Across the Muslim state's remote and impoverished south-east, women such as Ayse Ozgur are still prone to crimes of violence. (Smith, 2004)

The range of positions that are represented in these items is quite dramatic: one can find reference to both similarities ('secular democracy') and differences ('human rights violations') and one can read these items as supporting the bid or, on the contrary, as (implicitly) putting forward reasons for not supporting it. Sometimes historical events would be referenced to underscore the differences that exist between Europe and Turkey – for example, this from *The Guardian*'s account of the prejudices still present in Austria (but not elsewhere?):

> What Helmut is against, like two out of three Austrians, is Turkey joining the European Union. Gerhard, the landlord serving him his wine, joined in eagerly. 'This is Europe and we're in danger of losing our identity with all these people from Turkey and Africa. We Christians are losing our faith while the Muslims are getting more fundamentalist.'
>
> Both were keen to dwell on history. The place they were sitting, a hillside north-east of Vienna, was where 321 years ago last week the Polish King John

III, after a plea from the Vatican, marshalled a huge Roman Catholic army and went galloping down the mountain to save Christendom, Europe and Austria, routing the Turks, raising the 61-day Ottoman siege of Vienna, and halting the Turkish advance into the European heartland. (Traynor, 2004)

But, in giving space to these statements and positions, is the newspaper seeking to draw attention to a 'European' antipathy towards the Turks or simply an Austrian one? Is it seeking to show up the Austrians in an unfavourable light and, by implication, highlighting a more benevolent British position? Furthermore, was it using these statements as a device to illustrate how 'old prejudices [were] coming to the fore' (ibid.) or was it doing so and, simultaneously, undergirding the differences that were seen as important? The lack of clarity in these news items suggests that there is much scope for the press of different member states to define the issues in very different ways and through different domestic prisms.

We can observe this in France's *Le Figaro*, whose position in 2004 was broadly hostile to Turkish entry. In an editorial entitled 'Turkish poison', the paper called on the European Council to recognize that, 'historically, culturally and geographically, Turkey is not European' (Brezet, 2004). By contrast, in *Libération*, a newspaper that was generally less hostile to the prospect of Turkish membership, Alain Duhamel argued that the history of Turkey and Europe were intricately tied up with each other in ways which reflect the past relationship between states that now form part of the European Union. As he also pointed out, Turkey's 'history and geography have not prevented it from being admitted into the Council of Europe, to become a member of NATO . . . or an associate member of the Common Market as early as 1963' (Duhamel, 2004).

Here, as elsewhere, what one finds is the recurring tension between historically fixed positions – for example, on identity, borders, etc. – and positions that seek to transcend these. We find, then, fixed historical constructions of irreconcilable differences between Europe and Turkey and those who wish to make a case for a more progressive understanding of history as a dynamic process that is inherently linked with European integration and democratization. Such discussions inevitably also problematize the whole question of the shifting nature of 'identity': the Turkish question was also a discussion about European identity.

It is worth noting, though, that the British press was less likely to dwell on the issue of identity or even the essential make-up of the EU. This is a key difference between the British press and the press of other countries, since it emphasizes the extent to which identity and the essence of Europe was *not* an issue in Britain. Opposition to Turkey on religious, cultural or historical grounds was something that continental Europeans, in the main, talked about. What the British wanted, at least as far as Giscard d'Estaing was concerned, was to destroy the EU, to reduce it to 'a crippled trade bloc' (Evans-Pritchard, 2004). The Anglo-Saxons had no conception of Europe as a political and cultural project. For the British press, that Turkey was a large and poor Muslim country was no more than a statement of fact and, in itself, not a cause for rejection. It mattered little that Turkey was different, since any differences could be overcome, but, for the French, the differences were themselves an issue. As with the tensions highlighted in the French coverage, it was not about whether differences existed or were perceived to exist, but whether those differences mattered and/or could be overcome. As one *Guardian* leader expressed it:

> Jose Manuel Barroso, the president-designate of the European commission, was right to insist that Turkey must accept European values. Jean-Pierre Raffarin, the French prime minister, was wrong when he asked whether it was wise to let the 'river of Islam enter the riverbed of secularism?' The firm answer must be that Turkey is a secular state and no longer the sick man of Europe, and that the EU is not an exclusively Christian club. (*The Guardian*, 2004b)

As the various examples of news stories illustrate, the discussions surrounding the question of Turkey's accession to the EU is much more than a simple economic discussion. In the most recent enlargement, Romania and Bulgaria were both absorbed without any debate or concern. A decision to enlarge the EU, taken at a high level, was simply put into practice, and the concerns, if any, of the public never seemed to surface. Turkey, as the stories above show, is a different case, and it throws up questions about what the EU is, what it means to be European, what it means to be in Europe, and who should be in and who should be out. It also highlights the question that many in Turkey must now be asking – namely, what does Turkey have to do to stand a chance of being taken into the EU framework? Without clarity about what the EU is in practice – Is it only or mainly a trading bloc? Is it a Christian club? – the discussions replayed above are bound to continue.

Summary

As we have seen, there are different conceptions of the EU at play within different member states, and usually these find their way into the press of the different countries. At the heart of many of these discussions within member states and at the European level are issues of identity and the ways in which identity in the twenty-first century complicates formerly simple links between the individual and the nation-state. As more and more people migrate across borders, that sense of national exclusivity evaporates, and nation-states are forced to grapple with differences and divisions both within them and across the member states of a supranational organization. In recent years we have seen such points of difference become manifest: the controversy in France over the veil, the consequences of the Danish cartoons in 2008, and elements of Islamophobia during the 2009 European parliament elections. Under such conditions, how can the EU create a sense of a single European identity?

Does this mean that a common EU outlook does not or cannot exist? Does it signify that a European public sphere is unlikely to emerge or that a common European identity is never likely to be forged? Koenig and his colleagues conclude their work by suggesting that the differences they identified in their analysis – often replicating the differences identified here – point away from a vision of European commonness: the results, they write, do 'not encourage the development of a European public of individuals, of a European public sphere, but something at odds with the idea of a European public sphere – a Europe of different cultures and peoples who may or may not be in conflict with one another' (Koenig et al., 2006: 165).

Such a conclusion might be both too simplistic and too negative: too negative in implying that some forms of common European identities and outlooks may be still-born. Work by Bruter (2005) and Shore (2000) suggests that, over time and with the continual reference point of Europe/the European Union at play, some basic understandings and recognitions might begin to emerge. Even the debate about Turkey's bid to join the EU can be seen as a positive step towards defining the nature of Europe and its future trajectory and – and this is the key point – the need to reconsider the importance of difference in the twenty-first century. If, following Delanty (1995, 2005), there is a continual process of change at play, the events of 2004 will contribute in important ways to the future development of European identities, if only in alerting societies to the need to confront and deal with difference. Such a task may become more urgent when Europeans begin to acknowledge that economic and political power is shifting away from Europe to, for example, China and India and that the need to offer a united economic front is of more than just an academic interest and much more than a political dream.

9   Conclusions

Few would disagree with the view that Europe is a media-rich region, a region whose citizens have access to a wide range of media outlets for their information and entertainment at home, at work and on the move. Although there have been significant changes in the media landscape across Europe, in reality there has also been continuity and stability, with changes in terms of real consumption rather slower than in other regions such as North America. Europeans still spend most of their leisure time watching TV, reading newspapers and listening to their favorite radio stations. They also still go to the cinema and read magazines and books.

The advent of new media will undoubtedly have an impact on existing patterns of media consumption. Digital media, their portability, and the kinds of convergence that they bring about have already accelerated the fragmentation of European media with a whole new generation of consumers, the so-called digital natives, bypassing newspapers and television to source their news on the internet. More generally, the ways in which all people consume media content has changed, and media consumption has increased. Europeans consume more content, both linear and non-linear, have greater access to media and content, and are generally more immersed in media than before (see also Trappel et al., 2011).

The new wave of mainly online media is often seen as the preserve of the young, so representing another instance of the fragmentation of the media audience and something of a generation gap between the old and young. Since Europe has a larger proportion of older people than other regions, it will be interesting to observe the pace and speed of penetration of the new media and how they will be adopted by older generations. This might suggest that policy-makers at both the national and the regional level, as well as producers and manufacturers, need to develop a better understanding of how technologies come to be used by different (demographically defined) groups and within particular social settings. The overemphasis on new media might lead to exaggerated estimates of what the future might bring and so fail to appreciate the ways in which systems are bounded by socio-cultural, political and economic circumstances. Needless to say, in years to come we will continue to refer to various buzzwords, such as DTV, IPTV and mobile TV, just as we did in the past. The new media will continue to be new until they adapt to a format, direction and application that makes them appealing to the majority of European citizens – or, conversely, until European citizens have decided how best to use them. In most cases, Europeans have shown that what counts is the message and the content and not the medium. In other words, the media in Europe – regardless of the advent of the new media, the regulations of the European Union and the ambitions of the European Commission – are still shaped by the content they carry, the audiences they serve and the national frameworks that guide their developments.

As the media in Europe have expanded in the last two decades, the communications landscape of the region has become much more competitive, both nationally and internationally. There has been fierce competition for audiences and advertising revenues not only between different media, but also between off- and online media. There have been winners (the internet) and losers (newspapers). Indeed, there would be a major upset for the European media landscape and for its political and cultural life if newspapers were to go into terminal decline. Like public service broadcasters, newspapers have faced considerable problems and they have had to adapt and meet the challenges of new media, of globalization and of Europeanization. The new media and globalization, for instance, have both had an enormous impact on newspapers and public service broadcasters, which have played a critical role in the development of European societies. While these sorts of challenges simply illustrate that global issues affect all media systems and their features – and the pressures faced by publicly and privately funded organizations in a period of economic adjustment and/or downturn – they also demonstrate that the initiatives of the EU might not be able to overcome global forces so as to promote the sorts of values that reflect 'European' priorities. Nonetheless, the European media form an industry that is approaching a point of transition as a result of the introduction of new media and related services. However, the financial crisis of 2008–10 has slowed down the pace of developments, so there is increasing uncertainty over the revenue potential of new media and changes in consumer behaviour: in the first six months of 2009, Europe's biggest broadcasters experienced a decline in net TV advertising revenues of between 7.7 and 37.3 per cent (*Screen Digest*, 2009b). If the predictions of the pundits are correct, the biggest change in media and entertainment in the near to mid-term will be contraction. Consumption of media and entertainment may continue to rise, particularly as broadband and wireless distribution expands, yet it remains unclear whether European consumers are ready to pay for all this in an unfavourable economic climate. Some pay-TV operators (especially in Spain, France, Italy, Germany and Greece) are afraid that many customers might renege on their subscriptions.

Nevertheless, the convergence of different communication technologies and digitalization are expected to alter completely the way the citizens of Europe access and consume media content. This will have an enormous impact on the media business in general. The fact is that Europe has witnessed an impressive array of new developments in the last thirty years in terms of both the supply and the demand for media and media content; developments have resulted in many new players entering the industry and some, such as telecommunications companies, have taken the lead in the creation of networks and content.

The EU, and subsequently the European Commission, has widened its policy remit to cover the whole communications sector with an approach that has sought to create a framework favourable to the development and harmonization of the communications sector and, in the process, to *Europeanize* that sector. That said, the framework that it has tried to establish, and in many cases to update, remains vague, since its policy of harmonization is by default a policy full of compromises and without any real solutions to emerging problems. Although the 'Audiovisual Media Services Directive' aims to increase the scope of its provisions beyond television and to include online media, at this stage it is difficult to gauge whether it will be any more successful than the original TWF Directive – whether, in other words, it will do any better than previous efforts to overcome or supersede the national frameworks that guide domestic media.

To recap, the diversity that exists within the EU and among member states, as discussed in chapter 4, makes it difficult to harmonize the audiovisual or communication sectors. For instance, the AMS Directive – adopted in 2007 – should have been incorporated into the national legislation of the EU member states by 19 December 2009. Yet by that date only Belgium, Romania and Slovakia had notified the Commission of full implementation.

The last AMS Directive, though more pragmatic, is only one of the hundreds adopted, discussed or planned: the EU has adopted and/or revised a number of directives, ranging from television to electronic communications, from TV standards to telecommunications, and from creative content online to media literacy. The extent of areas of involvement suggests perhaps more than anything else that the EU is intent on creating a competitive communications structure in order to be able compete at the international level. No other international organization has the range, the flexibility, the adaptability and, most importantly, the legal instruments of the EU. While the European audiovisual or communications landscape has not yet been (and may never be) constituted, it has become, nevertheless, an important area for international policy cooperation. Overall, it must be acknowledged that the EU has at least succeeded in keeping the communications and media issues on the agenda.

However, the EU has not succeeded in making significant inroads in its attempts to rebalance the trade in cultural content. Hollywood studios continue to dominate the world market in general and the European market in particular. Europe is the major importer of US fiction programming, though the advent of the new media age has made the trade in content a much more complicated affair. Content can now 'travel' between different media, giving rise to different markets, legitimate and otherwise. In this case, the hardware and software aspects appear to be equally important. The case of feature films is illustrative. Feature films used to make money from box-office receipts, DVD sales and TV rights. Today, consumers can download their preferred movies directly from the internet. In the best-case scenario, they pay much less than they used to do when they went to the cinema or rented a DVD. In the worst-case scenario, consumers simply download content for free. The internet has already proved to be an imperfect place for the film and TV industries to make money. In other words, we may be entering a situation where the old models of media production and consumption, of sales and revenue streams, may no longer reflect the reality of consumer behaviour. Indeed, there are already voices which claim that evolving funding media models are way behind what web companies such as Google, YouTube and Yahoo are already achieving by giving away things for free (Anderson, 2009). YouTube, Google's video-sharing site, has always had the lion's share of the online video audience. Virtually all of the content there is free, and no one knows whether consumers/viewers will ever be prepared to pay for such services again. The point to note here is that technological change – driven hard by competing media business interests – has undermined the old ways of producing and consuming content and the attendant revenue streams, but there is, as yet, no indication that significant new 'business models' are on the horizon.

Until such new models are developed, older media organizations, such as public broadcasters, have to consider their futures very carefully. Since the mid-1980s, there has been a gradual withdrawal of the public sector from the communication and broadcasting field. In an era of ensuring that everything is done cost-effectively and the gradual withdrawal from the welfare-state model in which public broadcasting was regarded as an integral part of civil society, the future of public broadcasters seems uncertain. Convergence, digitalization, new systems of delivery, and economic downturns affecting licence fee levels, and advertising rates will almost certainly change the old rules of engagement and reignite debates about licence funding and state support for broadcasting, especially when most things are delivered for free. In this newer environment, it is conceivable that the public broadcasters might be forced to share their funding with other organizations that also claim to provide public service content.

Europe has already entered the 'third age' of political communication. The advent of the new media has affected the way politicians strive to reach, persuade and mobilize the public though a fragmented media landscape. But they do so using both the 'old' and the 'new' media. In effect, political parties have come to use and exploit more heavily the new media and the relevant technologies in their effort to improve their performance and their electoral chances. Political parties have seen their traditional positions as ideological poles eroded, and voters are no longer 'aligned' as they once were; furthermore, parties no longer have access to their 'own' media. In the face of these changes, political parties have come to appreciate the importance of the media and the need to deal with, and confront, the 'media's logic'. In the same way, the EU needs to communicate with its citizens in order to overcome the 'democratic deficit'. Members of the European Parliament are largely unknown in comparison with their domestic counterparts, the EU is geographically distant and shrouded in mystery, the deliberations of the European Parliament are less than riveting, and so on. This is perhaps why the organization of the European Union and its myriad bodies attracts such little allegiance – only 35 to 40 per cent bothered to vote in the European Parliament elections in 2009 – even though the work of the EU impacts in so many ways on so many people. The substance of the work of any domestic parliament or executive body is rarely the stuff that would make journalists wild with excitement and is hardly likely to be the stuff that news executives would demand for their front pages, and this applies even more so to the EU.

Clearly, the Commission wants and needs to improve communication and has provided key resources, such as websites, for journalists and the public to access relevant information. That is one of its challenges. The problem may be a lack of media interest in the work of the EU, though even that simple statement forces us to reconsider the whole news production process and its preference for the dramatic and personalized. For many, the EU is characterized by inefficiency, convoluted decision-making processes and a lack of implementation, and these difficulties have increased in magnitude with its expansion. Even the desire to reach 'compromises' and to adopt 'soft' approaches to thorny issues has not enamoured the institutions to the public at large. The campaign for the elections to the European Parliament in 2009 made one thing clearer than ever. Insofar as people have any intention of voting at all, most will do so on the basis of the performance of *national* politicians in dealing with *national* problems within *national* political systems. European citizens still tend to believe that EU politics has no bearing on their lives, and European politics is often presented by the media as an issue that is detached from national debates. This may change following the ratification of the Lisbon Treaty in 2009, but the fundamental issues of how to represent the European institutions to European citizens remain unresolved.

These patterns of voting behaviour are probably also related to the fact that a common European identity seems unlikely to be forged: there are different cultural, political and economic considerations that pull publics in quite different directions, as was seen in respect to the coverage of Turkey's bid to join the EU. An intriguing question, arising from Garnham's (2007) analysis of Jürgen Habermas's recent musings, is whether religion (and ethnicity) may become a point of contention across European countries. As more and more member states experience the rise of far right, nationalist and anti-immigration parties, the threat to the EU is a double one: from parties that want to pull out or see the end of the integration project to parties that wish to maintain some clearer sense of EU identity. As with much in this book, the future of the media in Europe is tied up in no small measure with the future of Europe and the EU itself.

Alongside the differences that create political tensions in Europe – differences that draw on culture as well as history, on language as well as demography – one should not overlook the competing interests of different member states. There is a belief that the EU consists of two, often antagonistic, sets of member states: the large and powerful members and their smaller and less powerful counterparts, particularly those who joined after the expansion of 2004 (Hegedus, 2006). The five largest states (the UK, France, Germany, Italy and Spain), for example, represent over 71 per cent of total TV revenue in Europe. There are those who believe that larger countries exercise a dominant influence in the EU and that the smaller countries have to follow. While it is true that, in certain respects, all countries have faced similar problems, it is also the case that the needs and ambitions of the larger European countries differ from those of the smaller ones: smaller member states cannot pursue developments in the communications field as easily as the larger ones, and the starting points for dealing with problems and issues are often very different, drawing, as they do, on factors of power, resources and market size (Traquina, 1998; Meier and Trappel, 1992; Burgelman and Pauwels, 1992). Smaller European countries, it is often argued, face both external and internal problems in their effort to formulate and implement their broadcasting policies. This is because the globalization of the audiovisual economy and the integrative action of the EU tend to promote the marginalization of both production and culture in smaller countries. Thus, the latter, who have a limited market for their national products – a factor which itself poses an obstacle to the profitability and survival of their audiovisual industries – have very few opportunities to exploit their media so as to be credible and profitable in a European single market. Moreover, the smaller states face internal difficulties which are a consequence of internal structural weakness, resulting in inadequate national policies, with plenty of irrationalities and paradoxes (Burgelman and Pauwels, 1992: 181).

Smaller European countries thus are not only influenced by their larger 'brother' nations (Tunstall, 2008: 259), they also have to act and react under different conditions to new developments (Meier and Trappel, 1992). Their policies have to take into account the policies of larger countries, rather than the other way round. The cost and the pace of digitalization, for instance, are modelled upon the needs and market size of the larger states. This is because their resources are limited and their market size, which is small for production and consumption, does not usually represent a worthwhile target for multinational corporations. Smaller countries and their media industries have to face not only the Anglo-American media but often also the inescapable presence of the larger neighbouring country, which (sometimes also) use the same language (Tunstall and Machin, 1999). The result is that smaller countries, in most cases, have gained little or nothing from the changes in the European media landscape (Meier and Trappel, 1992) but, rather, have had to adopt an interventionist regulatory approach (Puppis et al., 2009) and to follow and implement policies that do not really benefit them. This can produce extremely negative effects for their industries, such as heavy cross-ownership by local dominant groups or a sharp decline in the fortunes of their public broadcasters.

The same, we believe, applies to the Eastern and Central European countries. Most, if not all, Eastern European countries have adjusted to the regulations and norms of Western Europe and have tried to reform their media systems, their economies and their societies, and align them to the rhythms and priorities of their Western counterparts. They import from the USA and from the larger European countries, while importing little or almost nothing from each other or from smaller Western European countries. This latter fact to a large extent slows up, if not hinders, the development of a European public sphere and identity.

The media in Europe are going through processes of change which are unfolding in a very complex way. Yet it is important to recognize that these changes are taking place at different levels: at the national level, 'old' media are adapting to 'new' media, with consequences for media businesses, producers and consumers; at the European level, there are processes of change that take in such things as the efforts of the EU to harmonize policies, to create competitive industries, and to give birth to the European citizen; at the global level, the domestic and the European are often dwarfed by larger forces and transnational interests. With many American global companies such as Google, YouTube and Apple at the forefront of change, what will be left for the European media? Perhaps they need to start searching for audiences from other continents. As Europe is still considered to be a leading force in the world, it could exploit digital technologies to broadcast and publish on the internet in different languages, for example. It could, in other words, use digital technologies to spread its skills and the contents of its media workers across the globe. International broadcasters have already launched such services: Euronews is broadcast in seven different languages in Europe and elsewhere, France 2 launched an Arab channel in 2007, and the BBC also broadcasts in Arabic. Perhaps this can be done for India, Africa and other markets. In this way, Europe can project its image, its way of life and its culture to the world outside and also to itself. In this way, digital media may help it to become more aware of itself at the same time as it promotes itself across the globe. The new media and the convergence and digitalization of the communications systems may offer a new opportunity to, and for, a new Europe. This may be no more than a limited challenge to American dominance, but it may provide some inroads to a changing global media landscape. The real challenge for the European Union is to grasp the momentum and to create a true European media landscape; otherwise all its efforts, in the past as in the future, will be seen as no more than 'tilting at windmills'.

Appendix From the 'Television without Frontiers Directive' to the 'Audiovisual Media Services Directive': a short overview

Issue	TWF Directive (Directive 89/552/EEC, as amended by Directive 97/36/EC)	AMS Directive (Directive 89/552/EEC, as amended by Directive 97/36/EC and by Directive 2007/65/EC)
Definition	'Broadcaster' means the natural or legal person who has editorial responsibility for the composition of schedules of television programmes within the meaning of (a) and who transmits them or has them transmitted by third parties.	'Audiovisual media service' means a service as defined by Articles 49 and 50 of the Treaty which is under the editorial responsibility of a media service provider and the principal purpose of which is the provision of programmes in order to inform, entertain or educate, to the general public by electronic communications networks within the meaning of Article 2(a) of Directive 2002/21/EC. Such an audiovisual media service is either a television broadcast as defined in point(e) of this Article or an on-demand audiovisual media service as defined in point (g) of this Article; and/or audiovisual commercial communication. In other words, the AMS Directive covers all audiovisual media services – that means traditional television (linear service) and video-on-demand (non-linear services).
		'Media service provider' means the natural or legal person who has editorial responsibility for the choice of the audiovisual content of the audiovisual media service and determines the manner in which it is organised; under the new rules, EU countries can restrict the retransmission of unsuitable on-demand audiovisual content that may not be banned in its country of origin.

'Television broadcasting' means the initial transmission by wire or over the air, including that by satellite, in unencoded or encoded form, of television programmes intended for reception by the public. It includes the communication of programmes between undertakings with a view to their being relayed to the public. It does not include communication services providing items of information or other messages on individual demand such as telecopying, electronic data banks and other similar services.

'Television advertising' means any form of announcement broadcast whether in return for payment or for similar consideration or broadcast for self-promotional purposes by a public or private undertaking in connection with a trade, business, craft or profession in order to promote the supply of goods or services, including immovable property, rights and obligations, in return for payment.

'Television broadcasting' or 'television broadcast' (i.e. a linear audiovisual media service) means an audiovisual media service provided by a media service provider for simultaneous viewing; 'broadcaster' means a media service provider of television broadcasts; 'on-demand audiovisual media service' (i.e. a non-linear audiovisual media service) means an audiovisual media service provided by a media service provider for the viewing of programmes at the moment chosen by the user and at his individual request on the basis of a catalogue of programmes selected by the media service provider; 'audiovisual commercial communication' means images with or without sound which are designed to promote, directly or indirectly, the goods, services or image of a natural or legal entity pursuing an economic activity. Such images accompany or are included in a programme in return for payment or for similar consideration or for self-promotional purposes. Forms of audiovisual commercial communication include, inter alia, television advertising, sponsorship, teleshopping and product placement.

'Television advertising' means any form of announcement broadcast whether in return for payment or for similar consideration or broadcast for self-promotional purposes by a public or private undertaking or natural person in connection with a trade, business, craft or profession in order to promote the supply of goods or services, including immovable property, rights and obligations, in return for payment.

Issue	TWF Directive (Directive 89/552/EEC, as amended by Directive 97/36/EC)	AMS Directive (Directive 89/552/EEC, as amended by Directive 97/36/EC and by Directive 2007/65/EC)
	'Surreptitious advertising' means the representation in words or pictures of goods, services, the name, the trade mark or the activities of a producer of goods or a provider of services in programmes when such representation is intended by the broadcaster to serve advertising and might mislead the public as to its nature. Such representation is considered to be intentional in particular if it is done in return for payment or for similar consideration.	'Surreptitious audiovisual commercial communication' means the representation in words or pictures of goods, services, the name, the trade mark or the activities of a producer of goods or a provider of services in programmes when such representation is intended by the media service provider to serve as advertising and might mislead the public as to its nature. Such representation shall, in particular, be considered as intentional if it is done in return for payment or for similar consideration.
	'Teleshopping' means direct offers broadcast to the public with a view to the supply of goods or services, including immovable property, rights and obligations, in return for payment.	'Teleshopping' means direct offers broadcast to the public with a view to the supply of goods or services, including immovable property, rights and obligations, in return for payment.
Sponsoring	They must be clearly identified as such by the name and/or logo of the sponsor at the beginning and/or the end of the programmes.	Viewers shall be clearly informed of the existence of a sponsorship agreement. Sponsored programmes shall be clearly identified as such by the name, logo and/or any other symbol of the sponsor such as a reference to its product(s) or service(s) or a distinctive sign thereof in an appropriate way for programmes at the beginning, during and/or the end of the programmes.

Product placement	Sometimes addressed at national level but not in the Directive; by and large in a legal void.	'Product placement' means any form of audiovisual commercial communication consisting of the inclusion of or reference to a product, a service or the trade mark thereof so that it is featured within a programme, in return for payment or for similar consideration. Prohibited in principle, in particular for 'children's programmes, news, current affairs'. However, 'unless member states decide otherwise', 'admissible' in film, drama and sports.
Advertising: breaks (time between consecutive breaks)	Successive breaks separated by at least twenty minutes.	Deleted.
Advertising: non-linear	Not addressed.	The twelve-minute limit also applies to 'non-linear' (interactive) advertising.
Advertising: split screen	Not allowed.	Permitted, as advertising breaks no longer need to be 'separated' but only 'distinct' from programming (understood as allowing split-screen advertising).
Advertising: limit per hour	20 per cent (twelve minutes) per given clock hour limit on advertising and TV shopping.	Unchanged.
Advertising: daily limit	Three hours a day.	Deleted.

Appendix From the 'Television without Frontiers Directive' to the 'Audiovisual Media Services Directive': a short overview (*continued*)

Issue	TWF Directive (Directive 89/552/EEC, as amended by Directive 97/36/EC)	AMS Directive (Directive 89/552/EEC, as amended by Directive 97/36/EC and by Directive 2007/65/EC)
Promotion, distribution and production of television programmes	Member States shall ensure where practicable, and by appropriate means, that broadcasters reserve for European works, and broadcasters reserve at least 10% of their transmission time, excluding the time appointed to news, sports events, games, advertising teletext services and teleshopping, or alternately, at the discretion of the Member State, at least 10% of their programming budget, for European works created by producers who are independent of broadcasters.	Member States must ensure that not only television broadcasters but also on-demand audiovisual media services promote European works.
Religious programmes, documentaries, children's programmes, news	No interruptions when programme duration is less than thirty minutes.	Unchanged at thirty minutes.
Regulatory bodies		Because users have different degrees of choice and control over on-demand audiovisual media services, only a basic tier of rules applies to them. But the rules on advertising and protecting children are stricter for television broadcasts.

The new rules recognize both the existence and the role of national independent regulators. To ensure the correct application of the Directive, these regulators must cooperate closely both among themselves and with the Commission, notably on issues of jurisdiction. Member States will take appropriate measures to provide each other and the Commission with the information necessary for the application of the provisions of this Directive, in particular Articles 2, 2a and 3 thereof, notably through their competent independent regulatory bodies.

| Revision | . . . every two years thereafter, the Commission shall submit to the European Parliament, the Council and the Economic and Social Committee a report on the application of this Directive as amended and, if necessary, make further proposals to adapt it to developments in the field of television broadcasting, in particular in the light of recent technological developments. | As with the TWF, the Commission established the Contact Committee (now Article 29), to monitor the implementation of the Directive and the developments in the sector and as a forum for the exchange of views. It deals not only with the existing audiovisual policy but also with the relevant developments arising in this sector. The committee will also help the Member States with their national reports which have to be written every two years. . . . every three years thereafter, the Commission shall submit to the European Parliament, the Council and the European Economic and Social Committee a report on the application of this Directive and, if necessary, make further proposals to adapt it to developments in the field of audiovisual media services, in particular in the light of recent technological developments, the competitiveness of the sector and levels of media literacy in all Member States. |

Source: Based on European Commission, http://ec.europa.eu/avpolicy/reg/avms/index_en.htm.

Notes

Chapter 3 The New Media in Europe

1 The dial-up modem is already obsolete on account of its speed limitations (typically 56 kbit/s). The integrated services digital network (ISDN), at speeds of up to 144 kbit/s, offered some improvement, but generally not enough. Digital subscriber line (DSL) technology, which uses the same twisted-pair copper telephone lines, offers much higher speeds, suitable for multimedia and video applications. The term xDSL covers a number of types of DSL technology, including ADSL, SHDSL and VDSL. The most popular is ADSL (asymmetrical digital subscriber line), which has its bandwidth provision slanted in favour of downstream traffic. This asymmetry, combined with always-on access, makes ADSL ideal for web browsing, file downloads, video-on-demand, remote LAN access, etc. These applications typically have much greater download traffic than upload (ITU, 2006).

Chapter 4 Europeanizing the Media of Europe

1 The European Council in November 2008 rejected the Commission's proposals. The Commission planned to establish a new authority to serve as its main advisor on all European telecoms regulatory affairs. This body would have had the power to block remedies imposed by national regulators if they contradicted European regulations. The European Parliament had also rejected the Commission's proposal.

2 Media literacy is another issue which has received particular attention from the Commission. The interest is related to the concerns linked to illegal downloading (see also chapter 5). In August 2009, the Commission presented a recommendation on media education and called on the member states to promote media literacy across Europe through activities that help people access, understand and critically evaluate all media to which they are exposed.

3 The assessment is based on Articles 87 and 88 on state aid and Article 86(2) on the application of the rules of the EC Treaty and the competition rules, in particular, to services of general economic interest. The Commission has also adopted several relevant communications on the application of the state aid rules. The 2005 State Aid Action Plan has set out the objectives of reform in the context of the Lisbon Strategy for Growth and Jobs in the European Union. Also in 2005, the Commission adopted the so-called Services of General Economic Interest Package, clarifying the requirements of Article 86(2) of the EC Treaty (see CEC, 2008d).

Chapter 5 The Question of Content

1 Commission Regulation (EC) no. 1998/2006 of 15 December 2006 on the Application of Articles 87 and 88 of the Treaty to *de minimis* aid: http://eur-lex. europa.eu/LexUriServ/LexUriServ.do?uri=CELEX:32006R1998:EN:NOT.

Chapter 7 Public Communication in Europe

1 During the 2008 Irish referendum on the Lisbon Treaty, demonstrators carried placards with the word 'bully'.

2 See http://euractiv.com/en/priorities/eu-communication-policy/article-117502.

3 See *Plan D for Democracy, Dialogue and Debate*, http://ec.europa.eu/dgs/communication/pdf/communication_com_en.pdf; http://eur-lex.europa.eu/smartapi/cgi/sga_doc?smartapi!celexplus!prod!DocNum ber&lg=en&type_doc=COMfinal&an_doc=2005&nu_doc=494.

References and Bibliography

ACT, AER and EPC (2004) *Safeguarding the Future of the European Audiovisual Market: The Financing and Regulation of Publicly Funded Broadcasters*. Brussels: ACT, AER and EPC.

Amel, A. (2002) *The Personal Video Recorder: Market Assessment and Forecast*. London: Screen Digest.

Anderson, B. (1991) *Imagined Communities: Reflections on the Origin and Spread of Nationalism*. London: Verso.

Anderson, C. (2009) *Free: The Future of Radical Price*. New York: Hyperion.

Attentional, Oliver & Ohlbaum Associates, Rambøll Management and Headway International (2009) *Study on the Application of Measures Concerning the Promotion of the Distribution and Production of European Works in Audiovisual Media Services (i.e. including Television Programmes and Non-Linear Services)*. Available at: http://ec.europa.eu/avpolicy/info_centre/library/studies/index_en. htm#eurworks).

Bache, I., and George, S. (2006) *Politics in the European Union*. 2nd edn, Oxford: Oxford University Press.

Banerjee, T., Mulligan, M., and Thomas, N. (2008) *European Media Consumption: Understanding Trends in Online Media Behavior*. Available at: www.forrester.com.

Barnett, S. (2004) 'Media ownership policies: pressures for change and implications', *Pacific Journalism Review*, 10(2): 9–20.

Basnee, O. (2003) 'The (non-)coverage of the European Parliament', pp. 77–104, in M. Bond (ed.) *Europe, Parliament and the Media*. London: Federal Trust for Education and Research.

Bauer, M. W., Knill, C., and Pitschel, D. (2007) 'Differential Europeanization in Eastern Europe: the impact of diverse EU regulatory governance patterns', *Journal of European Integration*, 29(4): 405–23.

Bauman, Z. (2004) *Europe: An Unfinished Adventure*. Cambridge: Polity.

BBC (2004) *Building Public Value: Renewing the BBC for a Digital World*. London: BBC.

Beck, U. (1999) *What is Globalization?* Cambridge: Polity.

Becker, J. (2004) 'Lessons from Russia: a neo-authoritarian media system', *European Journal of Communication*, 19(2): 139–63.

Bellucci, L. (2010) 'National support for film production in the EU: an analysis of the Commission decision-making practice', *European Law Journal*,16(2): 211–32.

Berman, S. J., Abraham, S., Battino, B., Shipnuck L., and Neus, A. (2007) 'New business models for the new media world', *Strategy & Leadership*, 35(4): 23–30.

Bertrand, C. J., and Urabayen, M. (1985) 'European mass media in the 1980s', pp. 21–42, in E. M. Rogers and F. Balle (eds) *The Media Revolution in America and Western Europe*. Norwood, NJ: Ablex.

Billig, M. (1995) *Banal Nationalism*. London: Sage.

Blàzquez, C .J. F. (2008) *User-Generated Content Services and Copyright*. Strasbourg: European Audiovisual Observatory.

Bloomfield, M. (2008) 'Nothing but Blu skies', *Screen Digest*, 438: 96.

Börzel, T., and Risse, T. (2000) 'When Europe hits home: Europeanization and domestic change', *European Integration Online Papers*, 4(15). Available at: http://eiop.or.at/eiop/texte/2000-015a.htm.

Bouwman, H., Carlsson, C., Walden, P., and Molina, C. F. J. (2008) 'Trends in mobile services in Finland 2004–2006: from ringtones to mobile internet', *info*, 10(2): 75–93.

Brants, K., and De Bens, E. (2000) 'The status of TV broadcasting in Europe', pp. 7–22, in J. Wieten, G. Murdock and P. Dahlgren (eds) *Television across Europe: A Comparative Introduction*. London: Sage.

Brants, K., and van Praag, P. (2007) 'From accommodation to profession-alization? The changing culture and environment of Dutch political commu-nication', pp. 97–110, in R. M. Negrine, C. Holtz-Bacha, P. Mancini and S. Papathanassopoulos (eds) *The Professionalisation of Political Communication*. Bristol: Intellect Books.

Brezet, A. (2004) 'Le poison turc', *Le Figaro*, 15 October.

Broadcast Mobile Convergence Forum (2008) *The Status of National Licensing Frameworks for Mobile TV: A Country-by-Country Assessment*. Available at: www.bmcoforum.org.

Brown, L. (1995) 'The American networks', pp. 259–84, in A. Smith (ed.) *Television: An International History*. Oxford: Oxford University Press.

Bruter, M. (2005) *Citizens of Europe?* Basingstoke: Palgrave.

Bugdahn, S. (2005) 'Of Europeanization and domestication: the implementation of the environmental information directive in Ireland, Great Britain and Germany', *Journal of European Public Policy*, 12(1): 177–99.

Bughin, J., and Griekspoor, W. (1997) 'A new era for European TV', *McKinsey Quarterly*, no. 3: 90–102.

Buller, J. (2003) 'The Europeanization of national politics?', *Government and Opposition*, 38(4): 528–35.

Burgelman, J. C., and Pauwels, C. (1992) 'Audiovisual policy and cultural identity in small European states: the challenge of a unified market', *Media, Culture & Society*, 14(2): 169–83.

Burri-Nenova, M. (2007a) 'The new audiovisual media services directive: television without frontiers, television without cultural diversity', *Communication Market Review*, 44(6): 1689–1725.

Burri-Nenova, M. (2007b) 'The law of the World Trade Organization and the com-munications law of the European Community: on a path of harmony or discord?', *Journal of World Trade*, 41(4): 833–78.

Bush, V., and Gilbert, F. (2002) 'The web as a medium: an exploratory comparison of internet users versus newspaper readers', *Journal of Marketing Theory and Practice*, 10(1): 1–10.

Bustamante, E. (2004) 'Cultural industries in the digital age: some provisional conclusions', *Media, Culture & Society*, 26(6): 803–20.

Calhoun, C. (2003) 'The democratic integration of Europe: interests, identity, and the public sphere', pp. 243–74, in M. Berezin and M. Schain (eds) *Europe without Borders: Remapping Territory, Citizenship, and Identity in a Transnational Age.* Baltimore: Johns Hopkins University Press.

Castells, M. (2000) *The End of the Millennium.* 2nd edn, Cambridge: Polity.

Cave, M., and Nakamura, K. (2006) 'Digital television: an introduction', pp.1–22, in M. Cave and K. Nakamura (eds) *Digital Broadcasting: Policy and Practice in the Americas, Europe and Japan.* Cheltenham: Edward Elgar.

Cawley, A., and Preston, P. (2007) 'Broadband and digital "content" in the EU-25: recent trends and challenges', *Telematics and Informatics*, 24: 259–71.

CEC (Commission of the European Communities) (1983) *Realities and Tendencies in European Television: Perspectives and Options.* COM (83) 229 final, Brussels, 23 May.

CEC (1984) *Television without Frontiers: Green Paper on the Establishment of the Common Market for Broadcasting, especially by Cable and Satellite.* COM (84) 30 final, Brussels, 14 June.

CEC (1987) *Towards a Dynamic European Economy: Green Paper on the Development of the Common Market for Telecommunication Services and Equipment.* COM (87) 290 final, Brussels, 30 June.

CEC (1989) *Directive . . . on the Coordination of Certain Provisions Laid Down by Law, Regulation or Administrative Action in Member States concerning the Pursuit of Television Broadcasting Activities.* COM (89) 552, EEC, 3 October ['Television without Frontiers Directive'].

CEC (1992) *Pluralism and Media Concentration in the Internal Market: An Assessment of the Need for Community Action.* COM (92) 480 final, Brussels, 23 December.

CEC (1997a) *Directive . . . amending Council Directive 89/552/EEC on the Coordination of Certain Provisions Laid Down by Law, Regulation or Administrative Action in Member States concerning the Pursuit of Television Broadcasting Activities.* COM 97/36, EC final, Luxembourg, 30 June [amendment of 'Television without Frontiers Directive'].

CEC (1997b) *Explanatory Memorandum* (media ownership in the internal market). DG XV, Brussels, February.

CEC (1997c) *Green Paper on the Convergence of the Telecommunications, Media and Information Technology Sectors and the Implications for Regulation – Towards an Information Society Approach.* COM (97) 623 final, Brussels, 3 December.

CEC (1998a) 'Directive 98/84/EC of the European Parliament and of the Council of 20 November 1998 on the legal protection of services based on, or consisting of, conditional access, the European Parliament and the Council of the European Union', *Official Journal* L 320 , 28/11: 0054–0057.

CEC (1998b) *The Digital Age: European Audiovisual Policy*. Report from the High Level Group on Audiovisual Policy, chaired by Commissioner Marcelino Oreja, Brussels, October.

CEC (1999a) *Communication* from the Commission to the Council, the European Parliament and the Economic and Social Committee of the Regions, *The Convergence of the Telecommunications, Media and Information Technology Sectors, and the Implications for Regulation: Results of the Public Consultation on the Green Paper*, COM (1999) 108 final, Brussels, 3 March.

CEC (1999b) *Communication* to the European Parliament, the Council, the Economic and Social Committee and the Committee of the Regions, *The Convergence of the Telecommunications, Media and Information Technology Sectors, and the Implications for Regulation: Results of the Public Consultation on the Green Paper*, COM (97) 623, COM (99) 108 final, Brussels, 10 March.

CEC (1999c) European Commission, *Proposal for a Programme in Support of the Audiovisual Industry, MEDIA Plus, 2001–2005*, COM (1999) 658 final, Brussels, 14 December.

CEC (2001) *How Europeans See Themselves: Looking through the Mirror with Public Opinion Surveys*. Available at: http://ec.europa.eu/publications/booklets/eu_documentation/05/txt_en.pdf.

CEC (2003) *The Future of European Regulatory Audiovisual Policy*, COM (2003) 784 final, Brussels, 15 December.

CEC (2004) 'Guidelines on the assessment of horizontal mergers under the Council Regulation on the control of concentrations between undertakings', *Official Journal of the European Communities*, 31: 5–18.

CEC (2005a) *Proposal for a Council Framework Decision to Strengthen the Criminal Law Framework to Combat Intellectual Property Offences*, COM (2005) 276 final, Brussels, 12 July.

CEC (2005b) *Strengthening the Competitiveness of the EU Publishing Sector: The Role of Media Policy*. Commission Staff Working Paper, SEC (2005) 1287, Brussels, 7 October.

CEC (2006) *Plan D for Democracy, Dialogue and Debate*. Available at www.euractiv.com/en/opinion/eu-communication-policy/article-117502.

CEC (2007a) *Directive . . . amending Council Directive 89/552/EEC on the Coordination of Certain Provisions Laid Down by Law, Regulation or Administrative Action in Member States concerning the Pursuit of Television Broadcasting Activities*. 2007/65/EC, Strasbourg, 11 December ['Audiovisual Media Services Directive'].

CEC (2007b) *An EU Strategy for Mobile TV – Frequently Asked Questions*. MEMO/07/298, Brussels, 18 July.

CEC (2007c) *Media Pluralism in the Member States of the European Union*. Commission Staff Working Paper, SEC (2007) 32, Brussels, 16 January. Available at: http://ec.europa.eu/information_society/media_taskforce/doc/pluralism/media_pluralism_swp_en.pdf.

CEC (2007d) *Information Society and Media & Communications: Linking European Policies*. Luxembourg: Office for Official Publications of the European

Communities. Available at http://ec.europa.eu/information_society/activities/policy_link/brochures/documents/media.pdf.

CEC (2008a) *Progress Report on the Single European Electronic Communications Market 2007 (13th Report)*. COM (2008) 153, SEC(2008) 356, Brussels, 19 March.

CEC (2008b) *Eighth Communication on the Application of Articles 4 and 5 of Directive 89/552/EEC 'Television without Frontiers'*, as amended by Directive 97/36/EC, for the period 2005 2006 [SEC (2008) 2310], COM(2008) 481 final, Brussels, 22 July.

CEC (2008c) *Second Report on the Implementation of Directive 98/84/EC of the European Parliament and of the Council of 20 November 1998 on the Legal Protection of Services Based on, or Consisting of Conditional Access*, COM(2008) 593 final {SEC(2008) 2506} final, Brussels, 30 September.

CEC (2008d) *Communication from the Commission on the Application of State Aid Rules to Public Service Broadcasting*. Available at: http://ec.europa.eu/competition/state_aid/legislation/broadcasting_communication_en.pdf.

CEC (2008e) *Document Accompanying the Communication from the Commission to the European Parliament, the Council, the European Economic and Social Committee and the Committee of the Regions on Creative Content Online in the Single Market*, SEC(2007) 1710, Brussels, 3 January.

CEC (2009a) *Creative Content in a European Digital Single Market: Challenges for the Future: A Reflection Document of DG INFSO and DG MARKT*, Brussels, 22 October.

CEC (2009b) *Europe's Digital Competitiveness Report: Main Achievements of the i2010 strategy 2005–2009*, COM (2009) 390 final, Brussels, 4 August.

CEC (2009c) *Final Report on the Content Online Platform*, Brussels, May. Available at: http://ec.europa.eu/avpolicy/docs/other_actions/col_platform_report.pdf.

CEC (2010) *Ninth Communication on the Application of Articles 4 and 5 of Directive 89/552/EEC* ['Television without Frontiers'] *as amended by Directive 97/36/EC and Directive 2007/65/EC for the period 2007–2008*. COM (2010) 450 final, Brussels, 23 September.

Chalaby, J. K. (2002) 'Transnational television in Europe: the role of pan-European channels', *European Journal of Communication*, 17(2): 183–203.

Cole, A., and Drake, H. (2000) 'The Europeanization of the French polity: continuity, change and adaptation', *Journal of European Public Policy*, 7(1): 26–43.

Colombo, F. (2006) 'Technological innovation and media complexity: DTT in the light of a new theoretical prospect', pp. 21–36, in F. Colombo and N. Vittadini (eds) *Digitising TV: Theoretical Issues and Comparative Studies across Europe*. Milan: Vitae e Pensiero.

comScore (2007) 'comScore media matrix releases top 50 web rankings for June', press release, 16 July.

Corcoran, F. (2007) 'Television across the world', *New Review of Film and Television Studies*, 5(1): 81–95.

Council for Research Excellence (2009) *Video Consumer Mapping Study*. Available at: http://www.researchexcellence.com/vcmstudy.php.

Cox, B. (2004) *Free for All? Public Service Television in the Digital Age.* London: Demos. Available at: http://demos.co.uk.

Curtice, J. (2005) *The June 2004 Elections: The Public's Perspective.* London: Electoral Commission. Available at: www.electoralcommission.org.uk.

Curwen, P., and Whalley, J. (2008) 'Mobile television: technological and regulatory issues', *info*, 10(1): 40–64.

Daswani, M. (2009) 'Internet to overtake traditional TV in 2010', *WorldScreeen. com.* Available at: www.worldscreen.com/articles/display/20536.

Datamonitor (2006) *Technology Investment Drivers in the European Media Sector (Market Focus).* London.

Dawson, R. (2008) *Future of Media: Report.* London: Future Exploration Network. Available at: http://rossdawsonblog.com/Future_of_Media_Report2008.pdf.

DCMS and DBIS (Department for Culture, Media and Sport and Department for Business, Innovation and Skills) (2009) *Digital Britain: Final Report.* Cm 7650, London: TSO.

De Bens, E. (2007) 'Developments and opportunities of the European press industry', pp. 141–170, in W. A. Meier and J. Trappel (eds) *Power, Performance and Politics.* Baden-Baden: Nomos.

Deiss, R. (2002) 'Radio broadcasting market', *Statistics in Focus*, Theme 4, 34/2002. Luxembourg: Eurostat.

Delanty, G. (1995) *Inventing Europe: Idea, Identity, Reality.* Basingstoke: Macmillan.

Delanty, G. (2005) 'What does it mean to be a "European"?', *Innovation: The European Journal of Social Science Research*, 18(1): 11–22.

Deloitte (2007) *Turn on to Digital: Getting Prepared for Digital Content Creation and Distribution in 2012.* London: Deloitte.

Deloitte (2010) *Media Predictions 2010.* London: Deloitte.

Directorate-General for the Information Society and Media (2008) *E-Communications Household Survey.* Available at: http://ec.europa.eu/eurostat.

Donders, K., and Pauwels, D. (2008) 'Does EU policy challenge the digital future of public service broadcasting?', *Convergence: the International Journal of Research into New Media Technologies*, 14(3): 295–311.

Dougal, J. (2003) 'British press coverage of the European Union', pp. 55–62, in M. Bond (ed.) *Europe, Parliament and the Media.* London: Federal Trust for Education and Research.

Doyle, G. (1997) 'From "pluralism" to "ownership": Europe's emergent policy on media concentrations navigates the doldrums', *Journal of Information, Law and Technology*, no. 3. Available at: www2.warwick.ac.ukfac/soc/law/elj/jilt/1997_3/doyle/.

Doyle, G. (2002) *Media Ownership: The Economics and Politics of Convergence and Concentration in the UK and European Media.* London: Sage.

Doyle, G. (2007) 'Undermining media diversity: inaction of media concentrations and pluralism in the EU', *European Studies*, 24: 135–56.

Duhamel, A. (2004) 'Et si Chirac avait raison?', *Libération*, 15 December.

Dunkerley, D. (2002) *Changing Europe: Identities, Nations and Citizens*. London: Routledge.

Dyson, K., and Humphreys, P. (1988) *Broadcasting and New Media Policies in Western Europe*. London: Routledge.

Dziadul, C. (2008) *Eastern European Pay Television*. London: Screen Digest.

EAO (European Audiovisual Observatory) (2007a) *Television in 36 European States*, Vol. 1. Strasbourg: EAO.

EAO (2007b) *Television in 36 European States*, Vol. 2. Strasbourg: EAO.

EAO (2008a) *The Circulation of European Co-productions and Entirely National Films in Europe, 2001–2007*. Strasbourg: EAO.

EAO (2008b) 'Over 6,500 TV channels available in the European Union and candidate countries (Croatia and Turkey) in 2008', press release, Strasbourg, 15 October.

EAO (2008c) *Video on Demand in Europe: Second Survey of VoD Services as of January 2008*. Strasbourg: EAO.

EAO (2008d) *Trends in European Television*, Vol. 2. Strasbourg: EAO.

EAO (2009) *Trends in European Television*, Vol. 2. Strasbourg: EAO.

EBU (European Broadcasting Union) (2007) *Public Radio in Europe*. Geneva: EBU.

The Economist (2006) 'Regulation without frontiers; European television', 12 October: 68.

The Economist (2008) 'Just bury it', 21 June: 15.

EIAA (European Interactive Advertising Association) (2005) *Mediascope Europe 2004: Media Consumption Study*. Available at: www.eiaa.net.

EIAA (2008) *Digital Families Study*. Available at: www.eiaa.net.

EIAA (2009) *Mediascope Europe 2008: Media Consumption Study*. Available at: www.eiaa.net.

EIAA (2010) *Mediascope Europe 2010: Media Consumption Study*. Available at: www.eiaa.net.

Ellis, J. (2000) *Seeing Things*. London and New York: I. B. Tauris.

Elseewi, T. A. (2007) 'The Danish cartoon controversy: globalized spaces and universalizing impulses', *Global Media Journal*, 6(11): article no. 8. Available at: http://lass.calumet.purdue.edu/cca/gmj/fa07/graduate/gmj-fa07-grad-elseewi.htm.

Elvestad, E., and Blekesaune, A. (2008) 'Newspaper readers in Europe: a multilevel study of individual and national differences', *European Journal of Communication*, 23(4): 425–47.

eMarketer (2008) 'European IPTV homes skyrocket', 14 April.

eMedia Institute (2009) 'European digital TV market map'. Available at: www.e-mediainstitute.com.

ESC (Economic and Social Committee) (2000) *Pluralism and Concentration in the Media in the Age of Globalization and Digital Convergence*, Brussels, 29 March.

EurActiv (2008) 'Telecom giants scramble over fibre networks', 9 May. Available at: www.euractiv.com/en/infosociety/telecom-giants-scramble-fibre-networks/article-172299.

EurActiv (2009) 'Twittering not: MEPs fail to embrace internet craze', 20 May. Available at: www.euractiv.com/en/eu-elections/twittering-meps-fail-embrace-internet-craze/article-182511.

Euréval (Centre for European Evaluation Expertise) (2007) *Final Evaluation of the MEDIA Plus and MEDIA Training Programmes: Synthesis of the Final Report*. Paris: Euréval.

Eurobarometer (2007) *Audio Visual Communication: Analytical Report*. Flash Eurobarometer Series no. 199.

Eurobarometer (2008) *Eurobarometer 69: Europeans' State of Mind*. Available at: http://ec.europa.eu/public_opinion/archives/eb/eb69/eb69_ee_exe.pdf.

Europa (2008a) 'Mobile TV across Europe: Commission endorses addition of DVB-H to EU List of Official Standards', IP/08/451, Brussels, 17 March.

Europa (2008b) 'New figures show almost two thirds of EU television time is made in Europe', IP/08/1207, Brussels, 25 July.

Europa (2009a) 'EU member states on course for analogue terrestrial TV switch-off', IP/09/266, Brussels, 16 February.

Europa (2009b) 'How to transform the "digital dividend" into consumer benefits and up to €50 billion in economic growth for Europe?', IP/09/1112, Brussels, 10 July.

Europa (2009c) 'Time up for member states to tune TV rules to digital age', IP/07/1809, Brussels, 21 December.

Europa (2010) 'State aid: Commission clears annual financing regime for Dutch public service broadcasters after amendments', IP/10/52, Brussels, 26 January.

European Information Technology Observatory (2009) 'Record turnover for internet connections', press release, Berlin, 6 April.

European Journal of Communication (2007) *Special Issue: The Media and European Public Space*, 22(4).

Eurostat (2007) *Consumers in Europe: Facts and Figures on Services of General Interest*. Luxembourg: Office for Official Publications of the European Communities.

Eurostat (2008) 'Nearly 30% of individuals use internet banking; 60% of households have internet access', news release, 169/2008, 2 December. Available at: http://ec.europa.eu/eurostat.

Eurostat (2009) 'Nearly one third of individuals in the EU27 shopped on the internet in 2008: travel and clothes most popular purchases', news release, 43/2009, 27 March.

Evans-Pritchard, A. (2004) 'EU ignores critics and opens door to Turkey', *Daily Telegraph*, 16 December.

Featherstone, K., and Radaelli, C. (2003) 'Introduction: in the name of Europe', pp. 3–26, in K. Featherstone and C. Radaelli (eds) *The Politics of Europeanization*. Oxford: Oxford University Press.

Fernando B. (2009) 'Audience manufacture in historical perspective: from broadcasting to Google', *New Media Society*, 11(1& 2): 133–54.

Fidler, R. (1999) *Metamorphosis: Understanding New Media*. Thousand Oaks, CA: Sage.

Firmstone, J. (2008) 'The editorial production process and editorial values as influences on the opinions of the British press towards Europe', *Journalism Practice*, 2(2): 212–29.

Flavian, C., and Gurrea, R. (2008) 'Reading newspapers on the internet: the influence of web sites' attributes', *Internet Research*, 18(1): 26–45.

Fleishman Hillard (2009) *European Parliament Digital Trends*. Brussels: Fleishman Hillard. Available at: www.epdigitaltrends.eu.

Flockhart, T. (2010) 'Europeanization or EU-ization? The transfer of European norms across time and space', *Journal of Common Market Studies*, 48(4): 787–810.

Frieden, R. (2007) 'ITU world telecom 2006 report', *info*, 9(4): 81–3.

Füg, O. C. (2008) 'Save the children: the protection of minors in the information society and the audiovisual media services directive', *Journal of Consumer Policy*, 31(19): 45–61.

Galperin, H., and Bar, F. (2002) 'The regulation of interactive television in the United States and the European Union', *Federal Communications Law Journal*, 55: 61–84.

Garcia, D. L., and Surles, E. (2007) 'Media ownership and communications: enriching the research agenda', *Telecommunications Policy*, 31: 473–92.

Garde, A. (2008) 'Food advertising and obesity prevention: what role for the European Union?', *Journal of Consumer Policy*, 31(19): 25–44.

Garnham, N. (2007) 'Habermas and the public sphere', *Global Media and Communication*, 3(2): 201–14.

Gavin, N. (2000) 'Imagining Europe: political identity and British television coverage of the European economy', *British Journal of Politics and International Relations*, 2(3): 352–73.

Gavin, N. (2007) *Press and Television in British Politics: Media, Money and Mediated Democracy*. Basingstoke: Palgrave Macmillan.

George, L. (2007) 'What's fit to print: the effect of ownership concentration on product variety in daily newspaper markets', *Information Economics and Policy*, 19: 285–303.

Gilardi, F. (2005) 'The institutional foundation of regulatory capitalism: the diffusion of independent regulatory agencies in Western Europe', *Annals of the American Academy of Political and Social Science*, 598(1): 84–101.

Giscard d'Estaing, V. (2002) 'Turkey entry "would destroy EU"', *Le Monde*, 8 November. Available at: news.bbc.co.uk/2/hi/europe/2420697.stm.

Glenn, J. K. (2004) 'From nation-states to member states: accession negotiations as an instrument of Europeanization', *Comparative European Politics*, 2: 3–28.

Goetz, K. H., and Hix, S. (eds) (2000) *Europeanised Politics? European Integration and National Political Systems*. London: Frank Cass.

Goldberg, D., Prosser, T., and Verhulst, S. (1998) *EC Media Law and Policy*. London: Longman.

Golding, P. (2000) 'Forthcoming features: information and communications technologies and the sociology of the future', *Sociology*, 34(1): 165–84.

Graziano, P., and Vink, M. P. (eds) (2007) *Europeanization: New Research Agendas*. Basingstoke: Palgrave Macmillan.

Green Cowles, M., Caporaso, J., and Risse, T. (eds) (2001) *Transforming Europe: Europeanization and Domestic Change*. Ithaca, NY, and London: Cornell University Press.

Grigoriadis, I. (2003) 'Turkey, the EU and the 2004 milestone: is this time for real?', paper presented at conference on contemporary Turkey, South East European Studies Programme, University of Oxford, 14 March; Available at: www.sant. ox.ac.uk/esc/esc-lectures/turkey_report.pdf.

Gross, P. (2003) 'New relationships: Eastern European media and the post-communist political world', *Journalism Studies*, 4(1): 79–89.

Gross, P. (2004) 'Between reality and dream: Eastern European media transition, transformation, consolidation, and integration', *East European Politics and Societies*, 18: 110–31.

The Guardian (2004a) 'In bed with Europe', leader article, 8 September.

The Guardian (2004b) 'Getting closer', leader article, 25 September.

Hadley, R. (2008) *Pay TV in Western Europe: Market Sizings and Forecasts 2005–2013*. London: Analysys Mason.

Hafez, K. (2007) *The Myth of Media Globalization: Why Global Media is Not Truly Globalized*. Cambridge: Polity.

Hallin, D., and Mancini, P. (2004) *Comparing Media Systems: Three Modes of Media and Politics*. Cambridge: Cambridge University Press.

Hallin, D., and Papathanassopoulos, S. (2000) 'Political clientelism and the media: Southern Europe and Latin America in comparative perspective', *Media, Culture & Society*, 24(2): 175–95.

Hancock, D. (2008) 'Digital cinema: marker perspectives', paper presented in the conference Digital Cinema: Perspectives and Realities, organized by the Hellenic Audiovisual Institute, Athens, 11 June.

Harcourt, A. (1998) 'EU media ownership regulation: conflict over the definition of alternatives', *Journal of Common Market Studies*, 36(3): 369–89.

Harcourt, A. (2002) 'Engineering Europeanization: the role of the European institutions in shaping national media regulation', *Journal of European Public Policy*, 9(5): 736–55.

Harcourt, A. (2003) 'Europeanization as convergence: the regulation of media markets in the European Union', pp. 178–210, in K. Featherstone and C. Radaelli (eds) *The Politics of Europeanization*. Oxford: Oxford University Press.

Harcourt, A. (2005) *The European Union and the Regulation of Media Markets*. Manchester: Manchester University Press.

Harcourt, A. (2008) 'Introduction', pp. 13–24, in G. Terzis (ed.) *European Media Governance: The Brussels Dimension*. Bristol: Intellect Books.

Harcourt, A., and Picard, P. G. (2009) 'Policy, economic, and business challenges of media ownership regulation,' *Journal of Media Business Studies*, 6(3): 1–17.

Hardy, J. (2008) *Western Media Systems*. London: Routledge.

Harrison, J., and Woods, L. (2007) *European Broadcasting Law and Policy*. Cambridge: Cambridge University Press.

Hegedus, I. (2006) 'The mass media, political parties, and Europessimism in Hungary', *Mediterranean Quarterly*, 17(2): 72–83.

Heikkilä, H., and Kunelius, R. (2006) 'Journalists imagining the European public sphere: professional discourses about the EU news practices in ten countries', *Javnost – The Public*, 13(4): 63–80.

Helms, L. (2008) 'Governing in the media age: the impact of the mass media on executive leadership in contemporary democracies', *Government and Opposition*, 43(1): 26–54.

Herold, A. (2008) 'Country of origin principle in the EU market for audiovisual media services: consumer's friend or foe?', *Journal of Consumer Policy*, 31(19): 5–24.

Hitchens, L. (1994) 'Media ownership and control: a European approach', *Modern Law Review*, 57(4): 19–27.

Holtz-Bacha, C. (2007) 'Professionalisation of politics in Germany', pp. 27-46, in R. M. Negrine, C. Holtz-Bacha, P. Mancini and S. Papathanassopoulos (eds) *The Professionalisation of Political Communication*. Bristol: Intellect Books.

Host, S. (1999) 'Newspaper growth in the television era: the Norwegian experience', *Nordicom Review*, 20(1): 107–28.

Humphreys, P. (1996) *Mass Media and Media Policy in Western Europe*. Manchester: Manchester University Press.

Humphreys, P. (2002) 'Europeanisation, globalisation and policy transfer in the European Union: the case of telecommunications', *Convergence*, 8: 52–79.

Humphreys, P. (2007) 'EU audiovisual policy, cultural diversity and the future of public service broadcasting', pp. 183–212, in J. Harrison and B. Wessels (eds) *Mediating Europe: New Media, Mass Communications and the European Public Sphere*. Oxford: Berghahn.

Humphreys, P., and Padgett, S. (2006) 'Globalization, the European Union, and domestic governance in telecoms and electricity', *Governance*, 19(3): 383–406.

Humphreys, P., and Simpson, S. (2008) 'Globalization, the "competition" state and the rise of the 'regulatory' state in European telecommunications', *Journal of Common Market Studies*, 46(4): 849–74.

Humphreys, P., Gibbons, T., and Harcourt, A. J. (2008) *Globalization, Regulatory Competition and Audiovisual Regulation in 5 Countries: Full Research Report*. RES-000-23-0966, Swindon: ESRC.

IDATE (Institut de l' Audiovisuel et des Télécommunications en Europe) (2003) 'Thematic channels facing network digitisation', IDATE press release no. 256.

IDATE (2008) 'Advertising market evolution: the media advertising market represents 450 billion USD in 2007', *Idate News*, no. 406, February.

IDATE, TNO and IViR (2008) *User-Created Content: Supporting a Participative Information Society*. Montpellier: IDATE.

Informa (2007) *TV Trends 2007*. London: Informa Telecoms & Media.

Iordanova, D. (1995) 'Bulgaria: provisional rules and directorial changes: restructuring of national TV', *Javnost – The Public*, 2(3): 19–32.

Iosifidis, P. (1996) 'Merger control and media pluralism in the European Union', *Communications Law*, 1(6): 247–9.

Iosifidis, P. (1999) 'Diversity versus concentration in the deregulated mass media domain', *Journalism & Mass Communication Quarterly*, 76(1): 152–62.

Iosifidis, P. (2007a) 'The application of EC competition policy to the media industry', *International Journal on Media Management*, 7(3&4): 103–11.

Iosifidis, P. (2007b) 'Public television in small European countries: challenges and strategies', *International Journal of Media and Cultural Politics*, 3(1): 65–87.

Iosifidis, P. (2007c) 'Digital TV, digital switchover and public service broadcasting in Europe', *Javnost – The Public*, 14(1): 5-20.

Iosifidis, P., Steemers, J., and Wheeler, M. (2005) *European Television Industries*. London: BFI.

IP Network (2008) *Television 2008: International Key Facts*. Luxembourg: IP Network.

IPTV International (2008) 'Europe set for global market lead', January: 8–14.

ITU (International Telecommunication Union) (2006) *digital.life: ITU Internet Report 2006*. Geneva: ITU.

Jabko, N. (2006) *Playing the Market: A Political Strategy for Uniting Europe, 1985–2005*. Ithaca, NY: Cornell University Press.

Jakubowicz, K. (2007) 'Digital switchover in Central and Eastern Europe: premature or badly needed?', *Javnost – The Public*, 14(1): 21–38.

Johnson, D. (2007) 'Inviting audiences in', *New Review of Film and Television Studies*, 5(1): 61–80.

Journalism Studies (2009) *Special Issue: Questioning European Journalism*, 10(1).

Judge, E. (2009) 'Mobile phone users fail to get in tune with TV on the move', *The Times*, 17 April.

Julliard, J.-J., and Vidal, E. (2010) *Press Freedom in Ukraine: Temptation to Control*. Paris: Reporters without Borders. Available at: http://en.rsf.org/IMG/pdf/_rapport_ukraine_anglais.pdf.

JupiterResearch (2008) *Online Video in Europe: Managing TV Audience Fragmentation*. London: JupiterResearch.

Kaina, V., and Karolewski, I. P. (2009) 'EU governance and European identity', *Living Reviews in European Governance*, 4(2). Available at: www.livingreviews.org/lreg-2009-2.

Kaitatzi-Whitlock, S. (2008) 'The political economy of the media at the root of the EU's democracy deficit', pp. 25-47, in I. Bondebjerg and P. Madsen (eds) *Media, Democracy and European Culture*. Bristol: Intellect Books.

Kathimerini (2004) 'Adynamoi Europeoi' [Weak Europeans], 16 December.

Keane, J. (2009) *The Life and Death of Democracy*. Cambridge: Cambridge University Press.

Keane, M., and Moran, A. (2008) 'Television's new engines', *Television & New Media*, 9(2): 155–69.

Kelly, M., Mazzoleni, G., and McQuail, D. (eds) (2004) *The Media in Europe*. London: Sage.

Kershaw, I. (2008) *Hitler, the Germans, and the Final Solution*. New Haven, CT: Yale University Press.

Khan, U. (2009) 'Popularity of BBC iPlayer leads to renewed concerns internet could grind to a halt', *Daily Telegraph*, 7 January. Available at: www.telegraph. co.uk/technology/news/4143794/Popularity-of-BBC-iPlayer-leads-to-renewed-concerns-internet-could-grind-to-a-halt.html.

Kinzer, S. (2008) 'US must share power in new world order, says Turkey's controversial president', *The Guardian*, 16 August. Available at: www.guardian.co.uk/world/2008/aug/16/turkey.usforeignpolicy.

Kleinsteuber, J. H. (2007) 'A difficult road: the diffusion of digital radio and television in Europe', pp. 223–38, in W. A. Meier and J. Trappel (eds) *Power, Performance and Politics*. Baden-Baden: Nomos.

Knill, C., and Lehmkuhl, D. (2002) 'The national impact of European Union regulatory policy: three Europeanization mechanisms', *European Journal of Political Research*, 41: 255–80.

Koenig, T., Mihelj, S., Downey, J., and Gencel Bek, M. (2006) 'Media framings of the issue of Turkish accession to the EU: a European or national process?', *Innovation: The European Journal of Social Science Research*, 19(2): 149–69.

Kohler-Koch, B. (1999) 'The evolution and transformation of European governance', in B. Kohler-Koch and R. Eising (eds) *The Transformation of Governance in the European Union*. London: Routledge.

Kompare, D. (2006) 'Publishing flow: DVD box sets and the reconception of television', *Television & New Media*, 7(4): 335–60.

Koopmans, R., and Pfetsch, B. (2006) 'Obstacles or motors of Europeanization? German media and the transnationalization of public debate', *Communications*, 31: 115–38.

Kopper, G. G. (2007) *Practical Guidelines for Journalists: Reporting Europe – Rules and Context*. Dortmund: Erich-Brost-Institute for Journalism in Europe. Available at: http://www.aim-project.net/uploads/media/D9_guidelines.pdf.

Korres, G. M. (2007) 'Industrial and innovation policy in Europe: the effects on growth and sustainability', *Bulletin of Science, Technology & Society*, 27(2): 104–17.

Kroes, N. (2008) 'The way ahead for the broadcasting communication', speech at broadcasting conference, Strasbourg, 17 July. Available at: http://ec.europa.eu/cyprus/news/speeches/kroes_strasbourg_en.htm.

Kung, L., Picard, R. G., and Towse, R. (eds) (2008) *The Internet and the Mass Media*. London: Sage.

Kushner, D. (1999) 'Turkey and Europe: a relationship of passion and pain', *History of European Ideas*, 18(5): 683–95.

Ladrech, R. (1994) 'Europeanization of domestic politics and institutions: the case of France', *Journal of Common Market Studies*, 32(1): 69–88.

Laïdi, Z. (2008) *The Normative Empire: The Unintended Consequences of European Power*. Garnet Policy Brief no. 6. Available at: www.garnet-eu.org.

Lange, A., and Van Loon, A. (1991) 'Pluralism, concentration and competition in the media sector', *IDATE/IVIR*, December.

Lauristin, M. (2007) 'The European public sphere and the social imaginary of the new Europe', *European Journal of Communication*, 22: 397–412.

Lax, S. (2003) 'The prospects for digital radio: policy and technology for a new broadcasting system', *Information, Communication & Society*, 6(3): 326–49.

Lax, S., Ala-Fossi, M., Jauert, P., and Shaw, H. (2008) 'DAB: the future of radio? The development of digital radio in four European countries', *Media, Culture & Society*, 30(2): 151–66.

Lazar, M., and Paun, M. (2006) *Understanding the Logic of EU Reporting in Mass Media: The Case of Romania*. AIM in Europe working paper. Available at: www. aim-project.net/uploads/media/Romania_01.pdf.

Leadbeater, C. (2008) 'Democracy in the network age: time to WeThink', *openDemocracy*, 5 March. Avalable at: www.opendemocracy.net/article/charles_leadbeater/ WeThink.

Leiva, M., Trinidad, G., Starks, M., and Tambini, D. (2006) 'Overview of digital television switchover policy in Europe, the United States and Japan', *info*, 8(3): 32–46.

Lenschow, A. (2006) 'Europeanization of public policy', pp. 55–72, in J. Richardson (ed.) *European Union: Power and Policy Making*. Abingdon: Routledge.

León, B. (2007) 'Going digital: the Spanish experience', *Javnost – The Public*, 14(1): 77–92.

Létang, V. (2007) 'European TV homes get HD-ready', *Screen Digest*, 15 May: 147–8.

Light, C., and Lancefield, D. (2007) *Show Me the Money: Strategies for Success in IPTV*. London: PricewaterhouseCoopers.

Lippert, B., Umbach G., and Wessels, W. (2001) 'Europeanization of CEE executives: EU membership negotiations as a shaping power', *Journal of European Public Policy*, 8(6): 980–1012.

Livingstone, S. (2004) 'The challenge of changing audiences: or, what is the audience researcher to do in the age of the internet?', *European Journal of Communication*, 19(1): 75–86.

Lloyd, J. (2005) 'The epiphany of Joe Trippi', *Political Quarterly*, 76(1): 33–45.

Lodge, M. (2002) 'Varieties of Europeanisation and the national regulatory state', *Public Policy and Administration, Special Issue: Understanding the Europeanisation of Public Policy*, 17(2): 43–67.

Lööf, A. (2008) 'Internet usage in 2008 – households and individuals', *Eurostat Data in Focus*, 46/2008.

McQuail, D. (2005) *McQuail's Mass Communication Theory*. 5th edn, London: Sage.

McQueen, D. (2007) 'Convergence will change the telecoms game', *Financial Times*, 9 August.

Maier, M., Stromback, J., and Kaid. L. (2011) *European Political Communication: Campaign Strategies, Media Coverage, and Campaign Effects in European Parliamentary Elections*. London: Ashgate.

Mair, P., and Biezen, I. V. (2001) 'Party membership in twenty European democracies, 1980–2000', *Party Politics*, 7: 5–21.

Mancini, P. (2007) 'Political professionalism in Italy', pp. 111–26, in R. M. Negrine, C. Holtz-Bacha, P. Mancini and S. Papathanassopoulos (eds) *The Professionalisation of Political Communication*. Bristol: Intellect Books.

Mazower, M. (2005) *Salonica, City of Ghosts: Christians, Muslims and Jews, 1430–1950*. New York: Knopf

Mazzoleni, G. (1987) 'Media logic and party logic in campaign coverage: the Italian general election in 1983', *European Journal of Communication*, 2(1): 55–80.

Médiamétrie (2009) 'L'observatoire des Usages internet', *Communique de Presse*, 18 August.

Médiamétrie (2010) *2009: One Television Year in the World*. Paris: Médiamétrie.

Meier, W. A., and Trappel, J. (1992) 'Small states in the shadow of giants', pp. 129–41, in K. Siune and W. Tuetzschler (eds) *Dynamics of Media Politics: Broadcasts and Electronic Media in Western Europe*. London: Sage.

Meyer, C. (2007) *The Constitutional Treaty Debates as Revelatory Mechanisms: Insights for Public Sphere Research and Re-launch Attempts*. RECON Online Working Paper 2007/06. Available at: www.reconproject.eu/main.php/RECON_wp_0706.pdf?fileitem=5456963.

Meyer, L. (2006) 'Three scenarios for TV in 2015', *Communications & Strategies*, no. 62: 93–108.

Meyer-Stamer, J. (1996) 'Industrial policy in the EU: old dilemmas and new options', *European Planning Studies*, 4(4): 471–84.

Michalis, M. (1999) 'European Union broadcasting and telecoms: towards a convergent regulatory regime?', *European Journal of Communication*, 14(2): 147–71.

Michalis, M. (2007) *Governing European Communications: From Unification to Coordination*. Lanham, MD: Lexington Books.

Microsoft (2009) *Europe Logs On: European Internet Trends of Today and Tomorrow*. Available at: www.scribd.com/doc/14065700/Europe-Logs-On-Microsoft-Study.

Miller, T. (2008) 'Eastern Europe makes slow switchover progress', *New Media Markets*, 18 April: 5–7.

Mobile Media (2007) 'Operators face difficult choice in selecting a mobile TV business model', 8(14): 14–15.

Mobile Media (2008) 'Cellco: DVB-H not right for small countries', 9(6): 3.

Molsky, N. (1999) *European Public Broadcasting in the Digital Age*. London: FT Media and Telecoms.

Morgan, D. (1995) 'British media and European Union news', *European Journal of Communication*, 10(3): 321–43.

Morgan, D. (2004) 'Media coverage of the European Union', pp. 34–54, in M. Bond (ed.) *Europe, Parliament and the Media*. London: Federal Trust for Education and Research.

Murdock, G. (2000) 'Digital futures: European television in the age of convergence', pp. 35–58, in J. Wieten, G. Murdock and P. Dahlgren (eds) *Television across Europe: A Comparative Introduction*. London: Sage.

Murdock, G., and Golding, P. (1999) 'Common markets: corporate ambitions and communication trends in the UK and Europe', *Journal of Media Economics*, 12(2): 117–32.

Negrine, R. (1999) *Parliament and the Media: A Study of Britain, Germany and France*. London: Royal Institute of International Affairs/Cassell.

Negrine, R. (2008) *The Transformation of Political Communication*. London: Palgrave Macmillan.

Negrine, R., Kejanlioglu, B., Aissaoui, A., and Papathanassopoulos, S. (2008) 'Turkey and the European Union: an analysis of how the press in four countries covered Turkey's bid for accession in 2004', *European Journal of Communication*, 23: 47–67.

Neumann, I. B. (1999) *Uses of the Other: 'The East' in European Identity Formation*. Manchester: Manchester University Press.

Noam, E. (2008) 'TV or not TV?', *Financial Times*, 13 May.

Nord, L. (2007) 'The Swedish model becomes less Swedish', pp. 81–96, in R. M. Negrine, C. Holtz-Bacha, P. Mancini and S. Papathanassopoulos (eds) *The Professionalisation of Political Communication*. Bristol: Intellect Books.

O&O (Oliver & Ohlbaum) (2007) *Prospects for the European TV Content Sector to 2012*. London: O&O. Available at: www.oando.co.uk.

OECD (Organization for Economic Cooperation and Development) (2007) *Policy Considerations for the Audio-Visual Content Distribution in a Multiplatform Environment*. Working Party on Telecommunication and Information Services Policies. Paris: DSTI/ICCP/TISP (2006)3/FINAL, 12 January.

Ofcom (Office of Communications) (2006) *The International Communications Market 2006*. London: Ofcom.

Ofcom (2007) *Radio – Preparing for the Future, Phase 1: Developing a New Framework. Appendix B: Results of Audience Research*. London: Ofcom.

OJEC (*Official Journal of the European Communities*) (1990) 'Council Regulation 4064/89/EEC on the control of concentration between undertakings', L257/4, 30 September.

Olsen, P. J. (2002) 'The many faces of Europeanization', *Journal of Common Market Studies*, 40(5): 921–52.

O'Neil, B. (2009) 'DAB Eureka-147: a European vision for digital radio', *New Media and Society*, 11(1&2): 261–78.

Orgad, S. (2009) 'Mobile TV; Old and New in the Construction of an Emergent Technology', *Convergence*, 15(2): 197–214.

Örnebring, H. (2009) 'Introduction. Questioning European Journalism', *Journalism Studies*, 10(1): 2–17.

OSI (Open Society Institute) (2008) *Television across Europe: More Channels, Less Independence*. Budapest and New York: Open Society Institute.

Papathanassopoulos, S. (2001) 'The decline of the Greek Press', *Journalism Studies*, 2(1): 109–23.

Papathanassopoulos, S. (2002) *European Television in the Digital Age*. Cambridge: Polity.

Papathanassopoulos, S. (2005) 'Europe: an exemplary landscape for comprehending globalization', *Global Media and Communication*, 1(1): 46–50.

Papathanassopoulos, S. (2007) 'The Mediterranean/polarized pluralist media model countries: introduction', pp. 191–200, in G. Terzis (ed.) *European Media Governance: National and Regional Dimensions*. Bristol: Intellect Books.

Papathanassopoulos S., Negrine, R. M., Mancini, P., and Holtz-Bacha, C. (2007) 'Political communication in the era of professionalisation', pp. 9–27, in R. M. Negrine, C. Holtz-Bacha, P. Mancini and S. Papathanassopoulos (eds) *The Professionalisation of Political Communication*. Bristol: Intellect Books.

Pavlik, J. V., and Powell, A. D. (2003) 'New media', *Encyclopaedia of International Media and Communications*, 3: 225–33.

Perry, R. (2003) 'Priorities in information policy', pp. 63–76, in M. Bond (ed.) *Europe, Parliament and the Media*. London: Federal Trust for Education and Research.

Pfanner, E. (2006) 'EU grapples with proposal to set rules for new media', *International Herald Tribune*, 12 November.

Pfanner, E. (2010) 'The real world cup prize? Broadcast rights', *New York Times*, 23 May. Available at: www.nytimes.com/2010/05/24/business/media/24rights.html?_r=1.

Philpott, M. (2007) *IPTV: Challenges and Opportunities*. London: Ovum RHK.

Pitelis, C. N. (2007) 'European industrial and competition policy', *Policy Studies*, 28(4): 365–81.

Pons, J. F. (1998) 'The application of competition and anti-trust policy in media and telecommunications in the European Union', paper presented at the International Bar Association, Vancouver, 14 September. Available at: http://ec.europa.eu/competition/speeches/text/sp1998_041_en.html.

Pons, J. F., and Lucking, J. (1999) 'The euro and competition', *Competition Policy Newsletter*, 1: 1–16.

Povoledo, E. (2007) 'Free papers draw new audience in Italy', *International Herald Tribune*, 23 December.

Prosser, T. (2008) 'Self-regulation, co-regulation and the Audiovisual Media Services Directive', *Journal of Consumer Policy*, 31: 99–113.

Puppis, M. (2008) 'National media regulation in the era of free trade: the role of global media governance', *European Journal of Communication*, 23(4): 405–24.

Puppis, M. (2009) 'Media regulation in small states', *International Communication Gazette*, 71(1–2): 7–17.

Puppis, M., d'Haenens, L., Steinmaurer, T., and Künzler, M. (2009) 'The European and global dimension: taking small media systems research to the next level', *International Communication Gazette*, 71(1–2): 105–12.

PricewaterhouseCoopers (2009) *Global Entertainment & Media Outlook 2009–2013*. Available at: www.pwc.com/outlook.

Radaelli, M. C. (2000) 'Policy transfer in the European Union: institutional isomorphism as a source of legitimacy', *Governance: An International Journal of Policy and Administration*, 13(1): 25–43.

Rangone, A., and Turconi, A. (2003) 'The television (r)evolution within the multimedia convergence: a strategic reference framework', *Management Decision*, 41(1): 48–71.

Reding, V. (2008) 'Digital TV, mobile TV: let's push for open technologies in Europe and worldwide', speech given at DVB World Conference 2008, Budapest, 12 March.

Reding, V. (2009) 'Digital Europe – Europe's fast track to economic recovery', Ludwig Erhard Lecture, SPEECH/09/336, Lisbon Council, Brussels, 9 July.

Richardson, J. (2006) 'Policy-making in the EU: interests, ideas and garbage cans of primeval soup', pp. 3–30, in J. Richardson (ed.) *European Union: Power and Policy-Making*. Abingdon: Routledge.

Risse, T. (2003) 'An emerging European public sphere? Theoretical clarifications and empirical indicators', paper presented at the annual meeting of the European Union Studies Association, Nashville, 27–30 March. Available at: http://aei.pitt.edu/6556/01/001315_1.PDF.

Risse, T., and Grabowsky, J. K. (2008) *European Identity Formation in the Public Sphere and in Foreign Policy*. RECON Online Working Paper 2008/04. Available at: www.reconproject.eu/main.php/RECON_wp_0804.pdf?fileitem=16662546.

Robins, K. (1996) 'Interrupting identities: Turkey/Europe', pp. 61–86, in S. Hall and P. du Gay (eds) *Questions of Cultural Identity*. London: Sage.

Rooney, M. (2006) *Pace Micro Technology: IPTV White Paper*. London: Pace.

Rosenbaum, J. (2003) 'In the EU's image: transformation of broadcasting in five Central and Eastern European countries', paper presented at the annual meeting of the International Communication Association, Marriott Hotel, San Diego, 27 May. Available at: www.allacademic.com/meta/p111848_index.html.

Sassatelli, M. (2002) 'Imagined Europe: the shaping of a European cultural identity through EU cultural policy', *European Journal of Social Theory*, 5(4): 435–51.

Schiller, H. (2000) 'Digitalized capitalism: what has changed?', pp. 116–26, in H. Tumber (ed.) *Media Power, Professionals and Policies*. London: Routledge.

Schlesinger, P. (1987) 'On national identity', *Social Science Information*, 25(2): 219–64.

Schlesinger, P. (1999) 'Changing spaces of political communication: the case of the European Union', *Political Communication*, 16: 263–79.

Schlesinger, P. (2007) 'A cosmopolitan temptation', *European Journal of Communication*, 22: 413–26.

Screen Digest (2002) 'Replacing the VCR: home recording in the digital era', 1 January: 22–8.

Screen Digest (2005a) 'Germany's television prospects', January: 9–10.

Screen Digest (2005b) 'European video software markets: DVD spending beats VHS spending by more than eight to one', 1 July: 205–12.

Screen Digest (2006) 'Ownership of television content', March: 72.

Screen Digest (2007a) 'Rise of high definition TV channels', 25 January: 4–5.

Screen Digest (2007b) 'Digital cinema up and running', April: 109–16.

Screen Digest (2008a) 'Internet protocol TV market: France leads the IPTV pack in Europe', January: 13–20.

Screen Digest (2008b) 'Perspective', February: 64.

Screen Digest (2008c) 'Euro HDTV channels expand', February: 45–52.

Screen Digest (2008d) 'Video rental fades into history', April: 99.

Screen Digest (2008e) 'Cable/satellite PVRs sell on price', April: 104.

Screen Digest (2008f) 'Digital cinema poised on the cusp' June: 173–7.

Screen Digest (2009a) 'High-definition television in Europe: a clearer picture emerged during the past year', March: 77–84.

Screen Digest (2009b) 'Weathering the advertising storm', June: 171.

Screen Digest (2009c) 'European TV programme spending: turbulent conditions for investment in television content', June: 173–80.

Screen Digest, CMS Hasche Sigle, Goldmedia and Rightscom (2006) *Interactive Content and Convergence: Implications for the Information Society*. London: Screen Digest.

Servaes, J. (2000) 'The European information society: much ado about nothing?', *International Communication Gazette*, 64(5): 433–47.

Shore, C. (2000) *Building Europe: The Cultural Politics of European Integration*. London: Routledge.

Sidel, K. M., and McMane, A. A. (1995) 'Western Europe', pp. 123–52, in J. Merrill (ed.) *Global Journalism: Survey of International Communication*. White Plains, NY: Longman.

Sinclair, J. (2004) 'Television and the public interest', pp. 1–4, in J. Sinclair and G. Turner (eds) *Contemporary World Television*. London: BFI.

Siune, K. (1998) 'Is broadcasting policy becoming redundant?', pp. 18–26, in K. Brants, J. Hermes and L. van Zoonen (eds) *The Media in Question: Popular Cultures and Public Interests*. London: Sage.

Siune, K., and Hultén, O. (1998) 'Does public broadcasting have a future?", pp. 23–37, in D. McQuail and K. Siune (eds) *Media Policy: Convergence, Concentration and Commerce*. London: Sage.

Slaatta, T. (2006) 'Europeanisation and the news media: issues and research imperatives', *Javnost – The Public*, 13(1): 5–24.

Smaele, H. de (2007) 'More Europe: more unity, more diversity? The enlargement of the European audiovisual space', *European Studies*, 24: 113–34.

Smith, H. (2004) 'Human Rights Record Haunts Turkey's EU Ambitions', *The Guardian*, 13 December.

Sparks, C. (2000) 'Media theory after the fall of communism', pp. 35–49, in J. Curran and M. J. Park (eds) *De-Westernizing Media Studies*. New York: Routledge.

Special Eurobarometer (2008) *E-Communications Household Survey*. Special Eurobarometer no. 293. Brussels: European Commission.

Special Eurobarometer (2010) *E-Communications Household Survey*. Special Eurobarometer no. 335. Brussels: European Commission.

Splichal, S. (1994) *Media Beyond Socialism: Theory and Practice in East-Central Europe*. Boulder, CO: Westview Press.

Statham, P. (2007) 'Journalists as commentators on European politics: educators, partisans or ideologues?', *European Journal of Communication*, 22(4): 461–77.

Steemers, J. (2007) 'Europe: television in transition', pp. 57–78, in L. Artz and Y. R. Kamalipour (eds) *The Media Globe: Trends in International Mass Media*. Lanham, MD: Rowman & Littlefield.

Stevenson, R. L. (1994) *Global Communication in the Twenty-First Century*. New York: Longman.

Stråth, B. (2002) 'A European identity: to the historical limits of a concept', *European Journal of Social Theory*, 5(4): 387–401.

Subiotto, R. and Graf, T. (2003) 'Analysis of the principles applicable to the review of exclusive broadcasting licences under EC competition law', *World Competition*, 26(4): 589–608.

Sukosd, M. (2000) 'Democratic transformation and the mass media in Hungary: from Stalinism to democratic consolidation', pp. 122–64, in R. Gunther and A. Mughan (eds) *Democracy and the Media*. Cambridge: Cambridge University Press.

Taylor, C. (2004) *Modern Social Imaginaries*. Durham, NC, and London: Duke University Press.

Television Business International (2007) 'HD in Europe – not a clear picture', April: 1–4.

Thatcher, M. (2004) 'Varieties of capitalism in an internationalized world: domestic institutional change in European telecommunications', *Comparative Political Studies*, 37(7): 751–80.

Thompson, J. B. (1995) *The Media and Modernity*. Cambridge: Polity.

Thomson J. (2006) 'IPTV – market, regulatory trends and policy options in Europe', paper presented at the ITU–T IPTV Global Technical Workshop, 12–13 October.

Trappel, J., Meier, W. A., d' Haenens, L., Steemers, J., and Thomass, B. (2011) *Media in Europe Today*. Bristol: Intellect.

Traquina, N. (1998) *Western European Broadcasting, Deregulation, and Public Television: The Portuguese Experience*, Journalism and Mass Communication Monographs, no. 167.

Traynor, I. (2004) 'In 1683 Turkey was the invader: in 2004 much of Europe still sees it that way', *The Guardian*, 22 September.

Trenz, H. J. (2004) 'Media coverage on European governance: exploring the European public sphere in national quality newspapers', *European Journal of Communication*, 19(3): 291–320.

Tunstall, J. (2008) *The Media were American*. New York: Oxford University Press.

Tunstall, J., and Machin, D. (1999) *The Anglo-American Media Connection*. Oxford: Oxford University Press.

TV International (2007) 'Mobile TV and video revenues to reach US$8 billion by 2012', 15(21): 1–2.

TV International (2008a) 'Eastern Europe is growing fast, but digital switchover is far off', 16(2): 1–3.

TV International (2008b) 'Consolidation leads to greater competition as the French embrace new technologies', April: 4–7.

TV International (2009) 'Digital TV penetration in Eastern Europe to cross the half-way mark by 2013', 17(1): 3–6.

UMTS (Mobile TV Joint Work Group of the UMTS Forum and the GSM Association) (2008) *Sustainable Economics of Mobile TV Services*, 2nd White Paper. Available at: www.umts-forum.org.

Urban, A. (2007) 'Mobile television: is it just a hype or a real consumer need?', *Observatorio Journal*, 1(3): 45–58. Available at: http://obs.obercom.pt.

Vartanova, E. (2002) 'A global balancing act: new structures in the Russian media', *Media Development*, 49(1):13–17.

Vekeman, G. (2008) *The Telecom Sector in the EU*, Eurostat: Statistics in Focus, 38/2008.

Vidal-Hall, J. (2009) 'Handmaiden of democracy or everybody's football? The media in Central and Eastern Europe twenty years after 1989', *Eurozine*, 19 March. Available at: www.eurozine.com/articles/2009-03-19-editorial-en.html.

Vissol, T. (2006) *Is There a Case for an EU Information Television Station?* Luxembourg: European Commission.

WAN (World Association of Newspapers) (2008) 'World press trends: newspapers are a growth business', press release, Göteborg, Sweden, 2 June. Available at: www.wan-press.org/article17377.html.

Ward, D. (2004) *The European Union Democratic Deficit and the Public Sphere: An Evaluation of EU Media Policy*. Amsterdam: IOS Press.

Wenger, K. (2008) 'Europe is not programmable', pp. 56–60, in Institut für Auslandsbeziehungen and the Robert Bosch Stiftung in co-operation with the British Council and the Foundation for German-Polish Co-operation (eds) *Europe in the Media – Media in Europe: Culture Report Progress Europe*. Stuttgart: IFA.

Westcott, T. (2005) *European Programme Rights: Sport*. London: Screen Digest.

Westcott, T. (2007) 'The Business of Football on TV; Rights are now being split up to avoid monolithic operators', *Screen Digest*, December: 364.

Westcott, T. (2008) 'European football grows in value', *Screen Digest*, July: 200.

Wheeler, M. (2000) 'The "undeclared war", part II: The European Union's consultation process for the new round of the General Agreement on Trading Services/World Trade Organization on audiovisual services', *European Journal of Communication*, 15(2): 253–62.

Wheeler, M. (2004a) 'Tuning into the new economy: the European Union's competition policy in a converging communications environment', *Convergence*, 8: 98–116.

Wheeler, M. (2004b) 'Supranational regulation: television and the European Union', *European Journal of Communication*, 19(3): 349–69.

Wheeler, M. (2007) 'Whither cultural diversity: the European Union's market vision for the review of television without frontiers directive', *European Studies*, 24: 227–49.

Williamson, A. (2009) *MPs Online: Connecting with Constituents*. London: Hansard Society. Available at: www.hansardsociety.org.uk/blogs/publications/archive/2009/02/24/mps-online-connecting-with-constituents.aspx.

Woods, L. (2008) 'The consumer and advertising regulation in the television without frontiers and audiovisual media services directives', *Journal of Consumer Policy*, 31(19): 63–77.

Young, A. (2007) 'Trade politics aren't what it used to be: the European Union in the Doha round', *Journal of Common Market Studies*, 45(4): 789–811.

Index